PRAISE FOR MRS. SCHLAFLY &

WHO KILLED THE AMERICAN FAMILY?

Phyllis Schlafly has been, and continues to be, one of the most influential women in America. She stood virtually alone in the 1970s when the early feminist movement attempted to pass the Equal Rights Amendment to the US Constitution. It would have had a terrible social impact on our nation. Arrayed against her were two US Presidents, two First Ladies, the majority of congressmen and senators, most universities and the entire media. She stood like a rock in response to unmerciful criticism and scorn. From then to now, Phyllis has represented an unwavering voice of reason about marriage, parenthood, the defense of righteousness, and conservative thought. I admire her greatly and thank God for the impact she continues to have on our nation.

JAMES C. DOBSON, PH.D., PRESIDENT AND FOUNDER OR FAMILY TALK

My friend, Phyllis Schlafly, has been a prominent figure in the conservative movement for decades. With courage and tenacity she has led the charge against liberal feminists who have been at war with traditional values and the nuclear family of this country. *Who Killed the American Family?* is a brilliant analysis of the assault on the family, and it provides practical solutions for turning the tide in the culture war and reinstating the eminence of the American family.

DAVID LIMBAUGH, LAWYER, SYNDICATED COLUMNIST AND *NEW YORK TIMES* BEST-SELLING AUTHOR

With her characteristic courage and insight, the Iron Lady of the conservative movement indicts all those complicit in the forty-year war on the American family. Phyllis Schlafly exposes how feminists and globalists have worked in cahoots with the public school establishment, the welfare system, the divorce courts, the judges, and "free trade" activists to deconstruct the very heart of American identity and exceptionalism.

ROBERT W.PATTERSON, OPINION CONTRIBUTOR FOR *THE PHILDELPHIA INQUIRER*

Who Killed the American Family? goes beyond the clichés of both sides to offer a clear and powerful analysis of the forces that are destroying the family and the consequences that are already ensuing. Mrs Schlafly confronts important issues that are ignored by most advocates for the family. The result is the most penetrating account yet of the civilizational implications of radical ideologies that are not only dismantling the family but doing so quite intentionally and methodically and destroying freedom in the process.

STEPHEN BASKERVILLE, PROFESSOR OF GOVERNMENT AT PATRICK HENRY COLLEGE AND AUTHOR OF *TAKEN INTO CUSTODY: THE WAR AGAINST FATHERS, MARRIAGE, AND THE FAMILY*

WHO KILLED *THE* AMERICAN FAMILY?

WHO KILLED
THE AMERICAN
FAMILY?

BESTSELLING AUTHOR OF *A CHOICE NOT AN ECHO*

PHYLLIS SCHLAFLY

 WND Books

WHO KILLED THE AMERICAN FAMILY?

Published by WND Books®, Washington, D.C. WND Books is a registered trademark of WorldNetDaily.com, Inc. ("WND")

Book designed by Mark Karis

WND Books are distributed to the trade by:
Midpoint Trade Books
27 West 20th Street, Suite 1102
New York, New York 10011
WND Books are available at special discounts for bulk purchases. WND Books, Inc., also publishes books in electronic formats. For more information call
(541) 474-1776 or visit www.wndbooks.com.

Hardcover ISBN: 978-1-938067-52-5
eBook ISBN: 978-1-938067-53-2

Library of Congress Cataloging-in-Publication Data
Schlafly, Phyllis.
  Who killed the American family / Phyllis Schlafly.
     pages cm
  ISBN 978-1-938067-52-5 (hardcover)
1. Families--United States. 2. Family policy--United States. 3. Domestic relations--United States. I. Title.
  HQ536.S367 2014
  306.850973--dc23

                              2014020590

Printed in the United States of America
14 15 16 17 18 19 MV 9 8 7 6 5 4 3 2 1

CONTENTS

INTRODUCTION

When I was married in 1949, it was perfectly normal to quit my job (which I enjoyed) and begin a new life as a wife and full-time homemaker. We started out in a three-bedroom house with a white picket fence in a small Midwestern town and had six children. That was then the norm. Along with veterans returning from World War II (like my husband), we contributed to the baby boom. Many of my friends and neighbors had six children too.

That is not the norm anymore. A pregnant teenage girl receives more encouragement (and financial incentives) to collect welfare than to marry her child's father. His role is defined not by law or a marriage contract or the culture, but by a judge. Everyone seems to accept the notion that a judge, rather than parents, can determine the best interest of the child.

We hardly hear anyone today standing up for the proposition that traditional civil marriage is essential to society because it provides the legal construct under which a couple voluntarily accepts the rights and responsibilities for the resulting children. The state's vital interest in defining marriage is to maintain family autonomy for the benefit of the next generation.

Hillary Clinton popularized the slogan, "It takes a village to raise a child."[1] *Village* is the progressives' metaphor for the theory that the government, speaking through judges, psychologists, school personnel, and social workers, should make decisions about child rearing, not the parents.

Some states are moving to give judges the authority to name three or more legal parents of a child. The rationale is that only a judge can decide the best interest of the child, and if there are three adults with some relationship to the child, then a judge may designate all three as the legal parents. That might be one man paying child support and two lesbians spending it.

You may think that the court intervenes only when there is a nasty divorce conflict, or when the parents are drug addicts, or when someone fails to get adequate legal advice. But that is not true. No family is safe from the official busybodies.

Many divorced dads have discovered that they have no right to see their own kids. A judge decides what is demeaningly referred to as child support and visitation. Sadly, many of our social ills are attributable to children being cut off from a relationship with their dads.

The nuclear family used to be the basic institution of American society. It gave us a society in which people could make their own decisions without government supervision or financing. The nuclear family has been the essential building block of a free society with limited government. The nuclear family is not dependent on government supervision or handouts. There are other family types, but the nuclear family is the most independent and autonomous.

The word *nuclear* is used generally to refer to a central entity or "nucleus" around which others collect. The term *nuclear family*, then, refers to a household consisting of a father, a mother, and their children, all in one dwelling.

Americans who grow up in a nuclear family—one in which the parents are married—are more individualistic, self-supporting, and entrepreneurial than other people.

Some libertarians believe in writing their own marriage contract, but the law makes it impossible to make a binding or enforceable agreement about custody of your own children. Any such contract can be voided and replaced by the opinion of a judge or other government official.

In the 1930s Agatha Christie wrote a famous murder mystery novel titled *Murder on the Orient Express.* The question posed was, who committed the murder? The story's hero discovers that all the passengers on the train had motives and ultimately concludes they all had a hand in killing the victim. Likewise, many players had a hand in killing the American family.

This book explains the combination of forces that abolished the American family as we knew it in the 1950s. The many factors include changes in the law, in court decisions, in the culture, in education from elementary grades through college, and in the dictates of the intelligentsia who think they know how to run other people's lives. Any one of these factors would not have been enough to abolish marriage, but together they added up to a mighty force.

This book is not just another lament about the decline of marriage. That decline and its consequences are well documented elsewhere. Nor is it a book that blames the problem on the gays or on so-called deadbeat dads. Gays and lesbians have received most of the publicity about attacks on our marriage law, but they are vastly outnumbered by the feminists, the judges, the self-described experts, and others discussed in the pages ahead.

This book is about the attack on the American nuclear family by many forces, each with its own reason for wanting to abolish it. The wreckage of the American family renders us incapable of having limited government because government must step in to perform tasks formerly done by the nuclear family. The problem cannot be remedied just by prohibiting same-sex marriage or by telling dads to "man up." We must identify and go after all the forces that killed the American family.

Who Killed the American Family? explains why and how feminists, judges, lawmakers, psychologists, college professors and courses, government incentives and disincentives, and Democratic politicians seeking votes oppose the traditional American nuclear family as we knew it and as it was depicted on TV fifty years ago. Each antifamily act may seem minor, but added up, those acts and events are changing America for the worse. It is time to reverse the tide.

1

THE AMERICAN FAMILY WE ONCE KNEW

The American family used to be the fundamental institution of our stable, liberty-loving, and very successful society. It enabled us to build a prosperous middle class that was the envy of the world. The structure was based on defined gender roles: a breadwinner and protector husband and father who earned enough to support his family; a full-time homemaker whose principal duty was the care and upbringing of their own children; and children who were responsible to their own father and mother. Kids walked to school and received a pretty good education by the eighth grade. Today, that world seems to be gone or fast disappearing.

When the famous French commentator Alexis de Tocqueville traveled the United States in the mid-nineteenth century, he recognized that respect for marriage is almost uniquely American. He wrote: "There is certainly no country in the world where the tie of marriage is more respected than in America, or where conjugal happiness is more highly or worthily appreciated. . . . While the European endeavors to forget his domestic troubles by agitating society, the American derives from his own home that love of order which he afterwards carries with him into public affairs."[1]

It should be evident that the American nuclear family is a good thing, and laws, policies, and social conventions that undermine the family are bad things. All social statistics confirm that American-style marriage has been good for women, good for men, good for children, good for society, good for freedom, and good for our high standard of living. Real-life experience has given our lawmakers and judges a rational basis for concluding that marriage is a social good that should be protected and encouraged by laws and when challenged in the courts.

The traditional American nuclear family is the best gateway to major conservative goals: individual liberty, limited government, less government spending, and restraints on government meddling in our lives. The functioning traditional family doesn't need government handouts or supervision, child-care instructions, or bureaucrats and judges to dictate rules or resolve disputes.

The American family has deteriorated to such a sorry state today that its value is no longer obvious to younger Americans. Fifty years ago, it was considered shameful to have a baby out of wedlock. It is now so commonplace that it doesn't raise eyebrows. In 1950, only 4 percent of American babies were born to unmarried mothers. Today, 41 percent of American births are illegitimate.[2] "Single mother" became the nonjudgmental name for the unwed mother. More recently, she has been rebranded as "independent mother" to emphasize her lack of need for a husband or a father for her children.

The Great Depression of the 1930s, when millions of men were unemployed, didn't kill the American family. World War II, when we sent 16 million men to fight on faraway battlefields, requiring long absences from home, didn't kill it. What happened in the 1970s, '80s, and '90s to break up the family structure that seemed so secure in the 1950s and '60s?

This book connects the dots to explain how those changes happened and who is responsible for killing the traditional family. There is no single cause. The American family was destroyed by a combination of political activists, judges, economic theorists, self-proclaimed experts, and left-wing politicians—with different motives that produced the same result.

THE STRICT FATHER MODEL

Liberal University of California–Berkeley professor George Lakoff believes that conservative attitudes about politics and policies are produced by the traditional American family structure. Since he is eager to expand support for liberal/progressive policies, he tries to educate his fellow liberals about how the nuclear family made conservatism the dominant ideology.

In a 1995 essay, Lakoff portrayed conservatives as if they were a tribe in Borneo with alien practices and values. He argued that their political views, with which he disagrees, stem from their family structure, which he described as follows:

> The Strict Father Model. A traditional nuclear family with the father having primary responsibility for the well being of the household. The mother has day-to-day responsibility for the care of the house and details of raising the children. But the father has primary responsibility for setting overall family policy, and the mother's job is to be supportive of the father and to help carry out the father's views on what should be done. Ideally, she respects his views and supports them.
>
> Life is seen as fundamentally difficult and the world as fundamentally dangerous. Evil is conceptualized as a force in the world, and it is the father's job to support his family and protect it from evils—both external and internal. External evils include enemies, hardships, and temptations. Internal evils come in the form of uncontrolled desires and are as threatening as external ones. The father embodies the values needed to make one's way in the world and to support a family: he is morally strong, self-disciplined, frugal, temperate, and restrained. He sets an example by holding himself to high standards. He insists on his moral authority, commands obedience, and when he doesn't get it, metes out retribution as fairly and justly as he knows how. It

is his job to protect and support his family, and he believes that safety comes out of strength. . . .

The strict father provides nurturance and expresses his devotion to his family by supporting and protecting them, but just as importantly by setting and enforcing strict moral bounds and by inculcating self-discipline and self-reliance through hard work and self-denial. This builds character. For the strict father, strictness is a form of nurturance and love—tough love. . . .

Under the Strict Father approach, the father provides financial support for the family and there is no dependency on government. Keeping government out of family life promotes hard work, ingenuity, perseverance, and especially individual liberty.[3]

Lakoff disapproves of this lifestyle and seeks to discredit it. His ideas are a little goofy, and his description of the "strict father" is exaggerated, but he has identified aspects of the American family that conservatives admire and his fellow progressives despise.

The contrary family model is epitomized by the aforementioned slogan popularized by Hillary Clinton's book *It Takes a Village*. Conservatives reject the notion that the village (i.e., schools, government agencies, and family courts) should raise children; they believe this right and responsibility belong to parents.

Professor Lakoff believes that these family metaphors are the key to understanding politics. Liberals prefer what Lakoff calls the Nurturant Family, which he described thus:

The basic values in the progressive moral system are empathy and responsibility, both for oneself and others. This leads to a view of government as having certain moral obligations: providing protection and empowerment for everyone equally. This requires a vibrant commitment to the public—public infrastructure (roads, buildings, sewers), public education, public health, and so on. No private business can prosper at all without such public provisions. . . .

The progressive family has parents of equal authority. Their central moral role requires empathy with each other and their children; it requires self-responsibility and responsibility for the well being of other family members. This means open communication, transparency about family rules, shared decision-making, and need-based fairness.[4]

Lakoff and his liberal friends see these contrary visions of family structure as determinant of right-left politics. He wrote, "When this idealized family model is projected onto various governing institutions, we get conservative versions of them: conservative religion with a strict father God; a view of the market as Decider with no external authority over the market from government, unions, or the courts; and strictness in other institutions, like education, prisons, businesses, sports teams, romantic relationships, and the world community."[5]

The goal of the progressives is to break down the American family, destroy parental authority, deny right and wrong, reduce family autonomy, and get as many people as possible dependent on government programs. That's why liberals, especially feminists, wage a persistent attack on the institution of marriage and the traditional family structure.

The self-chosen label for the modern feminist movement, which emerged in the late 1960s and early 1970s, was "liberation," a word that signified the feminist goal of liberation from home, husband, family, and the care of children. They took their cue from the big mama of the feminist movement and author of *The Second Sex*, Frenchwoman Simone de Beauvoir, who famously labeled marriage "an obscene bourgeois institution."[6]

Most parents don't see politics as the cause or effect of the way they divide duties with their spouses or how they raise their children, but liberals and feminists do. The liberals and progressives believe that family structure is very political and even determinative of political attitudes.

The 1955 James Dean film *Rebel Without a Cause* was a popular teen-angst movie of that decade. It is about troubled teenagers, and the root of all their problems is weak or absent fathers. The advantages of the American nuclear family are presumed. James Dean,

Natalie Wood, and the others look to the fathers for strength and moral authority, but they do not get it. The moms try to fill the gap, but they cannot. They can help, nurture, approve, and encourage, but they cannot do what the teenagers desperately need from fathers. Viewers could conclude that the strict father model is essential for normal development to adulthood. But that was in the 1950s.

THE NUCLEAR FAMILY

In September 2012, husband-and-wife team Christopher Ryan and Cacilda Jethá engaged in a video debate about their book, *Sex at Dawn*. They argued that the human species did not evolve in monogamous, nuclear families, but rather, in small, intimate groups where "most mature individuals would have had several ongoing sexual relationships at any given time."[7] We are supposedly the descendants of these multi-male–multi-female mating groups and, even though we've constructed a radically different society from our hunter-gatherer forebears, the behavioral and psychological traits of our species that were developed in the distant past still manifest themselves today. Ryan, a psychologist, and Jethá, a psychiatrist, argue that understanding human sexual evolution this way helps explain our species' unique creativity inside (as well as outside) the marriage bed.

Ryan has written that his book should be very upsetting to social conservatives because, he argues, there is no such thing as traditional marriage. He says that primitive hunter-gatherer societies had no need for marriage. There were no individual dependencies, no property rights, no reason for jealousy, and no child knew who his father was. Girls were free and sexually liberated, like the ones famously (and inaccurately) described in Margaret Mead's *Coming of Age in Samoa*. According to Ryan, countries like Sweden have moved closer to this sexual utopia by adopting socialist policies, and as a result, Swedes have more relaxed ideas about monogamy and promiscuity. In the United States, you can find these jealousy-free attitudes at a Las Vegas swingers convention.

However, traditional American marriage does not mimic caveman behavior. Religion and law made marriage and modern civilization possible. Anthropologists say that 85 percent of human societies have allowed men to have multiple wives.[8] Genetic analysis shows that while 80 percent of females in ancient times reproduced, only 40 percent of males did.[9]

When social conservatives advocate laws protecting marriage, they are not doing it because they think that marriage instincts are innate. They do it because the institution of marriage depends on reinforcement from social norms, laws, and customs, as well as religion. Modern civilization depends on marriage and family units. If it were true that we would all behave like bonobos without marriage laws, then that is all the more reason to protect our marriage traditions.

It is sometimes argued that humans are not naturally monogamous, based on comparisons to the animal world. There are a couple of problems with this argument. The animals most similar to humans, as measured by DNA, are chimpanzees and bonobos, but they have radically different sexual practices. Those animals are incapable of cooperating on anything like a marriage. You never even see two chimps carrying a log together.[10]

The book *Explanation of Ideology: Family Structures and Social Systems*, by Emmanuel Todd, explains how different family structures correspond with different ideologies. These ideological structures created seven family types. Feudal England had the most absolute nuclear family. Married children lived on their own, not with their parents. Inheritance was determined by wills, and property usually went to the eldest son. People were free to choose their own spouses, except that cousin marriage was not permitted. The daughters and non-eldest sons were frequently on their own to make a new life for themselves. The clans were busted up by marriage outside the clan, and individual families had a high degree of autonomy.[11] This produced a degree of libertarian individualism very different from most other cultures.

There are two main types of families:

1. The American nuclear family: an autonomous unit consisting of dad, mom, and kids; dad is head of the household; Christian ideals prevail.

2. Old World families: arranged marriages, cousin marriages; rigid inheritance rules; household authority that includes the extended family; tribal culture.

According to Robin Fox, marriage between cousins was pervasive in the human past: "As an anthropologist," he wrote, "I am forced to face the fact that for the vast majority of our existence as a species, close cousin marriage must have been the norm, if for no other reason than that most of the time there was no one but cousins to marry. . . . Not only was it not forbidden, it was prescribed, often with a particular degree of detail."[12]

Cousin marriage is discouraged in the United States and generally in the West. Alex Tabarrok wrote in a popular economics blog:

In the United States consanguineous marriage (marriage between close relatives, often cousins) is frowned upon and in many states banned but it is common elsewhere in the world. Approximately 0.2% of all marriages are consanguineous in the United States, but in India 26.6% marriages are consanguineous, in Saudi Arabia the figure is 38.4% and in Niger, Pakistan, and Sudan a majority of marriages are consanguineous.[13]

It is widely believed that the argument against cousin marriage is the risk of birth defects, but actually that risk is not so large. The real problem with cousin marriage is that if everybody does it, the society develops into clans, making democracy extremely difficult.

Family types explain a great deal. A big advance in European civilization occurred about a millennium ago, when Christianity abolished cousin marriages. Islam has not done that. Families are very important in China and India, but they are not like the American nuclear family. The American nuclear family made America great, but few are now defending it against forces determined to destroy it. If America continues to have many immigrants with different family types, we are less likely to maintain American values of personal freedom, individualism, and limited government.

ATTACKS ON THE NUCLEAR FAMILY

Margaret Mead introduced anthropology to the world with her sensational 1928 book, *Coming of Age in Samoa*. It told a story of sexual freedom among young girls in the South Pacific islands and suggested they were happier and more fulfilled because they were not constrained by Western morals and culture. Mead's methodology and conclusions are very controversial. She was sharply criticized by anthropologist Derek Freeman, who claimed she'd been duped, that she was not objective, and that Samoan girls were nothing like her description.

Mead's work is often taught as implying that family and sex roles are cultural and arbitrary. But that was not her view; she wrote, "Men have always been the leaders in public affairs and the final authorities at home."[14]

Much of twentieth-century anthropology was dedicated to studying primitive tribes in the hope that we could learn from them. The premise was that all people are the same and our social customs are not necessarily better than anyone else's. This research was a big inspiration to feminists, Marxists, and others who were unhappy with Western social structures.

University of Pennsylvania economists Betsey Stevenson and Justin Wolfers argued in 2008:

> We believe that the answer lies in a shift from the family as a forum for shared production, to shared consumption. In case the language of economics lacks romance, let's be clearer: modern

marriage is about love and companionship. Most things in life are simply better shared with another person: this ranges from the simple pleasures such as enjoying a movie or a hobby together, to shared social ties such as attending the same church, and finally, to the joint project of bringing up children. . . .

So is marriage doomed? Marriage in which one person specializes in the home while the other person specializes in the market is indeed doomed. The opportunity cost of having women stay out of the labor force is likely to continue to rise—particularly as young women are surpassing men in educational attainment and higher education is becoming more important for market success.[15]

Stevenson and Wolfers have their own personal marriage-like arrangement. They have two kids together, but they have not legally married for tax reasons. Their deal was that she would do the breast-feeding while he would do all the diapers, and a full-time schoolteacher would do most of the child rearing.

The feminist movement started its attack on traditional marriage with Betty Friedan's 1963 book, *The Feminine Mystique*, which urged wives to leave their homes (called a "comfortable concentration camp"[16]), join the workforce, and become independent of men. *The Adventures of Ozzie and Harriet*, a traditional-couple sitcom of the 1950s, became an epithet. After Gloria Steinem persuaded President Jimmy Carter to change the name of his White House Conference on "the Family" to "Families," it became de rigueur to speak of different kinds of "families" instead of "*the* family."

The so-called Centre for the Modern Family has a website with surveys and "expert views," all designed to convince you that the traditional family is obsolete. And even *Wikipedia* now considers the traditional family a relic of the 1950s. Its contributors define *familialism* as:

An ideology that promotes the family of the Western tradition as an institution. Familialism views the nuclear family of one father, one mother, and their child or children as the central and primary social unit of human ordering and the principal unit of a functioning society and civilization. . . . Familialism advocates Western "family values" and usually opposes other social forms and models that are chosen as alternatives (i.e., single-parent, polygamy, LGBT parenting, etc.). . . .

Familialism is usually considered conservative or reactionary by its critics who argue that it is limited, outmoded, and unproductive in modern Western society.[17]

Familialism has been condemned as a destructive social construct imposed on Western culture. Its prevalence has been criticized, and its antagonistic relationship with LGBT culture has been noted.

In July 2012, the *New York Times* published a piece by Jason DeParle making the obvious, yet frequently denied, observation that children are a lot better off when they are reared by both parents than when a single mother has to make do on her own.[18] The *Times* could have headlined the story "Dan Quayle Was Right" if the *Atlantic* hadn't beaten them to it nineteen years before.

Katie Roiphe rushed to criticize. "It is disheartening to see that the *New York Times* has run yet another puritanical and alarmist rumination on the decline of the American family disguised as a straight-news story," railed Roiphe, a single mother who prefers feel-good puff pieces about single motherhood: "It's time to run a story about the resourcefulness, energy, and intensity of these homes, a fair, open-minded exploration of these new family structures and the independent, tough women who run them." She accused the paper of an ideological betrayal: "In the guise of writing a well-intentioned liberal piece, the *New York Times* is recycling truly retrograde and ugly moral judgments."[19]

DeParle's argument is essentially that two parents are better than one. That is true as far as it goes, but the difference between a single mother and a married couple is qualitative as well as quantitative. Children who grow up without a father are deprived of—pardon the cliché—a male role model. A close relationship with both parents helps children understand the differences between the sexes. A boy can learn to be masculine and a girl to be feminine. Those ideas defy feminist dogma, so they don't get past the editors of the *New York Times*.

There is a political as well as an ideological aspect to the left's disparagement of marriage and celebration of single motherhood. As pollster John Zogby noted in a *Forbes* column, the "marriage gap" between Democrats and Republicans is "even more dramatic" than the so-called gender gap.[20] The undeniable and possibly uncomfortable truths here are that kids do best on all measures with a biological mom and dad, and that married couples vote overwhelmingly Republican.

What the *New York Times* and its fellow liberals will not do is draw the obvious conclusions from those truths. They have a very strong incentive to destroy working-class marriages and to confuse the kids in the next generation because that is how Democrats get votes. Ann Coulter responded: "Children raised by single mothers commit 72% of juvenile murders, 60% of rapes, have 70% of teenaged births, commit 70% of suicides, and are 70% of high school dropouts."[21]

Scientific studies have consistently shown that kids do best with traditional families, a.k.a. intact biological families. That is no surprise, as that has been conventional wisdom for centuries. But for the last ten years, leftist, pro-LGBT professors have been saying otherwise, without evidence.

In 2012, two hundred PhDs and MDs signed a letter to the editors of the journal *Social Science Research* to complain about the truth being published without pro-LGBT spin: "We urge you to publicly disclose the reasons for both the expedited peer review process of this clearly controversial paper and the choice of commentators invited to submit critiques. We further request that you invite scholars with specific expertise in LGBT parenting issues to submit a detailed critique of the paper and accompanying commentaries for publication in the next issue of the journal."[22]

Most of the signers of the complaint were just sociologists with an interest in LGBT issues. If they were real scientists who had a legitimate disagreement, they would explain why the paper was wrong or do a better study. They probably would like to make the point that, under ideal conditions, lesbians and gays can make satisfactory adoptive parents, which may be true. But if we are to adopt laws and policies that promote LGBT parenting, we should look at data on how well it works in practice and stop pretending that LGBT parents do as well as natural parents. All evidence favors natural parents.

The 1950s were the high-water mark for the American nuclear family. Social policies favored it, evidence supported it, and no one apologized for it.

NAMES FOR FAUX SPOUSES

Elizabeth Weil explained the problem of what to call unmarried live-ins:

> Now that we've come to some consensus on same-sex marriage, let's move on to the next puzzle: what to call two people who act as if they are married but are not.
>
> "I went through a phase of just calling him Eric, even to people who didn't know who that was," said the master word-smith Ann Kjellberg, 50, editor of the journal *Little Star* and the literary executor of the poet Joseph Brodsky. Eric Zerof spent 15 years as her live-in not-spouse and is the father of Ms. Kjellberg's child. "I kept thinking, 'This should not be this hard!' I was very unhappy about the situation. I could never find a word I liked."
>
> One might imagine we would be less tongue-tied. The faux spouse is a pretty ho-hum cultural specimen for such a gaping verbal lacuna. But none of the word choices are good. Everyone agrees that partner sounds awful—too anodyne, empty, cold. Lover may be worse—too sexualized, graphic, one-dimensional. Boyfriend sounds too young. Significant other sounds too '80s. Special friend or just friend (both favored by the 65-and-over crowd) are just too ridiculous. . . .
>
> Demographers, tasked with counting the hombres, mujeres, and their relationships to one another, are not doing much better

than fusband. Until the 1970s, the American faux spouse was too rare and taboo to even try to track. In 1980, the United States Census Bureau made its first attempt at naming these creatures in order to count them. It really outdid itself lexicographically: "person of opposite sex sharing living quarters," abbreviated to POSSLQ and pronounced "possle cue." The CBS commentator Charles Osgood had his way with the acronym, publishing a poem riffing John Donne's "The Bait."

You live with me, and I with you,
And you will be my POSSLQ.
I'll be your friend and so much more;
That's what a POSSLQ is for.[23]

FAMILY IN OTHER COUNTRIES

Other countries respect what are called family values, but that doesn't mean what Americans mean by the traditional nuclear family. A *New York Times* article on India explained some of the family differences:

> The extended family is still the bedrock of Indian society. . . .
> That may be a fantasy, but matriarchal interference (call it guidance) is marriage Indian-style. When Indian women discuss the need to "adjust" to matrimony, they don't just mean adapting to a new husband. They mean moving in with his parents, grandparents and siblings, a custom that is still the norm, even in prosperous families. . . .
> Male children are favored in Indian society, and wives join the husband's family at the low end of the pecking order, often relegated to kitchen drudge work while the mother-in-law rules over the grandchildren. "We live with our parents until we are married, then we live with someone else's parents," Ms. [Etka] Kapoor [an Indian television and film producer] said. "There is pressure to give everything to the son. It's a source of conflict in so many homes."[24]

An outrageous sex crime in India received a lot of publicity, but the larger picture is that the overall status of women in India is much different from the status of women in the United States. The *New York Times* reported:

NEW DELHI—Harassed for years by her husband and his relatives, an Indian woman was finally kidnapped, raped, strangled and tossed into a ditch. For more than a year, the woman's father has tried without success to get the police to arrest those accused of killing her, including her husband, who were charged but remain at large. The father, Subedar Akhileshar Kumar Singh, an army officer, says he believes his daughter was killed because her in-laws were not satisfied with her dowry, according to an article on Thursday in *The Indian Express.* Such crimes are routine in this country, where researchers estimate that anywhere from 25,000 to 100,000 women a year are killed over dowry disputes. Many are burned alive in a particularly grisly form of retribution.[25]

Wikipedia says that India prohibited dowries in 1961, but dowry deaths continue: "Tradition in India also results in considerable acceptance of violence. A 2005 government survey found that 54% of women in India said that husbands were justified in beating their wives, with the most common justification being if they failed to show proper respect for their in-laws."[26]

A *New York Times* editorial read:

More broadly, India must work on changing a culture in which women are routinely devalued. Many are betrothed against their will as child brides, and many suffer cruelly, including acid attacks and burning, at the hands of husbands and family members. India, a rising economic power and the world's largest democracy, can never reach its full potential if half its population lives in fear of such unspeakable violence.[27]

The UK *Daily Mail* reported that a Muslim who raped a thirteen-year-old girl he groomed on Facebook was spared a prison sentence after a judge heard he went to an Islamic faith school where he was taught that women are worthless.

> Rashid had "little experience of women" due to his education at an Islamic school in the UK.
>
> After his arrest, he told a psychologist that he did not know having sex with a 13-year-old was against the law. The court heard he found it was illegal only when he was informed by a family member.
>
> In other interviews with psychologists, Rashid claimed he had been taught in his school that "women are no more worthy than a lollipop that has been dropped on the ground."[28]

Chinese families are also different. The BBC reported that China "passed a law requiring adult children to visit their elderly parents regularly or risk being sued."[29] Chinese Confucianism has always had great reverence for parents:

> In the "Hiao-king," Confucius is recorded as saying: "Filial piety is the root of all virtue. Of all the actions of man there are none greater than those of filial piety." To the Chinese, filial piety prompts sons to love and respect their parents, contribute to their comfort and bring happiness and honor to their name by honorable success in life. Filial piety includes the obligation of sons to live after marriage under the same roof with the father and to give him obedience as long as he lived. The will of the parents was declared to be supreme even to the extent that if the son's wife failed to please them he was obliged to divorce her. If a dutiful son found himself compelled to scold a wayward father he was taught to give the correction with the utmost meekness. The father does not forfeit his right to filial respect, no matter how great his wickedness.[30]

Sometimes Republican strategists argue that Asian Americans should be Republicans because of their strong families. But the majority of Asians voted for Barack Obama.[31]

BUT IT *DOESN'T* "TAKE A VILLAGE"

New research at the University of Michigan shows that it doesn't take a village to raise a child after all. U-M researcher Beverly Strassmann, professor of anthropology and faculty associate at the U-M Institute for Social Research (ISR), wrote, "In the African villages that I study in Mali, children fare as well in nuclear families as they do in extended families. There's a naïve belief that villages raise children communally, when in reality children are raised by their own families and their survival depends critically on the survival of their mothers."[32]

Strassmann found that, among the seventeen hundred children she followed, those whose mothers were dead were more than four times more likely to die by age five, and their overall risk of death was higher in polygamous than in monogamous families. This reflects the hazard of living with unrelated females whose own children are competing with those of co-wives for limited resources.

Clinton's *It Takes a Village* was supposed to be based on an African proverb. But even in African villages, kids do better in a nuclear family than when getting care from an extended family or others in the village.

***

Strong family structures exist all over the world, but the nuclear family developed only in Western Europe during the last millennium. A couple of the big causes were the medieval economic system of manorialism and the Christian abolition of cousin marriages, polygamy, and divorce. These forces combined to break down tribes and clans and to organize farms around self-sufficient nuclear families. The serfs developed a future-time orientation, a belief in the rule of law, and a regard for family autonomy.

Contrary to the feminist dog-in-the-manger attitude that homemaker wives are oppressed by the patriarchy, wives were always honored in the American nuclear family. After Alexis de Tocqueville made his famous trip across America in the 1830s, he wrote in his *Democracy in America*:

> As for myself, I do not hesitate to avow that although the women of the United States are confined within the narrow circle of domestic life, and their situation is in some respects one of extreme dependence, I have nowhere seen woman occupying a loftier position; and if I were asked, now that I am drawing to the close of this work, in which I have spoken of so many important things done by the Americans, to what the singular prosperity and growing strength of that people ought mainly to be attributed, I should reply: To the superiority of their women.[33]

Western Europe is also the origin of many great ideas, such as individualism, private property, personal freedom, and capitalism. America got these concepts from western European settlers, and the concepts are most appreciated in cultures with nuclear families.

America is now in the midst of a grand social experiment to abolish the nuclear family. It is being done with changes to marriage law, government incentives, public moral and cultural attitudes, immigration policy, and even tax and other economic policies. The trends started slowly in the 1960s, accelerated in the 1970s and '80s, and President Obama was reelected in 2012 in large part based on promises to continue those trends. The American people will have a chance to change course in the elections of 2014 and 2016.

2

FEMINISTS DISAVOW
THE FAMILY

When the feminists rushed into public attention in the 1970s, the general expectation was that their big issues would be equal pay for equal work and other policies to give political and financial advantages to women. However, the feminists' main punching bag turned out to be *The Adventures of Ozzie and Harriet*, the long-running TV sitcom about the daily life of a typical American family. "Ozzie and Harriet" became a favorite feminist epithet; the feminists tried to caricature their opponents as old fogeys. Other family-oriented TV sitcoms of that era, like *Father Knows Best* and *Leave It to Beaver*, also came under their scorn.

At first, it wasn't clear what those TV shows had to do with feminist goals such as amending the US Constitution. We gradually learned that the feminists were bent on using the Equal Rights Amendment (ERA) to destroy the values exhibited on those TV programs, especially marriage and the traditional American family.

The younger generation doesn't remember Ozzie and Harriet, but the feminists carried on so much against them that those names have gone into our language as synonyms for traditional gender roles and relationships. *Naples News* reported in 2013: "Southwest Florida is hatching some new reality TV stars. Two bald eagles—nicknamed Ozzie and Harriet—and their two offspring are becoming viral video sensations from their nest in Lee County."[1]

As mentioned in chapter 1, the feminists' direct attack on the American family was launched with the publication and big sale of Betty Friedan's 1963 book, *The Feminine Mystique*, which brought the antifamily notions of Simone de Beauvoir to an American audience. Beauvoir, a bitter intellectual who never married and had no experience with marriage, is recognized in college women's studies courses as the original spokeswoman for the feminist movement. Her book *The Second Sex* is a lengthy and tedious tirade against the full-time homemaker. Denying a woman's right to be a full-time homemaker, Beauvoir famously said, "We don't believe that any woman should have this choice. No woman should be authorized to stay at home to raise her children . . . precisely because if there is such a choice, too many women will make that one."[2] Any woman who did make that choice, she said, was a "parasite."

Labeling the full-time homemaker a "parasite," Freidan urged her to escape from the home and find a more fulfilling job in the workforce. She described the homemaker as suffering from an ailment "that has no name."[3] Indeed, it had no name because it was a figment of Friedan's imagination and a product of her own unhappy marriage.

Decades later, Ruth Bader Ginsburg, a radical, doctrinaire feminist, was confirmed as a justice of the Supreme Court by ninety-six senators who lacked the nerve to question her about her damaging paper trail. A report written by her, Brenda Feigen-Fasteau, and fifteen Columbia law students in 1977, entitled *Sex Bias in the U.S. Code*, was published by the US Commission on Civil Rights to persuade reluctant states to ratify the Equal Rights Amendment. The report identified one of ERA's goals as disavowing the American family:

> Congress and the President should direct their attention to the concept that pervades the Code: that the adult world is (and should be) divided into two classes—independent men, whose

primary responsibility is to win bread for a family, and dependent women, whose primary responsibility is to care for children and household. This concept must be eliminated from the Code if it is to reflect the equality principle.[4]

Feminism cultivates the attitude that a woman must put her own self-fulfillment above every other value. That attitude is not compatible with marriage and motherhood, and it does not produce happiness. Further, the feminists' goal is not achievement for women, or they would be lauding successful women such as Sarah Palin, Michele Bachmann, the late Margaret Thatcher, Diane Black, and Marsha Blackburn as role models. They do not. Not one of these women is a feminist.

If you are a feminist, perhaps you might like to move to Communist Cuba, which the media have proclaimed is the most feminist country in the Western Hemisphere. Cuba is the number-three country in the world for having women in parliament; nearly 49 percent of Cuba's members of parliament are female.[5]

The major goal of the women's liberation movement is to move all wives out of the home and into the labor force. The feminist view is that caring for children, even your own, is demeaning work for an educated woman.

So what are the feminists complaining about now that women are half of the labor force? They want workforce rules to be changed to be more female friendly. (These are the same feminists who claimed for years that there is no difference between males and females.) Feminists demand that the taxpayers provide high-quality day care and paid family leave, and that laws prohibit employers from ordering women to work overtime (as men are often required to do). They also want laws to force men to assume half of the household and baby-care duties, but they haven't achieved that goal yet.

The feminist goal is *not* fair or equal treatment for women, but gender interchangeability and the redistribution of power from men to women—not all women, of course; only to feminists who know how to play by rules they have invented.

Before the feminist movement burst on the scene in the 1970s, there were literally hundreds of US laws that gave advantages or protections to women based on society's common-sense recognition of the facts of life, human nature, and obvious differences between men and women. These included the obligation of the husband to support his wife and provide her with a home, the prohibition against statutory rape, the Mann Act (which protected women from being trafficked), special protections for widows (one state gave widows a property tax exemption and another prescribed triple penalties against anyone who cheated a widow), and laws that made it a misdemeanor to use profanity in the presence of a woman.

Feminists oppose respect and benefits for full-time homemakers. Their antifamily, anti-marriage, anti-motherhood, anti-full-time-homemaker ideology continues to be articulated by their icon, Gloria Steinem. In an ABC radio interview on January 16, 2003, she asserted that married women are not "whole people," with "their own names" and "their own lives," and that a woman becomes a "semi-person" when she marries. She still spouts the 1960s feminist line that wives pay "the price of marriage" by giving up their own identities and names and adopting "their husband's identity."

Feminists are not interested in gender equality. Their goals are the feminization and subordination of men in order to dismantle the "patriarchy." Their constant whine is that women are "victims." They have launched a broadside attack on such basic precepts as equality under the law, judicial neutrality, presumption of innocence until proven guilty, and proof beyond a reasonable doubt as the standard of evidence required for conviction of a crime.

A 1991 Ninth Circuit Court of Appeals decision replaced the common law "reasonable man" standard with a "reasonable woman" test, embracing the feminist notion that men and women don't see the same events in the same way. The court declared that the old common law standard "tends to systematically ignore the experiences of women."[6]

The feminists want the victim rather than the law to define the offense. It used to be against the law to speak "any obscene, profane, indecent, vulgar, suggestive or immoral message" to a woman or girl. Feminists repealed that law, but now they argue that it's just as actionable for a man to call a woman *honey* or *baby* as to call her a *bitch*. They demand an "unreasonable woman" rule. Feminists seek to establish the standard that offenses against women should be defined (not objectively, but subjectively) on the basis of how a woman feels instead of on what a man really did.

Those who try to understand the peculiar ideology and goals of the feminists would find it instructive to watch a couple of their favorite movies. *The Hours* (2002) is a dreary and depressing tale that exalts selfishness and makes heroines out of three women who betray their marital promises, abandon faithful husbands, flout moral standards, and walk out on the duties of motherhood. Feminists like this movie because they admire a woman who seeks her own identity apart from any man.

But *The Hours* actually dramatizes the folly of feminist ideology. The movie shows that the narcissistic pursuit of personal happiness by the three female leads, Virginia Woolf, Laura Brown, and Clarissa Vaughan, produces only loneliness and even leads to suicide.

Another favorite feminist movie, which a CBS-TV movie critic proclaimed "the best picture of the year by far," was *Mona Lisa Smile* (2003). It was a sanctimonious, feminist homily preaching salvation through modern art and making one's own career choices—as long as they do not include marriage and motherhood. The movie proved again that the feminists are an unhappy bunch whose lifestyle leads to loneliness. The heroine, played by Julia Roberts, ends up single and jobless on a slow boat to Europe, having tossed aside the latest of her faithless lovers.

INFLUENCE OF MARXISM

Since some feminist leaders had early training in Marxism, notably Betty Friedan and Bella Abzug, it is relevant to note the Communist view of marriage. Karl Marx urged "Abolition of the family!" in his 1848 *Communist Manifesto*. He argued that the family is based on "capital" and "private gain," which were dirty words in his lexicon. He particularly objected to parents being able to educate their children, and he called the "hallowed co-relation of parent and child . . . all the more disgusting."[7]

Marx and Friedrich Engels theorized that family structure was essential to the development of Western civilization, and that marriage was partially a system for the orderly inheritance of property. Marx believed that social revolution would eliminate the need for private property, so marriage and family would no longer be needed. The Russian Revolution introduced a grand experiment to restructure the family.

> The Russian Central Executive Committee of Soviets ratified the Code on Marriage, the Family, and Guardianship in October 1918, one year after the Bolsheviks took power. . . . Revolutionary jurists believed children, the elderly, and the disabled would be supported under socialism by the state; housework would be socialized and waged; and women would no longer be economically dependent on men. The family, stripped of its social functions, would "wither away."[8]

These changes created more problems than they solved, and the family did not wither away. A few years later, the Soviets had to pass laws reversing some of these changes.

The *New Yorker* in 2013 published a glowing tribute to the late Shulamith Firestone, one of the radical feminist leaders in the late 1960s and early 1970s. The eight-thousand-word article, called "Death of a Revolutionary," identified the Marxist roots of the feminist movement for which Betty Friedan became the driving force. The *New Yorker* credentialed Firestone's feminism by publishing pictures of her at the beach, reading Simone de Beauvoir's *The Second Sex* and marching with Gloria Steinem. The publication also credited Firestone with changing the 1920s women's movement, whose goal was women's right to vote, into the radical, antifamily movement of the 1970s led by Friedan. The *New Yorker's* words:

> Firestone was best known for her writing. . . . *The Dialectic of Sex* reinterpreted Marx, Engels, and Freud to make a case that a "sexual class system" ran deeper than any other social or economic divide. The traditional family structure, Firestone argued, was at the core of women's oppression. "Unless revolution uproots the basic social organization, the biological family—the vinculum through which the psychology of power can always be smuggled—the tapeworm of exploitation will never be annihilated," Firestone wrote. She elaborated, with characteristic bluntness: "Pregnancy is barbaric" . . . childhood is a "supervised nightmare." . . .
>
> "The end goal of feminist revolution must be, unlike that of the first feminist movement, not just the elimination of male privilege but of the sex distinction itself: genital difference between human beings would no longer matter culturally." . . .
>
> She envisioned a world in which women might be liberated by artificial reproduction outside the womb; in which collectives took the place of families.[9]

THE MARRIAGE GAP

Fewer and fewer Americans are getting married. Married couples now represent the minority of American households. For the first time ever, the majority of women are living without a husband. One factor driving this trend is the changing ratio of college-educated women to college-educated men. Fewer college-educated women are able to find college-educated men to marry.

Many of these women are choosing not to marry at all rather

than marry a non-college-educated man who may earn less income. Funny thing about women: even when they hold well-paying and prestigious jobs in the workforce, they still want a husband who earns more so they can drop out of the workforce at any time. Thirty years ago, wives earned more than their husbands in only 16 percent of marriages, but now it's 25 percent and continuing to rise.[10]

Many non-college-educated men are not interested in marrying college-educated women, so they find it increasingly difficult to get married. Thirty years ago, only 6 percent of men without college degrees had never married. Now it's about 18 percent and still rising. The problem is that there are fewer and fewer women without college degrees for them to marry. And even those women are trying to marry college-educated men with better financial prospects.

It's increasingly difficult for a husband without a college degree to support a wife, because millions of well-paying blue-collar jobs have moved overseas to low-wage countries. In America, twice as many black women as black men have university degrees, and 70 percent of black women have no husband.[11]

Most men are not eager to be full-time or even part-time stay-at-home dads. When the wife is the family breadwinner and also does the household duties, she often decides that she simply does not need a husband.

Feminist Katie Roiphe resents the disapproval she gets from others because she is a single mom:

> Conservatives will no doubt be elaborately hysterical over the breakdown of morals among the women of Lorain, but they will be missing the major point, which is that however one feels about it, the facts of American family life no longer match its prevailing fantasies. . . . One has to recognize that marriage is very rapidly becoming only one way to raise children.[12]

The breakdown of the American family will not be reversed by blaming the morals of single moms. There are just too many cultural and financial trends favoring that lifestyle. As long as we encourage women to follow Europe in accepting what they regard as "a rational recognition of the vicissitudes of love," we will have more single moms and all the consequential and expensive social problems. Those trends cannot be changed unless we stop providing incentives for single motherhood.

In 2012 the *Los Angeles Times* reported that father-daughter dances and mother-son ball games, cherished hallmarks of Americana, were banned in a Rhode Island school district after they were targeted by the American Civil Liberties Union (ACLU). The ACLU asserted that such events violate the state's gender-discrimination law. The ACLU challenged their existence following a complaint from a single mom who said her daughter was prevented from attending a father-daughter dance in the Cranston Public Schools district.[13] The ACLU explained:

> The school district recognized that in the 21st Century, public schools have no business fostering the notion that girls prefer to go to formal dances while boys prefer baseball games. This type of gender stereotyping only perpetuates outdated notions of "girl" and "boy" activities and is contrary to federal law. [Parent-teacher organizations] remain free to hold family dances and other events, but the time has long since passed for public school resources to encourage stereotyping from the days of Ozzie and Harriet.[14]

Even the ACLU is targeting poor old Ozzie and Harriet!

Many feminists not only seek to promote their own feminist views of sex and relationships; they want to destroy traditional marriage so they can achieve their goals. Getting full-time homemakers out of the home has been a longtime and primary feminist goal. Feminists fear career competition from men who have the advantage of stay-at-home wives. One particularly aggressive study, titled "Marriage Structure and Resistance to the Gender Revolution in the Workplace," was quoted in a recent *Eagle Forum Legislative Alert*: the study asserted there is resistance to the gender revolution in the workplace from married male employees who have stay-at-home wives. The men with the stay-at-home wives were more likely to see the benefits of such an arrangement and less likely to favor affirmative action for women at work. The study was intended to show the necessity of destroying the traditional family if women are to reach their ambitions.[15]

Sheryl Sandberg, the COO of Facebook, received extraordinary publicity about her book called *Lean In: Women, Work, and the Will to Lead*. She's a forty-three-year-old billionaire and mother of two who is eager to give advice to other women. She wants to liberate women from the stereotypes of gender, so her book is larded with the usual feminist propaganda. She seems to believe that women who opt out or "lean back toward home" are victims of sexism and social stereotyping, not exercising a natural or intelligent choice.

Sandberg presents numbers that she asserts prove current discrimination against women. Of the 195 independent countries in the world, only 17 are led by women. Women hold just 20 percent of seats in parliaments globally.[16] We don't know if she would mandate undemocratic quotas to achieve equal numbers.

New data from the Pew Research Center shared with the *Atlantic* found that the vast majority of married mothers do not want to work full time, and that married mothers who cut back at work to accommodate their families' needs tend to be happier.[17]

Feminist antagonism toward smart women who leave the workforce to take care of their children was on display when the social media erupted with a torrent of attacks on the *New York Times* for the first sentence of its obituary of Yvonne Brill. According to the *Times*, Brill, a brilliant rocket scientist who invented a propulsion system to keep communications satellites from slipping out of their orbits, "made a mean beef stroganoff, followed her husband from job to job and took eight years off from work to raise three children."[18] The attacks on the *Times*' alleged sexism were so virulent that the *Times* removed the offensive mention of "beef stroganoff" from its website.[19]

Some women have combined a successful career with the role

of wife and mother. But that kind of success requires a cooperative husband, whom the feminists usually lack, as Gloria Steinem noted in a bitter comment when she launched a documentary about her life. Sneering at the two women she apparently despises the most, she attempted to demean Sarah Palin and Michele Bachmann as women "only a man could love."[20] That's right; men do love the nonfeminists.

The most scholarly book written about the feminist movement is *Domestic Tranquility: A Brief Against Feminism* by F. Carolyn Graglia. She read all those tiresome books and articles by feminist leaders Betty Friedan, Germaine Greer, Kate Millett, Gloria Steinem, and Simone de Beauvoir, and concluded that the principal goal of feminism from the get-go has been "the status degradation of the housewife's role."[21] Its leaders seek to make being a homemaker economically untenable and socially disdained. Mrs. Graglia documented the fact that all branches of feminism have been united in the belief that a woman can find identity and fulfillment only by a career in the workforce.

Acquiescence in devaluing the role of full-time homemaker has become part of our culture, taught in women's studies courses and endlessly reiterated in the media. Politically correct dogma teaches that modern women should all be in the workforce because being *only* a homemaker is a wasted life and an impediment to a successful career, and that caring for one's own babies is not worth the time of an educated woman.

In November 2009, feminists used their wide access to the media, led by Maria Shriver as spokesperson, to reproach Americans who stuck to "an outdated model of the American family." They gave fulsome publicity to *The Shriver Report: A Woman's Nation Changes Everything*, published by the left-wing think tank, the Center for American Progress. The four-hundred-page *Shriver Report* boasted that we are now living in a "woman's world," and "emergent economic power gives women a new seat at the table—at the head of the table."[22] The female left argues for women to be independent of men, self-supporting, sexually uninhibited, and liberated from the obligations of marriage and the duties of motherhood.

However, the result is that women are chronically dissatisfied. The National Bureau of Economic Research reports, "As women have gained more freedom, more education, and more power, they have become less happy."[23]

New York magazine in 2013 dumped a new wave of feminist scorn on the full-time homemaker by labeling her the "Retro Wife." *Retro* refers to women who want to take us back to the Ozzie and Harriet era of the 1950s. The magazine described (in obvious feminist distress) the story of a thirty-three-year-old woman with a super education who walked away from her high-profile, high-paid position to care for her two toddlers. Even though she identifies herself as "a flaming liberal," she is nevertheless content with her new domestic lifestyle.

The author of *New York*'s article was devastated. She whined, "Feminism has fizzled . . . This is the revelation of the moment . . . a cause of grief for some, fury for others" because "what was once feminist blasphemy is now conventional wisdom." The grieving author admitted, "Mothers instinctively want to devote themselves to home more than fathers do." She concluded, "This is not the retreat from high-pressure workplaces of a previous generation but rather a more active awakening to the virtues of the way things used to be."[24]

The *New York* article spun off a lot of writing by feminists who vented their anger at being reminded of gender differences. Feminist Taylor Marsh described it like this: "*New York* magazine is one giant conservative fake-out that could have been posted on NRO or any conservative political magazine."[25] (Marsh is the author of a one-woman show titled *Weeping for J.F.K.*) Even *Forbes* magazine joined the pack to attack the Retro Wife, stating that she "threatens America's economy" and makes us feel "like we are stepping back in time."[26] We assume that means stepping back to the time of Ozzie and Harriet.

Another writer for *New York* magazine, Jonathan Chait, offered his helpful advice to feminists who complain that husbands don't do their share of household chores. In his response, headlined "A Really Easy Answer to the Feminist Housework Problem," he wrote, "The assumption of much of the feminist commentary surrounding household chores assumes that there is a correct level of cleanliness in a heterosexual relationship, and that level is determined by the female. I think a little cultural relativism would improve the debate. . . . Feminists want women to work like men do, right? Why not try living like men, too? Put down the duster. It'll be okay." Chait suggests that women should just act like men and ignore the lack of super household cleanliness. After all, don't feminists argue gender interchangeability? Before he was married, Chait says, he was content to live in a group house with newspapers for carpeting and pizza boxes stacked to the ceiling. And, "We didn't dust. Ever."[27]

DEVALUING FATHERS

Men have been adversely affected by the oppressive omnipresence of feminism in school, college, and the media. One Chicago law school student blogged: "I firmly believe one of the consequences of the feminist revolution has been that men in my generation are raised without a strong self-identity, and in essence grow up to be little more than boys looking for mothers."[28]

A major purpose of feminist ideology is to devalue fathers. Barbara Kay addressed this feminist bias in the *New York Daily News*:

> Why do fathers matter so much? Because fatherhood makes men out of boys, for one thing. And because typically they offer children a just as necessary but different kind of love and guidance from what mothers bestow.
>
> Mothers give their children unconditional love. It can be argued that children need their mother's love more in infancy and very early childhood than they need their father's. But from the moment they step into the world beyond their doorstep, their need for a father or father figure grows exponentially. They need his protection and guidance in handling the complexities and

competing demands of school, adult authorities and sometimes difficult peers. Fathers give boys a role model for manliness and girls respect for themselves. Fathers give children strategies for negotiating their way in the world. They set standards to be respected. Their love may even seem conditional on those standards being met. That's a good thing.

Father absence is devastating for children. Exhaustive peer-reviewed research confirms that the absence of a father is the single most reliable predictor for a whole roster of negative outcomes: low self-esteem, parental alienation, high school dropout (71% are fatherless), truancy, early sexual activity, promiscuity, teen pregnancy, gang membership, imprisonment (85% of jailed youth are fatherless), drug abuse, homelessness (90% of runaway children have an absent father), a 40 times higher risk of sexual abuse and 100 times higher risk of fatal abuse. . . .

Why haven't the facts around fatherlessness made a dent in the family law system? In a word, ideology. Judges aren't trained in sociology or psychology, but they take courses in "social context"—and the people who write their training manuals toe the feminist line that where children are concerned, mothers mainly have rights, while fathers mainly have responsibilities.[29]

President Obama's campaign ad called "The Life of Julia" shows how the feminists and their friends are trying to make fathers unnecessary. Julia has a child. But there is no father in the ad. With the aid of government, Julia enjoys life as a single mother.

THE DAY CARE BATTLES

Feminist ideology teaches that a major example of the oppression of women by the patriarchy is society's expectation that mothers should care for their own babies. According to Betty Friedan, the duties of a housewife and mother are "endless, monotonous, unrewarding" and "peculiarly suited to the capacities of feeble-minded girls."[30] This ideology led directly to feminist insistence that taxpayers provide (in Ruth Bader Ginsburg's words) "a comprehensive program of government supported child care."[31] Feminists made strenuous efforts to achieve the goal of federally financed day care for all children by congressional legislation in 1971, 1977, 1989, and 1997, and by Barack Obama in 2013.

Articulating vintage feminism in the 1973 *Harvard Educational Review*, Hillary Clinton wrote disparagingly about wives who are in "a dependency relationship" which, she said, is akin to "slavery and the Indian reservation system."[32]

The feminists are at war with Mother Nature, and Mother Nature is still winning. A 2013 Pew Research Center national poll reported that 61 percent of mothers said they would prefer to work part time or not at all, whereas 75 percent of men preferred full-time work.[33] The gender gap the feminists gripe about is a good gender gap because it gives babies what they most need: face time with their own mothers.

The average workweek for nonagricultural wage and salary female workers 16 years and older in 1995 was 35.8 hours while for men it was 42.1 hours.[34] Women, on average, choose fewer hours of work and less demanding specialties even after they train for careers. The reason they make these choices, and consequently earn less than men do, is that some, maybe most, of them have babies, and as Pew's research has demonstrated, most mothers prefer the mommy track. Despite the long-running feminist propaganda that baby care isn't worth the time of an educated woman and that this burden, imposed by the patriarchy, should be lifted from their shoulders by taxpayers, most women still want time off from a workforce job to be with their children.

FEMINIST DEMANDS FOR DAY CARE

In 1970, the National Organization for Women (NOW) published a comprehensive pamphlet setting forth feminist demands, called "Revolution: Tomorrow Is NOW." NOW demanded that "child care must become a political priority" for "all economic and social groups," and endorsed the Comprehensive Child Development bill (known as the Mondale-Brademas bill), which would have created a multibillion-dollar national day care system. It was passed by Congress in 1971 but famously vetoed by President Richard Nixon. The feminists have been crying about that veto ever since. As late as 2012, feminists used some of their media time on C-SPAN to lambaste Nixon for that veto. Even Rep. Nancy Pelosi, on April 29, 2013, was still whining about Richard Nixon's 1971 veto of day care forty-two years earlier.

Despite his many faults, Nixon understood the radical anti-family nature of turning the raising of preschool children over to the government. His veto message stated:

> Good public policy requires that we enhance rather than diminish both parental authority and parental involvement with children— particularly in those decisive early years when social attitudes and a conscience are formed, and religious and moral principles are first inculcated. . . . The legislation would create, ex nihilo, a new army of bureaucrats. . . . For the Federal Government to plunge headlong financially into supporting child development would commit the vast moral authority of the National Government to the side of communal approaches to child rearing over the family-centered approach.[35]

Although feminists are still complaining about President Nixon's veto of an expensive federal program to make day care a middle-class entitlement, his action was popular then and still is. The majority of Americans don't want their tax dollars to pay for babysitters for other people's children.

When the feminists gathered for their huge tax-funded conference in Houston in November 1977, called International Women's Year, taxpayer-paid day care for all children was one of their four hot-button issues. The others were ratification of the Equal Rights Amendment, taxpayer-funded abortion, and the gay rights agenda.

The massive media coverage of the IWY conference, which told the country the antifamily goals of the feminist movement, turned out to be a political and public relations disaster for feminism.

In 1989 the feminists orchestrated a massive third attempt to make day care a new middle-class entitlement. As Yogi Berra would say, it was déjà vu all over again. Government day care was supported by all the elites of the feminist movement. They wanted the family pattern to include a comprehensive program of taxpayer-paid child care.

The Children's Defense Fund led the battle for what was then called the ABC bill (Act for Better Child Care), a demand that the government take over the raising of children. The chief guru of that federal day care lobby was Edward Zigler, a psychology professor at Yale University and director of Yale's Bush Center for Child Development and Social Policy. He advocated a national day care system costing $75 to $100 billion annually. Zigler wanted day care centers to function as "schools of the twenty-first century" and "family resource centers." He wanted day care to extend as long as the workdays of mothers and fathers and to provide before- and after-school care as well as summer care for children up to age twelve. He deplored the "hodge-podge of profits, nonprofits, and family daycare homes" and the fact that 60 percent to 75 percent of day cares are not registered with the government. But the American people still opposed turning their babies over to government care.

In 1997 Hillary Rodham Clinton staged what a White House spokesman called a "focused comeback" to proclaim what she described as a "frontier issue." She followed the usual liberal for-mula: proclaim a "crisis," wrap it in "children," and try to intimidate Congress into funding a new middle-class entitlement.

Hillary's day care "crisis" was carefully orchestrated by all the bigwigs of the Clinton administration before an exclusive audi-ence in the East Room of the White House. Attendees included government officials who could influence public policy on day care, reporters expected to write favorably about day care, a few academic types paraded as "experts," and a large number of day care providers who could be turned into lobbying troops to gather the cash spoils of federally subsidized day care. The audience also included two Democratic senators who liked to pose as models of family propriety: Ted Kennedy and Chris Dodd.

Marian Wright Edelman, president of the Children's Defense Fund, the chief lobby for the "village" to raise children, said she hoped that Hillary's conference would be a launching pad for significant reinvestments in day care. In the Clintonian lexicon, *village* is the code word for "government," and *investment* is a synonym for "taxes."

However, the feminists lost again because Americans just don't want to pay taxes to provide babysitters for other people's children. American mothers and fathers prefer tax cuts or tax credits so they can spend their own money and make their own child-care decisions. The 1988–90 debate ended with modest tax credits for children. No doubt it came as a shock to the feminists when *Time* magazine reported that "a majority of both men and women still say it is best for children to have a father working and a mother at home."[36]

Bernard Goldberg lifted the curtain on how the media peddle the feminist promotion of day care in his best-selling book *Bias*. He wrote that "the most important story you never saw on TV" is "the terrible things that are happening to America's children" because "mothers have opted for work outside of the house over taking care of their children at home."[37]

A Heritage Foundation report by Jenet Jacob Erickson, PhD, concluded:

> The more time children spend in any of a variety of non-maternal care arrangements across the first 4.5 years of life, the more externalizing problems and conflict with adults they manifest at 54 months of age and in kindergarten, as reported by mothers, caregivers, and teachers. . . . More time in care not only predicts problem behavior measured on a continuous scale but at-risk

(though not clinical) levels of problem behavior, as well as assertiveness, disobedience, and aggression. It should also be noted that these correctional findings also imply that lower levels of problems were associated with less time in child care.[38]

The US Department of Labor, Bureau of Labor Statistics, reported in 2009 that nearly one in four children with a working mother goes to day care, and that seven in ten mothers with children under age eighteen are in the labor force. Children who spend longer hours (thirty hours a week) in day care are more likely to exhibit problematic social behaviors, including aggression, conflict, poorer work habits, and risk-taking behaviors throughout childhood and into adolescence.

The negative effects of day care are more persistent for children who spend long hours in center-care settings. Although high-quality day care has some positive effects, it does not reduce the negative effects associated with long hours in day care. Mothers whose children are in full-time day care show a decrease in sensitivity toward their children during their early years.

Perhaps as an attempt to shift public discussion away from the Obamacare train wreck as well as toady to the feminists, in 2013 Barack Obama announced support for universal tax-paid day care for preschoolers, now rebranded as pre-K, at an annual cost of $75 billion.

Day care lobbyists always cite the Perry Preschool Project, conducted fifty years ago in Ypsilanti, Michigan, as their model. But the Perry Project was very expensive (nineteen thousand dollars a year per child in today's dollars), was taught by highly trained teachers, and has never been replicated, so it is not scientifically credible. One additional fact, which came to light only in 2013, is that the 123 kids in the project all had stay-at-home moms. And the project included daily home visits.

Another fabulously expensive day care project into which taxpayers have poured $8 billion is Head Start. In 2010, the Department of Health and Human Services released the findings of its Impact Study, which tracked Head Start kids through kindergarten and first grade. Head Start showed little or no positive effect and some harmful effects. In 2013, the liberal Brookings Institution admitted that the supposed benefits of pre-K programs often "don't last even until the end of kindergarten." Brookings' lead research analyst commented, "I see these findings as devastating for advocates of the expansion of state pre-K programs."[39]

It's time to get the facts about day care's past failures before we "invest" any more taxpayer money in the hopes that pre-K will raise school achievement. How about a study to find out if kids do better in school if they live with their own mother and father, like the kids in the famous Perry Project?

The better way to support the educational development of young children is to provide a tax credit to married parents of children of an eligible age. This could then be used to pay for preschool, other educational services, or educational materials that parents could use with the child at home. Such a tax credit would reinforce the policy that parents, rather than government, have the primary right to raise their own children.

Sen. Elizabeth Warren (D-MA) attracted a lot of free publicity for her book *The Two-Income Trap: Why Middle-Class Mothers and Fathers Are Going Broke*.[40] Her thesis is that the middle class is having a hard time in the present economy because the two-income family (when wives enter the labor force) really has less spendable income than the traditional one-income family after paying for the basics. Her reasons? Because the two-income couple bought a house they could not afford with only 3 percent down, a second car, and day care for a kid or two. Her solution? Don't have children, because they cost money, and it's mostly parents with kids who are filing for bankruptcy.

THE DOGMA OF ABORTION

Abortion is the litmus test of whether or not you are feminist. Feminists have even made it the test of whether a political candidate is pro-women or is waging a "war on women." Resolutions passed by the National Organization for Women (NOW) repeatedly include language proclaiming that abortion is a basic fundamental right of every woman.

Abortion law traditionally had been in the domain of the states, as was nearly all criminal law. Beginning in 1967, seventeen states weakened their antiabortion laws in various ways. The tide turned against abortion in 1970, as pro-abortion bills were introduced and defeated in thirty-three states. Even the New York legislature repealed its two-year-old abortion-on-demand law (only to have the repeal vetoed by Gov. Nelson Rockefeller). In November 1972, proabortion referenda were defeated in North Dakota by 78 percent and in Michigan by 61 percent.

Then, on January 22, 1973, the US Supreme Court, in the preeminent act of judicial supremacy, struck down the antiabortion laws of all fifty states. As Justice Byron White wrote in dissent, *Roe v. Wade* was "an exercise of raw judicial power. . . . I find nothing in the language or history of the Constitution to support the Court's judgment."[41] For the next forty years, hard-fought battles about abortion were waged in Congress, state legislatures, and candidates' campaigns for public office.

In January 2013, *Time* magazine clobbered the feminists with a sensational cover proclaiming in oversize type: "40 Years Ago, Abortion Rights Activists won epic victory with *Roe v. Wade*. THEY'VE BEEN LOSING EVER SINCE." Detailing the success of various federal and state laws, *Time* asserted, "obtaining an abortion is now more difficult than at any point since the 1970s."[42] Pro-life activists have successfully lobbied for regulations that limit access, require waiting periods or ultrasounds, impose safety regulations on clinics, and require minors to get a parent's permission. Fewer doctors are willing to perform abortions, and fewer abortion clinics are open for business. Gallup polls report that support for abortion rights is fading, particularly among young Americans. More people now identify themselves as pro-life rather than pro-choice.

Then, in 2014 a federal court upheld a Texas law that prohibits abortion unless the abortionist has hospital privileges within thirty miles, so that the abortionist can remain available to handle any complications he or she causes instead of letting those costs fall on the taxpayers in emergency rooms. This is the most effective law that states can pass to reduce abortions; nineteen abortion clinics have closed in Texas because of this law.

Nevertheless, the feminists still consider abortion the fundamental, irreducible first commandment of feminism. It's usually shrouded in words such as choice, or reproductive freedom, or privacy, or even equal rights, but to feminist leaders, abortion is much more than that. It is the keystone of feminist power over men. As Gloria Steinem opined, the "right of reproductive freedom . . . attacks the very foundation of patriarchy."[43] Supreme Court Justice Anthony Kennedy, writing for the court in *Casey v. Planned Parenthood*, explained the centrality of abortion to feminism: "The ability of women to participate equally in the economic and social life of the Nation has been facilitated by their ability to control their reproductive lives."[44]

The abortion dogma has a strong antimale element. Feminists persuaded the Supreme Court to rule not only that the father has no say-so as to whether his own baby is killed, but even that the woman has a constitutional right *not* to tell her husband that his baby is being killed. This last point is hard to defend and is widely misunderstood, even by the author of the opinion. Here is an excerpt from a *Fresh Air* interview with . . .

GROSS: In *Casey v. Planned Parenthood*, which was a decision in Pennsylvania about a state's right to add restrictions on access to abortion, you had harsh words for Judge Alito. This was before he was a Supreme Court justice, but he had written part of the decision in *Casey*. In his decision he upheld a certain restriction, which was that a woman had to seek her husband's approval before getting an abortion. A wife had to seek her husband's approval. And in your decision in the Supreme Court overturning that aspect of the decision, you called that view repugnant to our present understanding of marriage and to the nature of the rights secured by the Constitution. Women do not lose their constitutionally protected liberty when they marry. Can you elaborate on that at all?

O'CONNOR: No. I don't think I'll try.[45]

Whether you agree with abortion or not, *Casey* was one of a series of anti-marriage and anti-father decisions by the US Supreme Court. Judge Alito had wanted only to uphold a requirement for spousal notification, not permission. O'Connor wrote in *Casey* to justify wives not ever telling their husbands about aborting their own child, and O'Connor was not willing to defend her radical antifamily opinion.

Here is an example of the gender asymmetry of abortion law. Although a woman has the constitutional right to kill her unborn baby without even notifying the baby's father, the father can be prosecuted for first-degree murder if he gives the mother a pill to cause an abortion. The *New York Post* reported: "The 28-year-old son of a Florida fertility doctor has been charged by federal authorities with tricking his girlfriend into taking a pill used to induce labor and cause an abortion, killing the fetus she was carrying. John Andrew Welden was indicted Tuesday by a federal grand jury on charges of product tampering and first-degree murder and faces up to life in prison if convicted of the murder charge."[46]

The new Federal Reserve Board chairman, Janet Yellen, coauthored an economic study in 1996 that blamed the breakdown of the American family on the increased availability of abortion and contraceptives. Not that she is against these changes, as she is a typical liberal and said that "attempts to turn the technology clock backward by denying women access to abortion and contraception . . . would almost surely be . . . counterproductive."[47] Yellen wrote:

[Feminist sociologist Lillian Breslow] Rubin [1969], who studied working-class whites in San Francisco in the late 1960s, found that courtship was brief and quite likely to involve sexual activity. In the event of pregnancy, marriage occurred. One of her subjects expressed the matter succinctly and with the absence of doubt with which many social customs are unquestionably observed: "If a girl gets pregnant you married her. There wasn't no choice. So I married her." . . .

A second model illustrates another reason why the previous support system could have been eroded by the advent of female contraception and legal abortion. The fact that the birth of the baby is now a *choice* of the mother has implications for the decisions of the father. The sexual revolution, by making the birth of the child the *physical* choice of the mother, makes marriage and child support a *social* choice of the father. This second model explores how the decisions of the father depend upon the decisions and options of the mother. The logic of this model corresponds to what one contributor to the Internet wrote to the Dads' Rights Newsgroup: "Since the decision to have the child is solely up to the mother (see *Roe v. Wade*), I don't see how both parents have responsibility to that child. . . . When one person has the decision-making power, they alone have the responsibility to provide and care for that decision."[48]

A FEW HAVE SECOND THOUGHTS

Media and feminists continue to chant the lie that women are paid only seventy-seven cents for every dollar earned by men. However, most women really like the so-called wage gap because they want to marry a man who earns more than they do.[49]

Back in the 1980s, Susanna Mancini, a twenty-seven-year-old successful, well-paid lawyer, married her boyfriend and bore him two children. "She kept working when her first child was born and was promoted to a more senior position in Citibank after her second child arrived." Eventually, however, her career "succumbed," as Reuters oddly put it. This was no tragedy but a hypergamous happy ending. Mancini left the labor force because her husband was doing so well that he could afford to support the whole family: "She quit in 2005 when her six-digit income was overtaken by his seven-digit one."[50]

For Mancini, that was real liberation. She told the press, "There was a real opportunity to do other things that did not require being chained to a desk." In fact, an increasing number of affluent women with affluent husbands are casting off the chains of professional work. A Federal Reserve study reported that between 1993 and 2006, there was a decline in the workforce of college-educated women with similarly educated spouses.[51]

For women with lower levels of education, the picture is markedly different, as Charles Murray describes in *Coming Apart: The State of White America, 1960–2010* (Crown Forum, 2012). One-income households have become common at the lower end of the socioeconomic spectrum, but the reason is not hypergamy. Women are less likely to be married at all, and men are less likely to be in the labor force.

The feminist revolution that swept across America in the 1970s promoted the dream of a land in which at least half of corporate officers, Fortune 500 CEOs, partners in law firms, and doctors would be women. The feminist movement was always elitist; it was about getting political and corporate power for highly educated women.

But a funny thing happened on the way to achieving that promise. Feminism was mugged by the reality that most women don't seek those goals. How some of the best and the brightest are rejecting the career track laid out for them by the feminists was detailed in a 2003 article entitled "The Opt-Out Revolution" by Lisa Belkin in the persistently feminist *New York Times Magazine*. That's the same publication that earlier featured a cover glamorizing the feminists' number-one role model as Saint Hillary Clinton in radiant white robes.

Ms. Belkin described a group in Atlanta, all of whom had graduated from Princeton about twenty years earlier; earned advanced degrees in law or business from other prestigious institutions, such as Harvard or Columbia; and waited until their thirties to marry and have children because their careers were so exciting.

These women were typical of what was happening in America. For the last couple of decades, roughly half of MBAs, JDs, and MDs have been granted to women. In the feminist game plan, these are the very women who should rise to the top of the business and professional world, wielding the fantasy power attributed to the so-called 1 percent. As one of them told Ms. Belkin, what she wanted when she graduated was to be "a confirmed single person, childless, a world traveler."[52]

But of these ten Princeton graduates interviewed by Ms. Belkin at a book club meeting, five were not employed outside the home, one was in business with her husband, one was employed only part time, two were freelance, and the only one with a full-time job had no children. At the time of that interview, only 16 percent of corporate officers were women, only eight Fortune 500 companies had female CEOs, and only 38 percent of Harvard Business School 1980s female graduates were working full time.[53]

Feminist ideology for years has preached that women's failure to cross those thresholds of power is because women are held down by a "glass ceiling" imposed by a discriminatory and oppressive patriarchy. But these smart, talented, successful women told Ms. Belkin that they'd opted out of their accelerating careers voluntarily.

A cover story in the *Atlantic* magazine, July–August 2012, went viral under the title "Why Women Still Can't Have It All." The author, Anne-Marie Slaughter, a former State Department official, delivered a fatal blow to the feminist dogma that it's possible to pursue a demanding foreign policy career and raise a family simultaneously. Feminists teach that a career in the workforce is the only life worthy of an educated woman, and children should be just an afterthought. But when her teenage boys were going through a "rocky adolescence," she decided to value family over professional advancement.

However, still a feminist at heart, Slaughter wrote that the only real route to her goal of closing the leadership gap is to elect a woman president and fifty women senators to ensure that women are equally represented in the ranks of corporate executives and judicial leaders. Only then, she wrote, will we have "a society that works for everyone." Slaughter elaborated on her change of heart and career:

> Women of my generation have clung to the feminist credo we were raised with, even as our ranks have been steadily thinned by unresolvable tensions between family and career, because we are determined not to drop the flag for the next generation. But when many members of the younger generation have stopped listening, on the grounds that glibly repeating "you can have it all" is simply airbrushing reality, it is time to talk.[54]

Why you can't read such politically incorrect news in women's magazines was entertainingly explained in a book, *Spin Sisters: How the Women of the Media Sell Unhappiness and Liberalism to the Women of America*, by Myrna Blyth, who was editor-in-chief of *Ladies' Home Journal* for two decades. The Spin Sisters are the high-profile women in the media, both those who control the profitable women's magazines and the anorexic female hosts on television. They are all busy selling American women the ideology of victimhood, the attitude that women's lives are full of misery and threats, and that they suffer from a constant state of stress that keeps them unable to cope with life's ordinary irritations.

The whole premise of female victimhood is false. American women today live longer, healthier lives than ever, filled with a multitude of opportunities for education, travel, and employment. But the Spin Sisters have marketed victimhood for their own career advancement and a luxurious lifestyle.

Women's magazines of the 1950s and 1960s were helpful and hopeful; women didn't need Zoloft or Prozac. Ms. Blyth's magazine, *Ladies' Home Journal*, built its original circulation on the positive slogan, "Never underestimate the power of a woman." Today's Spin

Sisters tell women that they are living in a treacherous and stress-filled world, confronted by threats from everything from abusive husbands to contaminated foods in their refrigerators. Women's worry list of fears and woes includes everything from the weight of the world's problems to the weight of extra fat on themselves. A typical article in a women's magazine is "The Health Hazard in Your Handbag."[55]

Ms. Blyth describes how the Spin Sisters on the major networks (Barbara, Katie, Diane, Connie, etc.) are not really rivals but a Girls' Club with a mission. Abortion is their bonding factor; the Spin Sisters will never allow any challenge to it to emerge on their television screens or their magazine pages. Liberalism/progressivism is a large part of what women's magazines are selling.[56]

3

OUTLAWING THE FAMILY

The primary purpose of marriage is for a man and a woman voluntarily and jointly to assume the moral and legal responsibility for those little bundles of helpless humanity that appear in the course of human behavior. The connection between mother and baby is biological and obvious. Marriage connects the baby to his biological father.

Marriage is a status defined by law that is voluntarily accepted before witnesses. Bride and groom each promise to take the other "to have and to hold from this day forward, for better, for worse, for richer or for poorer, in sickness and in health, forsaking all others, to love and to cherish, till death do us part." Marriage as the union of a man and a woman is a centuries-old matter of law in the United States, which came to us from British law dating back centuries. Traditional marriage of a husband and a wife is fortified by a network of legal rights and duties spelled out in more than a thousand federal laws, some four hundred state laws, and thirty-seven state constitutional amendments.

Congress reinforced this historic definition in 1996 by enacting the Defense of Marriage Act (DOMA), signed by President Bill Clinton. It provides that when any federal law refers to marriage or spouse, "the word 'marriage' means only a legal union between one man and one woman as husband and wife, and the word 'spouse' refers only to a person of the opposite sex who is a husband or a wife," and also that no state can be forced to accept another state's different definition of marriage.[1] The Government Accountability Office compiled 1,138 federal rights and responsibilities that are contingent on this law's definition of marriage. The GAO report lists these federal laws in many categories, including taxation, Social Security, welfare, veterans, federal employees, and private employees. The GAO report states that the man-woman marital relationship is "integral" to the Social Security system and "pervasive" in our system of taxation.[2]

The 2012 Republican National Platform adopted in convention in Tampa, Florida, stated what Republicans believe are good policy and popular opinion:

> The institution of marriage is the foundation of civil society. Its success as an institution will determine our success as a nation. It has been proven by both experience and endless social science studies that traditional marriage is best for children. . . . The success of marriage directly impacts the economic well-being of individuals. Furthermore, the future of marriage affects freedom. The lack of family formation not only leads to more government costs, but also to more government control over the lives of its citizens in all aspects.[3]

When DOMA was challenged in court, President Obama refused to defend it, even though the US Constitution commands the president to "take Care that the Laws be faithfully executed."[4]

The 2013 Supreme Court marriage decisions involved the definition of marriage. In *United States v. Windsor*, Justice Samuel Alito explained in dissent that the court was redefining marriage in a way that de-emphasized or ignored children and their relationship to their parents, and instead concentrated on the sex and the sexual desires of the adults. He called this part of the campaign to devalue procreation and biological kinship so that marriage can include same-sex spouses:

> While modern cultural changes have weakened the link between marriage and procreation in the popular mind, there is no doubt that, throughout human history and across many cultures, marriage has been viewed as an exclusively opposite-sex institution and as one inextricably linked to procreation and biological kinship.
>
> The other, newer view is what I will call the "consent-based" vision of marriage, a vision that primarily defines marriage as the solemnization of mutual commitment—marked by a strong emotional attachment and sexual attraction—between two persons. At least as it applies to heterosexual couples, this view of marriage now plays a very prominent role in the popular understanding of the institution.
>
> Indeed, our popular culture is infused with this understanding of marriage. Proponents of same-sex marriage argue that because gender differentiation is not relevant to this vision, the exclusion of same-sex couples from the institution of marriage is rank discrimination.[5]

In the last couple of decades in the United States, changes have chipped away at marriage law to the point that children and parental responsibilities have little to do with marriage. After marriage law was decoupled from parenthood, gays argued that any two people who want to live together ought to be able to marry, and they are trying to make this a civil rights issue.

The *New York Times* boasts that "the United States is becoming a post-marital society," creating "new forms of semi-marriages," blurring the lines between marriage and cohabitation, and imitating European types of "Marriage Lite."[6] But marriage should not be redefined to mean merely two consenting persons agreeing to share quarters and start applying to the government and to employers for economic benefits. Marriage of a husband and wife should continue to be recognized as the essential unit of a stable society wherein husbands and wives commit to provide for the rearing of their children.

Children learn the most important lessons about how to relate to the opposite sex from observing how their parents interact with them and with each other in their daily lives. These crucial lessons will be denied to children raised by same-sex couples, who will never teach by their own example how to live with the opposite sex. It is very difficult to absorb these lessons from books or television or conversations with one's peers.

UNILATERAL DIVORCE

The American family was hit with a major attack in 1969 by a dramatic change in California's divorce law. Divorce is a matter of state, not federal, law. Before that time, in all states except Nevada, divorce required one spouse to present evidence of some fault in the other spouse. The court required such evidence of fault because marriage was considered a solemn contract, entered into before witnesses. Under the new California divorce law, signed by Gov. Ronald Reagan, dissolving the marriage contract became almost like checking a box for "Bye-bye; I'm out of here." Between 1969 and 1980, the number of divorces per year rose from 639,000 to 1,189,000.

Ronald Reagan's son Michael wrote in his book *Twice Adopted*: "Dad later said that he regretted signing the no-fault divorce bill and that he believed it was one of the worst mistakes he ever made in office. That law set into motion one of the most damaging social experiments in the history of our nation."[7]

The new California law, eagerly pushed by feminists and by divorce lawyers, was euphemistically but inaccurately called "no-fault" divorce; its proper name should have been "unilateral" divorce. It enables one spouse to get a divorce without the consent of, even over the objections of, the other spouse. The spouse trying to preserve the marriage always lost.

The argument for unilateral divorce was that it would end the acrimony in marriage breakups and possibly false assertions (about adultery, abandonment, violence, and so forth). But unilateral divorce did not eliminate false charges and countercharges; it simply transferred the nastiness to battles over child custody and financial support.

Divorce imposes heavy human costs, particularly on children. Michael Reagan wrote eloquently about his parents' divorce: "Divorce is where two adults take everything that matters to a child—the child's home, family, security, and sense of being loved and protected—and they smash it all up, leave it in ruins on the floor, then walk out and leave the child to clean up the mess."[8]

What the children of divorce have always known is now confirmed by research that shows that the adverse impact of divorce on children is often deep and long lasting, and it increases over time.

The feminist push for unilateral divorce was not merely to achieve easy and rapid liberation from marriage for housewives allegedly confined to the dead-end life of household duties; it was essential to the feminist goals of independence from men and empowerment of women. It served the major feminist goal of attempting to move all wives, whether divorced or still married, into the labor force. F. Carolyn Graglia summed up the new divorce law:

> Through the enactment of no-fault divorce, society warned women that they were expected to abandon their child-rearing role, cease being financially dependent on their husbands, and become self-supporting. Because they viewed the traditional family as women's oppressor, the feminist champions of no-fault divorce argued that women must pursue the careers which, feminists are convinced, can be the only source of identity and self-fulfillment. With this ideology, feminists rejected the value of the female role, the rewards and importance of motherhood, and the worth of children to a degree never before witnessed in our society.[9]

Feminist writer Lenore Weitzman concluded that the "present legal system" makes it clear that instead of expecting to be supported, a woman is now expected to become self-sufficient.[10] Society tells mothers it is unsafe to devote themselves to raising children. Feminist Leslie Bennetts, author of *The Feminist Mistake*, advises women not to stay home with their children. Her argument is that when a wife opts out of the workforce, she sets herself up to be abandoned by a philandering husband and left penniless.[11]

At first, unilateral divorce appeared to be a gift to husbands who sought to reclaim their youth by abandoning a longtime wife and taking a trophy wife who was younger, thinner, and better looking. Often he didn't even have to cough up alimony because the feminists had spread the notion that alimony was demeaning and women should be independent and support themselves.

The big-government liberals welcomed this movement with open arms. The American people were resisting tax increases, so the liberals could fatten the federal treasury by adding to the labor force all the women from whose wages the tax collector would get his cut. Big government was the biggest financial winner of the movement of wives into the labor force.

As the years went on and feminist ideology permeated the family courts, it began to be wives who far more frequently walked away from marriage. Now, wives initiate two-thirds of divorces. To understand why, follow the money.

The federal government took control of child support and made the laws severe and onerous. Local agencies and courts found it much more profitable to give child custody to the ex-wife so that the ex-husband (who presumably has a larger income) can be forced to pay for an army of psychologists, psychiatrists, custody evaluators, parenting classes, and other court-appointed busybodies who make their income by helping a judge rule what is in "the best interest of the child."

Feminists, who had complained for years that their husbands failed to do 50 percent of household and child-care duties, took the position that, after divorce, the wife should have sole custody of the children. Wives who had tired of marriage and its obligations discovered that they could divorce with or without any reason, keep the kids and most of their ex-husbands' income, and live a life free from marriage obligations.

Easy divorce also changed the attitude of young people: *We won't get married because it risks too much disappointment*, or, *We'll get married, but, of course, divorce is always an easy option.* Couples who assume the availability of divorce are less likely to work hard to make a marriage permanent. Couples seduced by feminist ideology no longer assume marriage is a commitment "till death do us part."

California's mistake spread rapidly across the United States during the 1970s. Unilateral divorce was enacted in nearly every other state. The number of divorces increased dramatically. Most religious leaders remained strangely silent. The state of New York was the last holdout against unilateral divorce, requiring mutual consent of both spouses if a divorce were to be granted, unless one spouse could prove the other guilty of a major fault. New York finally adopted unilateral divorce in 2012.

Not only were traditional divorce laws abolished, but the feminist anti-marriage network fanned out in state after state to repeal the laws designed to respect morality and preserve marriage, such as the laws against adultery, fornication, sodomy, alienation of affection, and even the laws that made it a husband's duty to support his wife and children.

Unilateral divorce violates the US Constitution, Article I, Section 10, which prohibits the states from passing "any Law impairing the Obligation of Contracts." The Fifth and Fourteenth Amendments also guarantee that "no person be deprived of life, liberty or property without due process of law." Unilateral divorce violates agreements that were properly and publicly made before witnesses. How can there be "due process" if the spouse who wants to save the marriage is guaranteed to lose? In a divorce, one person loses a part of his or her life, such as regular access to his or her children; loses liberty (often even the right to attend a child's play or sporting event); and most definitely loses property and income. Yet there is no case in which a divorce was denied by a state or federal court due to constitutional issues.

Two law professors, Margaret Brinig from Notre Dame University and Douglas Allen from Iowa, conducted a study to find out why women are 66 percent more likely to file for a divorce than men. They studied forty-six thousand divorce cases filed in four states—Connecticut, Virginia, Montana, and Oregon—asking why women filed for divorce. The results of their questions were published in *These Boots Are Made for Walking: Why Most Divorce Filers Are Women*. Contrary to their expectations, women were not seeking divorce because of mistreatment, domestic violence, the husband's adultery, or even money problems. Some women gave reasons such as "because I've outgrown him" or "because I don't need him." Brinig and Allen found that the most powerful reason why wives initiate divorce is "because I will win." Wives divorce specifically to "gain full control over the children."[12] The women were confident they would receive a preferential child custody decision and the money to go with it.

Chateau Heartiste, an acerbic commentator on male-female relations, wrote:

> One thing you have to understand about the divorce industrial complex if you want to know how and why things traveled this far down the circles of post-nuptial hell: The spiteful degenerates who advocated for no-fault divorce and punitive alimony and child support, and the blood-sucking parasites who inevitably followed in their wake, never had fairness in mind. What they wanted, ultimately, was the reconstruction of society to extend and enshrine total female freedom of access and removal of accountability in the marital and sexual markets.[13]

LAWYERS ATTACK MARRIAGE

A broadside attack on traditional marriage has been carried on for years by the American Law Institute (ALI), an association of liberal lawyers and academics who write model laws and then try to bamboozle state legislatures into passing them. The American Law Institute has no official authority, but the media describe it as a prestigious private organization that has immense influence on the writing of our laws. The ALI's proposals are a threat to marriage and to the traditional rights of husbands, wives, fathers, and children. The ALI would give the rights and privileges of married couples to any sexual roommates, same-sex or two-sex couples.

The American Law Institute issued a ponderous document of recommendations in 2000 called *Principles of the Law of Family Dissolution*, which was a devastating legal assault on marriage. The ALI defined domestic partnerships as "two persons of the same or opposite sex, not married to one another, who for a significant period of time share a primary residence and a life together as a couple."[14] The institute would treat these arrangements just like marriage. When breaking up, the cohabitants should be entitled to a division of property and alimony-like payments, as well as share in the custody of any children. This deal would validate homosexual relationships and make them comparable to married couples. The ALI would demolish marriage as the crucial building block of our social order and make marriage just one living arrangement among many.

The American Law Institute would also give rights of child custody, child support, and distribution of marital property "without regard to marital misconduct." The proposals are part of a long-running ALI campaign to persuade the courts that "rights" should have nothing to do with morality. This line now runs through most activist court decisions. Thus, *Goodridge v. Dept. of Public Health* quotes *Lawrence v. Texas* quotes *Planned Parenthood v. Casey* in stating: "Our obligation is to define the liberty of all, not to mandate our own moral code."[15] But in rejecting any moral code, supremacist judges are mandating public approval of an immoral code. It's no wonder that some activist judges have tried to ban the Ten Commandments!

The ALI's *Principles of the Law of Family Dissolution* would solidify and codify the changes brought about by the sexual revolution. The ALI protects many interests of cohabiting by unmarried heterosexual couples, thereby diminishing incentives to marry. The institute also validates the rearing of children by same-sex couples through recognition of co-parenting agreements and the creation of custodial rights in a partner of the legal parent, despite objections by the biological parent.

The ALI accepts the fact that the traditional family is in decline and fails to make any attempt to resurrect it. All family forms are equal, the ALI concludes, or at least are good enough. F. Carolyn Graglia described and explained the institute's anti-marriage proposals in a definitive article on the ALI's *Principles of the Law of Family Dissolution*.[16]

COURTS APPROVE ILLEGITIMACY

Government's definition of marriage is society's way of establishing the clear relation and responsibility of the father as well as the mother for caring for their children. That purpose was ignored by Lyndon Johnson's Great Society. Beginning with LBJ's War on Poverty and its vast expansion of welfare, the welfare system has channeled most handouts to mothers, making the husband and father irrelevant to the family's economic well-being. It should come as no surprise that this encouraged illegitimacy because, as Ronald Reagan is reported to have said, if you subsidize something, you will get more of it.

The courts promoted illegitimacy by a series of decisions. In a wrongful death case in 1968, the US Supreme Court ruled, "Legitimacy or illegitimacy of birth has no relation to the nature of the wrong allegedly inflicted on the mother." The dissent, recognizing that this decision overturned previous law, argued, "the state has power to provide that people who choose to live together should go through the formalities of marriage."[17]

In a 1973 case, the court ruled that "a state may not invidiously discriminate against illegitimate children by denying them substantial benefits accorded children generally."[18]

These decisions were blows to the ancient precepts that when a man marries a woman, he takes responsibility for the resulting kids. The ruling goes against the idea that women should get a marriage contract before having kids. The upshot of these cases was to assure women that they will get child support money even if they never marry, and to interfere with the state's ability to use its laws to discourage out-of-wedlock births.

HOMOSEXUALS ATTACK MARRIAGE

Americans were shocked in 2003 when the Massachusetts Supreme Judicial Court ruled four to three to legalize same-sex marriages in the case called *Goodridge v. Dept. of Public Health*. The court acknowledged that for three centuries we have defined marriage as "the legal union of a man and woman as husband and wife." Then the court impudently ruled that there is no "rational basis" for that definition, and it ordered this new definition of marriage: "the voluntary union of two persons as spouses." With elitist arrogance, the slim, four-person majority bragged: "Certainly our decision today marks a significant change in the definition of marriage as it has been inherited from the common law, and understood by many societies for centuries."[19]

Justice Anthony Kennedy had opened the door to this travesty in 2003 with his far-out reasoning in *Lawrence v. Texas*. Citing a European court ruling (since he couldn't cite the US Constitution), he overturned a US Supreme Court precedent of only seventeen years earlier.[20] The dissenting Supreme Court justices in *Lawrence v. Texas* warned that this case "is the product of a law-profession culture that has largely signed on to the so-called homosexual agenda," and that the court is imbued with the "law profession's anti-anti-homosexual culture."[21]

The gay lobby has been trying to position same-sex marriage as a logical expansion of the civil rights movement. It isn't. Gays already have the liberty to live their lives as they choose, set up housekeeping, share income and expenses, make contracts and wills, and transfer property. They can even have a marriage ceremony before some clergy member or justice of the peace willing to perform it; there is no law banning same-sex marriage in any state; there are only requirements to get a state-issued marriage license, which apply to everyone. But now they are also demanding respect and social standing for a lifestyle that others believe is immoral. They want to silence all criticism of their behavior, and they are fighting for the right to teach about homosexuality in the schools. That amounts to the minority forcing its views on the majority.

The Massachusetts same-sex marriage court decision posed the question for our nation: Are Americans willing to submit to what Thomas Jefferson predicted would be "the despotism of an oligarchy" if judges are allowed to be "the ultimate arbiters of all constitutional questions"? The dissenting judges in this case recognized this: "The power to regulate marriage lies with the Legislature, not with the judiciary." Commentator Micah Clark caught lesbian journalist Masha Gessen on a radio program admitting that homosexual activists are not merely trying to access the institution of marriage—they want to radically redefine and eventually eliminate marriage. Here are Gessen's words:

> It's a no-brainer that [homosexual activists] should have the right to marry, but I also think equally that it's a no-brainer that the institution of marriage should not exist. . . . Fighting for gay marriage generally involves lying about what we are going to do with marriage when we get there—because we lie that the institution of marriage is not going to change, and that is a lie. The institution of marriage is going to change, and it should change.[22]

Attorney David Boies argued for same-sex marriage at the US Supreme Court, and he repeated his argument on NBC-TV's *Meet the Press*:

At the very beginning of this case, we said we needed to prove three things. We needed to prove, first, that marriage was a fundamental right. And I think we did that, and even the defendants agreed with that, because the Supreme Court has ruled that fourteen times in the last hundred years. Second, we needed to prove that depriving gay and lesbian citizens of the right to marry [each other] seriously harmed them, and seriously harmed the children that they were raising. And we proved that too, not only through our witnesses but through the defense witnesses. . . .

But we believe that, even if you simply apply the rational basis test, there is no rational basis to justify this ban. And that's because of the third thing that we proved, which was that there was no evidence, none, that allowing gays and lesbians to marry harms the institution of marriage or harms anyone else. . . .

And I think one of the things that's important is that the evidence is that having a loving couple that are married is great for children. Everybody agreed with that. But the evidence is that's true whether it's a gay couple or a straight couple. And it's true whether it's an adopted couple or a biological couple. . . . That's the evidence. The evidence is absolutely clear that, if you have a loving, adopted couple, it is no worse off at all than a biological couple.[23]

No, he did not prove any of those things. All studies show that kids do best with their natural parents.

After Canada legalized same-sex marriage, there was no rush down the aisle to the altar. Out of 34,200 self-identified homosexual couples, only 1.4 percent obtained marriage licenses. The editor of *Fab*, a popular gay magazine in Toronto, explained, "I'd be for marriage if I thought gay people would challenge and change the institution and not buy into the traditional meaning of 'till death do us part' and monogamy forever."[24] The 1984 McWhirter-Mattison study reported in *The Male Couple* that most homosexual couples with relationships lasting more than five years incorporated a provision for outside sexual activity.[25]

If personal desire is to become the only criterion for public recognition of marriage, and if equal rights and nondiscrimination require us to be neutral about who is eligible for marriage, how then can we deny marriage to those who want to marry a child or a sibling or a cousin or more than one wife? All those practices are common in some other countries.

The US Supreme Court did not rule in *United States v. Windsor* that there is a constitutional right to same-sex marriage, but the gays and the federal court judges started behaving as though they did, and the advocates of traditional marriage retreated into ominous silence.

It wasn't just that the Supreme Court ruled that the Defense of Marriage Act (DOMA) is unconstitutional. It was the way that the five-to-four majority insulted the advocates of DOMA by falsely asserting that "only those with hateful hearts could have voted 'aye' on this Act." As Justice Scalia wrote in dissent, this decision was a "jaw-dropping . . . assertion of judicial supremacy over the people's Representatives in Congress and the Executive."

THE EQUAL RIGHTS AMENDMENT

The Equal Rights Amendment (ERA), a proposed amendment to the US Constitution, was born in the era of the women's suffrage amendment and first introduced into Congress in 1923. For nearly fifty years, all those Congresses had the good judgment to leave the ERA buried in committee.

After the radical feminist movement was born, the ERA was voted out of Congress on March 22, 1972, and sent to the states for ratification. The amendment was passionately debated across America from 1972 to 1982, rejected by the American people, and declared dead by the US Supreme Court after the end of its second time limit on June 30, 1982.

A radical feminist organization, the National Organization for Women (NOW), stormed the halls of Congress, secured signers for a discharge petition, and forced the ERA out for a vote. Apparently convinced that NOW represented all women, the House passed the

ERA by an overwhelming margin on October 21, 1971, and the Senate did likewise on March 22, 1972, sending the amendment to the states and setting a time limit of seven years for three-fourths of the states (thirty-eight) to pass ratification resolutions.

Women were falsely led to believe that the Equal Rights Amendment would put women in the US Constitution. But as anyone can see from its text, the ERA would not put women in the Constitution—it would put "sex" in the Constitution. Section 1 of the amendment's text reads: "Equality of rights under the law shall not be denied or abridged by the United States or by any State on account of sex."

The Equal Rights Amendment had a righteous name and awesome political momentum. Within the first year, the ERA was ratified by thirty states, so it needed only eight more states to become part of the US Constitution. Supporting the amendment were all those who had pretensions to political power from left to right—from Ted Kennedy to George Wallace—and three US presidents: Richard Nixon, Gerald Ford, and Jimmy Carter, plus two very activist First Ladies: Betty Ford and Rosalynn Carter. The ERA was actively supported by the majority of Congress, all governors, most of the pushy women's organizations, a consortium of thirty-three women's magazines, numerous Hollywood celebrities, and 99 percent of the media. But the American people rejected the amendment. Over the ten years during which the ERA was actively debated, I wrote a hundred issues of the *Phyllis Schlafly Report* and fliers about the ERA, which staked out the battleground: the legal rights that women would lose if the amendment were ever ratified.

The Stop ERA campaign showed that the Equal Rights Amendment was a fraud. While pretending to benefit women, it actually would be a big takeaway of rights that women then possessed, such as the right of an eighteen-year-old girl not to be drafted and sent into military combat and the right of a wife to be supported by her husband. The facts came straight from the writings of the pro-ERA legal authorities: Yale Law School professor Thomas I. Emerson's

100-page article in the *Yale Law Journal*, articles by Harvard professor Paul Freund, and ACLU lawyer Ruth Bader Ginsburg's 230-page book *Sex Bias in the U.S. Code.* Those documents confirmed the opponents' arguments that ERA would draft women into military combat, abolish a husband's duty to support his wife, take away Social Security benefits from wives and widows, and cause many other kinds of legal mischief.

The ERA's opponents showed that the amendment would give enormous power to the federal courts to define the words in the Equal Rights Amendment: specifically, "sex" and "equality of rights." Section 2 of the ERA would give vast new powers to the federal government and to the courts over all laws that allow traditional and reasonable differences of treatment on account of sex: marriage, divorce, alimony, adoptions, abortion, homosexual laws, sex crimes, property rights, private and public schools, Boy and Girl Scouts, prison regulations, and insurance.

The ERAers could not show *any* benefit to women, not even in employment, since US employment laws were already sex-neutral. The federal equal-pay-for-equal-work law was passed in 1963. The ERAers said their amendment would put women into the Constitution. But again, the Constitution doesn't mention men or women; it uses only sex-neutral words, such as "we the *people*," *person, citizen, inhabitant, elector, president,* and *senator.* ERA advocates argued that the amendment would and should make all federal and state laws as blind to sex differences as we are blind about race differences (except, of course, for affirmative action).

After 1975, the ERAers won only five more states, but five other states rescinded their previous ratifications. The ERAers were running out of time since their seven-year time limit was scheduled to expire on March 22, 1979.

International Women's Year (IWY) became the feminists' plan to win ratification in the remaining states. Bella Abzug, then a member of Congress, persuaded Congress to appropriate $5 million for a tax-funded IWY convention in Houston in November 1977. The

International Women's Year convention opened in Houston with three First Ladies on the platform (Mrs. Ford and Mrs. Carter were joined by Lady Bird Johnson) and featured every feminist you ever heard of; three thousand members of the media were on hand to provide total press and television coverage.

But that extensive media coverage exposed the American people to the feminists' real goals and the radical effects of the ERA: the drafting of girls, a militant attack on marriage, taxpayer funding of abortions, government day care, and the gay rights agenda. The Equal Rights Amendment would put the entire feminist, anti-marriage agenda into the US Constitution, with power to federal courts to enforce it. ERAers argued that since abortion happens only to women, it is sex discrimination to deny taxpayer funding for abortions. And, since the word used in the ERA is "sex" (not women), the amendment would require us to grant same-sex marriage licenses.

A couple of months later, a reporter asked the governor of Missouri, "Governor, are you for ERA?" He replied, "Do you mean the old ERA or the new ERA? I was for equal pay for equal work, but after those women went down to Houston and got tangled up with the abortionists and the lesbians, I can tell you ERA will never pass in the Show-Me State."[26]

When the feminists realized they could not win thirty-eight states by the seven-year deadline, they ran to President Carter for help. He persuaded Congress to pass an ERA time extension that changed "within seven years" in the original ERA resolution to *ten* years, three months, eight days, seven hours, and thirty-five minutes, so that the time limit was extended to midnight on June 30, 1982, the time of the mandatory adjournment of the Illinois State Legislature. Congress passed this extension by only a simple majority vote instead of the two-thirds majority required for constitutional amendments. The American people were so turned off by the dishonesty of the time extension that the Equal Rights Amendment never scored another victory, even though it has since been voted on about twenty-five times, in state legislatures, in Congress, and in several statewide referenda. Political cartoonists had a field day, describing the time extension as giving three more innings to a baseball game that was not tied up.

In *Idaho v. Freeman*, the federal court ruled that the time extension was *un*constitutional, and that the rescissions *are* constitutional.[27] The feminists appealed. The US Supreme Court ruled that the lawsuit was "moot" because the ERA was *dead* regardless of whether we use the original time limit of March 22, 1979, or the extended time limit of June 30, 1982.[28]

The Equal Rights Amendment is a stunning example of how the grass roots can rise up and defeat the entire establishment. A bunch of dedicated women defeated the ERA in the era when there were no friendly TV and radio talk show hosts, no Rush Limbaugh talking about feminazis, no "fair and balanced" Fox News, no "No Spin Zone," no Internet, no e-mail, not even fax machines.

The spectacular defeat of the ERA, which no one predicted, saved Americans from a constitutional mandate that all federal and state laws must abolish all gender and sex roles and embrace sex interchangeability.

VIOLENCE AGAINST WOMEN ACT

Most people think of domestic violence as tragic cases of men beating up women. Assault and battery are crimes that should be prosecuted and punished. But domestic violence doesn't mean only criminal conduct. Feminists have expanded the definition of domestic violence to include an endless variety of legal actions that are made punishable because of *who* commits them. The feminist aim is to break up marriages, not solve problems.

The Violence Against Women Act (VAWA) is a gender-specific title that is pejorative and sex-discriminatory. VAWA means violence *by men against women*. VAWA does not include violence by women against women, or women against men. A Texas VAWA grant application made it sex specific: "Grant funds may not be used for the following: Services for programs that focus on children and/or men."[29]

The term *domestic violence* has morphed into *domestic abuse*, a far broader term. Domestic abuse doesn't have to be violent—it doesn't even have to be physical. The feminists' mantra is, "You don't have to be beaten to be abused."

VAWA was passed in 1994 as Bill Clinton's payoff to the feminists who supported him for president in 1992. Remember the Super Bowl Hoax, the ridiculous claim that "the biggest day of the year for violence against women" is Super Bowl Sunday, when domestic violence increases "by 40 percent"? That falsehood and other bogus statistics were conclusively refuted by the scholarly research of Dr. Christina Hoff Sommers.[30]

Domestic violence has become whatever the woman wants to allege, with or without evidence. Examples of claims of domestic abuse include name-calling, constant criticizing, insulting, belittling the victim, blaming the victim for everything, ignoring or ridiculing the victim's needs, jealousy and possessiveness, insults, put-downs, gestures, facial expressions, looking in a certain way, body postures, and controlling the money. A Justice Department–funded document published by the National Victim Assistance Academy stated a widely accepted definition of "violence" that includes such non-criminal acts as "degradation and humiliation" and "name-calling and constant criticizing."[31] The acts need not be illegal, physical, violent, or threatening.

The domestic violence checklist typically provided by family courts to women seeking divorce and/or sole child custody asks questions like has the other parent has ever done or threatened to do any of the following: blamed all the problems on you, followed you, embarrassed you or put you down, or interrupted your eating or sleeping. Such actions are not illegal or criminal; no one has a right not to be insulted. But in the weird world of the domestic violence industry, acts that are not criminal between strangers become crimes between members of a household, and such actions can be punished by depriving a man of his fatherly rights, putting him under a restraining order, and even jailing him. Family courts mete out punishment based on gender and relationships rather than on acts.

Creating a special category of domestic-violence offenses creates a new level of crimes for which punishment is based on who you are rather than what acts you commit, and the "who" in the view of VAWA and the domestic-violence lobby is always the husband, father, or boyfriend. There's been no accountability or oversight for VAWA's ten-plus years of spending nearly a billion dollars a year. There is little evidence that VAWA has benefited anyone except the radical feminists on its payroll.

A 1979 book called *The Battered Woman* by Lenore Walker is credited with establishing feminist theory on domestic violence and in originating what is called the "battered woman syndrome." This book is all hearsay without credible statistical data. Walker admitted that her generalizations were based on "a self-volunteered sample" of women who contacted her after hearing her speeches or interviews.[32] She mentioned the large study of domestic violence undertaken by the National Institute of Mental Health, but failed to tell her readers that its final conclusion was that women initiate violence in intimate relationships at least as often as men do.

Nevertheless, Walker's unscientific book had a big impact in spreading the propaganda that the "battered" are always women, that "batterers" are always men, and that "battering" is not necessarily a violent or even a physical act. She admitted, "Most of the women in this project describe incidents involving psychological humiliation and verbal harassment as their worst battering experiences, whether or not they had been physically abused."[33] While psychological abuses can be hurtful, they are subjective, and it is absurd to pretend that verbal abuse is done only by men against women and not vice versa.

As an example of "battering," Walker defended the woman who admitted she "began to assault Paul physically, before he assaulted her," but "Paul had been battering her by ignoring her and by working late, in order to move up the corporate ladder." So, trying to do a better job of supporting his family was construed as domestic abuse. Like many feminists, Walker is not trying to improve marriage but to destroy it. She urged that "psychotherapists must encourage breaking the family apart."[34]

A woman seeking help from a VAWA-funded center is not offered any options except to leave her husband, divorce him, accuse him of being a criminal, and have her sons targeted as suspects in future crimes. VAWA ideology rejects joint counseling, reconciliation, and saving marriages. It also refuses to recognize that alcohol and illegal drugs contribute significantly to domestic violence, a peculiar assumption contrary to all human experience. Numerous studies confirm a high correlation between domestic violence and alcohol or drug abuse.

VAWA forces Soviet-style psychological reeducation on men and teenage boys. The accused men are not given treatment for real problems (such as counseling for drug or alcohol addiction), but are assigned to classes where feminists teach shame and guilt because of an alleged vast male conspiracy to subjugate women.

VAWA funds the reeducation of judges and law enforcement personnel to teach them feminist stereotypes about male abusers and female victims, how to game the system to empower women, and how to ride roughshod over the constitutional rights of men.

VAWA encourages women to make false allegations and then petition for full child custody and a denial of fathers' rights to see their own children. It also promotes the unreserved use of restraining orders, which family courts issue merely on the woman's say-so.

The groundwork for the Violence Against Women Act was laid by Gloria Steinem's nonsense, such as, "The patriarchy *requires* violence or the subliminal threat of violence in order to maintain itself,"[35] and Andrea Dworkin's tirades of hate such as, "Under patriarchy, every woman's son is her betrayer and also the inevitable rapist or exploiter of another woman."[36]

Feminist ideology teaches that domestic violence is not a matter of the misbehavior of *some* men who may be bad individuals or drunks or psychologically troubled, but that *all* men share the blame for domestic violence because they benefit from a patriarchy that empowers men and keeps women subservient. VAWA is based on the unscientific notion that all men are potentially if not actually abusive, and that all women are victims or in danger of becoming victims.

Sixty-seven feminist and liberal organizations supported a lawsuit to try to get private allegations of domestic abuse heard in *federal* courts so they could collect civil damages against men and institutions with deep pockets. Fortunately, the Supreme Court, in *United States v. Morrison*, declared unconstitutional VAWA's section that would have permitted that additional mischief.[37]

No VAWA programs promote intact families or better male-female relationships. The act has no provision for addressing problems within the context of marriage. Instead, VAWA promotes divorce and provides women with weapons, such as the restraining order and free legal assistance, to get sole custody of their children. Since 1994, VAWA has dished out massive grant money that empowers a network of feminist organizations. The Violence Against Women Act is known as "feminist pork" because it puts up to $1 billion a year of US taxpayers' money into the hands of the radical feminists.

An American Bar Association document called "Tool for Attorneys" provides lawyers with a list of suggestive questions to encourage their clients to make domestic-violence charges. Knowing that a woman can get a restraining order against the father of her children in an *ex parte* proceeding without evidence and that she will probably never be punished for lying, domestic-violence accusations have become a major tactic for securing sole child custody.

Worse, feminists have persuaded most states to adopt *mandatory arrest* laws. That means, when the police arrive at a disturbance and lack good information on who is to blame, even if there is no sign of violence and the woman doesn't want the man arrested, the police are nevertheless legally bound to arrest somebody. Three guesses who is usually arrested.

Feminists have also lobbied most states into passing *no-drop prosecution* laws. Those laws make the prosecutor legally bound to go forward with prosecution even if the woman recants her charges or wants to drop them. Studies show that women do recant or ask to drop the charges in 60 percent of criminal allegations, but the law requires prosecution against the man to proceed regardless. The Violence Against Women Act provides the woman with free legal counsel to pursue her allegations, but not the man to defend himself. He is on his own to find and pay a lawyer—or struggle without one.

VAWA has a built-in incentive for the woman to make false charges of domestic violence because she is rather sure she will never be prosecuted for perjury. Charging domestic violence practically guarantees she will get custody of the children and sever forever the father's relationship with his children, even though the alleged violence had nothing whatever to do with any abuse of the children. Judges are required to consider allegations of domestic violence in awarding child custody, even though no evidence of abuse is ever presented.

Professor Martin Fiebert of California State University at Long Beach compiled a bibliography of 286 scholarly investigations, 221 empirical studies, and 65 reviews or analyses that demonstrate that women are as physically aggressive, or more aggressive, toward their partners as men.[38] Studies by the leading domestic violence researchers found that half of all couple violence is mutual, and when only one partner is physically abusive, the abuse is as likely to be initiated by the woman as by the man.[39] Even so, the Violence Against Women Act has dozens of passages in its lengthy text that exclude men from its benefits. For starters, the words "and men" should be added to those passages, and the law's title should be changed to Partner Violence Reduction Act.

Intimate partner violence is twice as likely to occur in two-income households compared to those where only one partner is employed, according to a study made at Sam Houston State University by assistant professor of criminal justice Cortney A. Franklin and Tasha A. Menaker and supported by the Crime Victims' Institute: "When both male and females were employed, the odds of victimization were more than two times higher than when the male was the only breadwinner in the partnership, lending support to the idea that female employment may challenge male authority and power in a relationship."[40]

Voluminous documentation to dispel the feminist myths that have perpetuated VAWA are spelled out in a lengthy report called *Family Violence in America* published by the American Coalition for Fathers and Children, and in a series of reports issued by an organization called RADAR (Respecting Accuracy in Domestic Abuse Reporting).[41]

The feminists' determination to punish men, guilty or innocent, is illustrated by the capricious April 4, 2011, "Dear Colleague" letter issued by the feminists in the Department of Education's Office for Civil Rights. It's not a law (Congress would never pass it), and it's not even a regulation required to be published in the *Federal Register*; it's just a peremptory order to scare colleges into compliance by pretending it's an implementation of the law known as Title IX.[42]

This letter orders colleges to use a "preponderance of the evidence" standard of proof in sexual harassment and sexual assault cases, replacing the traditionally accepted "clear and convincing" standard of proof. The new rule means that the feminist academics sitting in judgment on male college students need to be only 50.01 percent confident a woman is telling the truth, whether or not she has any credible evidence.

The way the Duke Lacrosse players' reputations and college education were destroyed is typical of feminist control of university attitudes. The prosecutor who falsely accused the men was disbarred, but there were no sanctions against the professors and college administrators who rushed to public judgment against the guys.

Dr. Stephen Baskerville's landmark book *Taken into Custody: The War Against Fatherhood, Marriage and the Family* (Cumberland House, 2007) poignantly describes how attorneys advise divorced wives seeking child custody to accuse the father of abuse and thereby obtain a restraining order barring him from the family home.

Taken into Custody provides a copiously documented description of society's injustices to children who have been deprived of their fathers and to fathers who have been deprived of their children. His book is "must" reading on how family courts and taxpayers' money are promoting divorce, cheating fathers, and imposing incredible harm on children.

NEW SORTS OF PARENTS

The Iowa State Supreme Court ruled on May 3, 2013, that an Iowa agency's refusal to list both spouses in a lesbian marriage as parents on their children's birth certificates violates their constitutional rights and must stop. All six justices who participated backed the ruling. Justice David Wiggins said the likely explanation for treating lesbian parents differently was "stereotype or prejudice."[43]

Surrogate births, same-sex parenthood, and assisted reproduction are changing society by creating new possibilities for nontraditional households and relationships. California state senator Mark Leno sponsored a law to allow a child to have multiple parents, asserting, "The bill brings California into the twenty-first century, recognizing that there are more than Ozzie and Harriet families today."[44] Leno thus reaffirmed in 2013 that the Ozzie and Harriet marriage is still the *bête noire* of the feminists. Leno explained further:

> This bill would authorize a court to find that a child has 2 presumed parents notwithstanding the statutory presumption of parentage of the child by another man. The bill would authorize the court to make this finding if doing so would serve the best interest of the child based on the nature, duration, and quality

of the presumed or claimed parents' relationships with the child and the benefit or detriment to the child of continuing those relationships. . . .

This bill would provide that a child may have a parent and child relationship with more than 2 parents. . . .

This bill would, in the case of a child with more than 2 legal parents, require the court to allocate custody and visitation among the parents based on the best interest of the child, including stability for the child.[45]

Governor Jerry Brown signed the law in 2013 allowing a judge to rule that a child has three or more parents. Some say such legislation recognizing more than two parents of a child was probably inevitable because of the complicated childbearing situations taking place today. Leno claimed, "The definition of family is evolving."[46] A couple of law professors issued a plea for the rejection of this three-parent law, saying, "When it comes to parenting, three's a crowd."

The big problem is the breakdown of the family unit. Babies are increasingly born outside of marriage, leading to legal battles over who the baby's father is. Same-sex couples are making babies with the eggs, sperm, and wombs of unrelated individuals who are usually separated from the baby's life.

Leno and his allies are anti-liberty and anti-equality. His proposal gives a judge extremely broad discretion to disrupt the most fundamental family relationships based on his own personal prejudices. Nothing could be more contrary to concepts of liberty and equality. This bill would not have protected any children. The primary purpose was to let lesbians interfere with natural parents and wipe out the rights of fathers. A divorced mom could get a lesbian spouse, and soon the dad is just one of three or four parents under the law. All this is completely within the discretion of a family court judge, who is allowed to enforce his or her personal prejudices.

Lesbian marriage is all about forcing kids to grow up without their fathers. They talk about equality and rights, but they are dead set against equalizing moms and dads in family law, and dead set against the rights of kids to have fathers. Three-parent families take us farther down that road.

The same-sex marriage movement led to kids having three or more legal parents and the destruction of the family as we know it. Fox News reported that a Miami-Dade circuit judge approved an adoption allowing three people—a gay man and a married lesbian couple—to be listed on the birth certificate of their twenty-three-month-old daughter. If we reject the mom-dad family, then the legal parents become whatever names lawyers and judges conspire to put on the birth certificate.

The *New York Times* reported on more wacky trends in destroying the family: nonromantic parenting partnerships.[47] Neither Ms. Hope nor Mr. Williams is interested in a romantic liaison. But they both want a child, and they're in serious discussions about having, and raising, one together. Mr. Williams is gay, and the two did not know of each other's existence until they met on Modamily.com, a website for people looking to share parenting arrangements.

Mr. Williams and Ms. Hope are among a new breed of online daters, looking not for love but rather a partner with whom to build a decidedly nonnuclear family. And several social networks, including PollenTree.com, Coparents.com, Co-ParentMatch.com, and MyAlternativeFamily.com, as well as Modamily, have sprung up over the past few years to help them.

Libertarians say people should be able to make whatever contracts they want for their nonstandard arrangements. They seem committed to their kids, so why not let them pursue their goofy plans? Because the law makes it impossible. Even a legal document is not necessarily binding. "Courts will operate on the basis of what is in the best interest of the child," says Bill Singer, a lawyer in Belle Mead, New Jersey, who specializes in nontraditional families. "Although a judge might look at an agreement to see what the intention of the parties was, it is not controlling."[48]

There is no chance of states passing a law to enforce co-parenting contracts, because our legislatures are dominated by feminists, liberals, LGBTQIA sympathizers, and other statists. The parents will always be subject to a judge tearing up their contract and forcing a completely different arrangement based on the judge's own bias about the best interest of the child. Jennifer Roback Morse wrote: "We are replacing the natural pre-political concept of biological parenthood with an artificial, government-created concept of parenthood that is entirely socially constructed. Instead of the government simply recognizing and recording the pre-political reality of biological parenthood, we are giving agents of the state the authority to construct parenthood, all in the best interests of the child, of course."[49]

Some people are under the mistaken impression that the homosexual lobby is pushing for some sort of libertarian goal to keep government busybodies out of the bedroom. It is definitely not. The gay lobby is bringing us one of the most antilibertarian, antifamily laws California has ever passed. The three-parent law gives judges the power to redefine families as they see fit. Not even the Communists attempted anything so extreme.

A summer 2012 *New York Times* article described this new DNA social order:

> It is an uncomfortable question that, in today's world, is often asked by expectant mothers who had more than one male partner at the time they became pregnant. Who is the father? With more than half of births to women under 30 now out of wedlock, it is a question that may arise more often. Now blood tests are becoming available that can determine paternity as early as the eighth or ninth week of pregnancy, without an invasive procedure that could cause a miscarriage. Besides relieving anxiety, the test results might allow women to terminate a pregnancy if the preferred man is not the father—or to continue it if he is.[50]

So the women of the future can eschew marriage, have promiscuous sex lives, get pregnant, get a DNA test to determine the father, get a court order for income statements and child support, and get an abortion if the money is not good enough.

LIBERTARIAN ATTACK ON MARRIAGE

The Libertarian Party claims to be "The Party of Principle: Minimum Government, Maximum Freedom,"[51] and it argues that the state should get out of the marriage business. Some libertarians urge that we let marriage be merely a contract between two people. Why let the government issue marriage licenses and control who can get one? The Libertarians ignore the fact that when marriage breaks up, the divorce process brings the whole coercive machinery of government into micromanaging the lives and property of the divorcing couples and their children. The divorce has to be enforced against the reluctant spouse, and thousands of details about child custody, financial support, the family home, and division of property and income fall into the hands of family court judges.

The Libertarian Party Platform describes the Libertarian goal:

Personal Relationships. Sexual orientation, preference, gender, or gender identity should have no impact on the government's treatment of individuals, such as in current marriage, child custody, adoption, immigration or military service laws. Government does not have the authority to define, license or restrict personal relationships. Consenting adults should be free to choose their own sexual practices and personal relationships.[52]

The California platform appears to spell out a Libertarian vision:

Marriage. We support the rights of individuals to form private relationships as they see fit, either by contract or by mutual agreement. We regard marriage as one such private relationship. The State of California should not dictate, prohibit, control, or encourage any such private relationship. To implement this principle, we advocate: . . . The repeal of all marriage and marriage dissolution laws and their replacement by contracts where desired by the parties. . . . The right of all consenting adults to form marriage contracts without regard to gender, sexual preference, degree of consanguinity, or number of parties to said contracts.[53]

This would *not* take the government out of the marriage business. A couple could agree to a marriage and make their own decision about property, but the socially more important part is to agree on the custody of any resulting kids. For example, they could agree to joint child custody in case of divorce and to separately support the kid, but unfortunately, US courts will not enforce such contracts. Child custody is totally at the discretion of a family court judge, and child support is based on formulas related to the income tax system.

The courts will not enforce any contract for the care and custody of kids, even if agreed to by both parents. All divorcing or unmarried parents are subject to having their lives micromanaged by judges who have personal opinions about the best interest of children and have the power to enforce those views.

The Libertarian approach presumes that the only interested parties are consenting adults. But the main point of marriage law is to protect the interests of the resulting kids, and they are certainly not consenting to the arrangement. If the Libertarians really followed their principles of minimum government and maximum freedom, they would support parents making enforceable contracts for the care and custody of their kids. There is no evidence that the Libertarian Party supports these basic freedoms. Doug Mainwaring warns about the very antilibertarian effect of same-sex marriage:

> Same-sex marriage will lead to greater government intrusion into all of our lives. I firmly believe that those who are the prime movers of same-sex marriage legislation want to see government have more control. When families are weakened, as is the case with so many fatherless families, children are brought up looking

to government, not family, for help and sustenance. We run the risk of turning into the Obama administration's dream for America and Americans, as displayed in last year's "Life of Julia." Throughout her life, Julia's most important relationship was with the government. I can't imagine a more *Twilight Zone*–like future for our progeny.[54]

If our government cannot define marriage as the union of one man and one woman, it follows that there can be no law against polygamy, a practice that is totally demeaning and harmful to women. The first platform adopted by the Republican Party, in 1856, condemned polygamy and slavery as the "twin relics of barbarism." The 2008 Republican Party Platform called for "a constitutional amendment that fully protects marriage as a union of a man and a woman, so that judges cannot make other arrangements equivalent to it." The 2012 Republican Party Platform proclaimed: "The institution of marriage is the foundation of civil society. Its success as an institution will determine our success as a nation. It has been proven by both experience and by endless social science studies that traditional marriage is best for children."[55]

We thought our nation had definitely settled the polygamy issue a century and a half ago, but it has raised its ugly head. The American Civil Liberties Union (ACLU) is on record as supporting polygamy. The ACLU's feminist president, Nadine Strossen, stated in a speech at Yale University in June 2005 that the ACLU defends "the right of individuals to engage in polygamy."[56] And on October 15, 2006, in a high-profile debate against Supreme Court Justice Antonin Scalia, Strossen stated that the ACLU supports a constitutional right to polygamy.

The massive immigration that the United States has accepted in recent years includes large numbers of immigrants from Third World countries whose residents practice polygamy as well as marriage to children and cousins. We wonder if they are continuing these customs in America and, if they are, whether they are prosecuted by US authorities for violating US laws. We know that they have continued their cruel practice of genital mutilation of girls.

President Obama's nominee for a commissioner of the Equal Employment Opportunity Commission (EEOC), a lesbian law-school professor named Chai R. Feldblum, signed a radical manifesto that endorsed polygamous households (i.e., "in which there is more than one conjugal partner"). Signed in 2006, this manifesto, entitled "Beyond Same-Sex Marriage: A New Strategic Vision for All Our Families & Relationships," argues that traditional marriage "should not be legally and economically privileged above all others."[57]

President Obama's regulatory czar, Cass Sunstein, cowrote a book in 2008 with economist Richard H. Thaler, called, *Nudge: Improving Decisions about Health, Wealth and Happiness*, in which he argues that traditional marriage discriminates against single people by imposing "serious economic and material disadvantages." Sunstein asks, "Why not leave people's relationships to their own choices, subject to the judgments of private organizations, religious and otherwise?" Earlier in the book, we are told, "Under our proposal, the word marriage would no longer appear in any laws, and marriage licenses would no longer be offered or recognized by any level of government."[58]

Suddenly, polygamy took center stage on December 13, 2013, when a federal district court judge in Utah ruled in favor of a constitutional right by a television celebrity to continue a polygamous arrangement with the equivalent of multiple common-law wives.[59] That supremacist judge invalidated an essential part of a Utah statute that prohibited a married person cohabitating with another person. Unless reversed on appeal, this opens the door to widespread polygamy-type arrangements.

Then, on December 20, another federal judge in Utah declared a constitutional right to same-sex marriage, and Utah began marrying same-sex couples, even though the people of Utah had previously amended their state constitution to prohibit this.[60]

Traditional marriage is essential to a stable society. It is essential to maintain government's proper role in defining it and protecting it. Government has and should have a very important role in defining who may get a license to marry. In America, it is and should be a criminal offense to marry more than one person at a time, or to marry a child or a sibling, even though such practices are common in some foreign countries.

UN TREATY ON WOMEN

Having failed in their effort to persuade Americans to put the Equal Rights Amendment (ERA) into the US Constitution, despite spending millions of dollars and enjoying the support of Big Media, three presidents, and dozens of prominent politicians of both parties, the feminists then tried to give us an even more dangerous ERA through ratification of a UN Treaty on Women enforced by busybody bureaucrats from foreign countries. This treaty has the pretentious label of Convention on the Elimination of All Forms of Discrimination Against Women (CEDAW).[61] It was signed by Jimmy Carter in 1980 and is constantly promoted by Bill and Hillary Clinton, but the US Senate has wisely never ratified it.

The notion is downright ridiculous that American women—the most fortunate class of people who ever lived—should submit to a treaty that dictates uniform rules for 185 other nations, many of which treat women badly. Ratification of CEDAW would be craven kowtowing to the radical feminists, exceeded only by the treaty's unlimited capacity for legal mischief.

Article 2 reiterates that the treaty would "eliminate discrimination against women by any person, organization or enterprise," including "laws, regulations, customs and practices." Our "customs" should be none of our government's business, much less the business of the United Nations.[62]

Article 5 would require us "to modify the social and cultural patterns of conduct of men and women" and to "ensure" that we are following United Nations dictates about "family education."[63]

Article 10 would make it a federal responsibility to ensure "the elimination of any stereotyped concept of the roles of men and women at all levels and in all forms of education . . . by the revision of textbooks and . . . teaching methods."[64] We certainly don't want the UN to revise our textbooks! Remember, the feminists consider it a "stereotype" that children should be raised by a mother and father married to each other.

Article 11 would chain us to the feminist goal that wages should be paid on subjective notions of "equal value" (i.e., the discredited feminist notion called "comparable worth") rather than on the free market or on US legal standards of equal pay for equal work. The UN would also require us to "establish" a federal "network of child-care facilities."[65]

Article 16 would require us to allow women "to decide freely and responsibly on the number and spacing of their children."[66] The text doesn't use the word *abortion*, but CEDAW's compliance committee has interpreted this feminist jargon to mean approval of abortion and has pressured thirty-seven nations to legalize or increase access to abortion. The CEDAW committee has held that nations should provide public funding of abortion, and it has even criticized nations that have laws to allow medical professionals to opt out of providing abortions. The European Parliament in 2002 adopted a report calling for removal of all limitations to abortion, citing CEDAW as its authority. Some pro-abortion US senators claim that they can paper over this problem by inserting an "understanding," but an "understanding" in regard to a treaty has no legal force whatsoever.

Article 16 also orders a massive interference with US laws as well as with our federal-state balance of powers by obligating the federal government to take over all family law, including marriage, divorce, child custody, and marital property.

Article 17 creates a monitoring committee in charge of "progress." This consists of "23 experts," on which the United States might have one vote out of twenty-three.[67] The current committee includes representatives from Algeria, Cuba, and Bangladesh, and a vice chairman from Zimbabwe. No doubt the committee members will always be "experts" in feminist ideology and tactics, such as Hillary Clinton, Barbara Boxer, or a president of NOW.

CEDAW's international "experts" have already issued negative reports about the practices of countries that were foolish enough to ratify the treaty. The committee criticized Ireland for "promoting a stereotypical view of the role of women in the home and as mothers," Belarus for "such symbols as a Mother's Day" because it promotes "a negative cultural stereotype," and Slovenia because "less than 30 percent of children under three years of age . . . were in formal day care."[68]

UN TREATY ON THE RIGHTS OF THE CHILD

The United Nations Convention on the Rights of the Child was unanimously adopted by the UN General Assembly on November 20, 1989, and signed by more than a hundred foreign governments. President George Bush did not sign the treaty, and the Senate has never ratified it. There are dozens of excellent reasons to reject it.

If the text of the UN treaty were proposed as new federal legislation, the bill would never pass. It would be unacceptable to the American people because it would give the federal government too broad a grant of power over our children, families, and schools, and it would be unconstitutional because of vagueness and federal interference with states' rights.

The UN Convention on the Rights of the Child purports to be a comprehensive listing of *all* rights of the child, and is based on the concept that a child's rights originate with the UN treaty itself or with the government. The logical conclusion is that a child would have no rights except those in the treaty. What government gives, government also can take away.

The treaty purports to give the child the right to express his own views freely in all matters (Article 12), to receive information of all kinds through "media of the child's choice" (Article 13), to exercise freedom of religion (Article 14), to be protected from interference with his correspondence (Article 16), to have access to information from national and international sources in the media (Article 17), to use his "own language" (Article 30), and to have "rest and leisure" (Article 31).

What do all these rights mean? How will they be enforced, and against whom? Does this mean that the child can refuse to do his homework and household chores because they interfere with his "right" to rest and leisure? Can he demand a government-paid lawyer to file a lawsuit against his parents?

Does this mean that a child has the right to use his native language in school and cannot be required to speak English? Can he demand the right to watch television in order to receive media reports from national and international sources? Can a child assert his right to say anything he wants to his parents at the dinner table? Will the government assist the child in joining a cult or selecting a different church from the one his parents attend?

These are just a few of the dozens of brand-new "rights of the child" scattered throughout the fifty-four articles of the UN treaty. Despite a vague reference to undefined "rights and duties of parents," the treaty does not recognize any specific parental right to make decisions for their minor children.

Article 28 prescribes that "the education of the child shall be directed to" such things as "the principles enshrined in the Charter of the United Nations"; respect for "the national values of the country . . . from which he or she may originate, and for civilizations different from his or her own" (that means adopting the controversial curricular approach known as "global education" or "multiculturalism"); "equality of sexes" (that means promoting the same Equal Rights Amendment that was rejected by the American people); and "the development of respect for the natural environment" (one of the most politically charged issues in the United States).

The UN treaty recognizes that private schools may exist, but only so long as they teach the above curriculum and otherwise conform to government standards.

This treaty would probably require us to set up a national system of day care. Article 18 says that the government "shall ensure the development of institutions, facilities and services for the care of children . . . of working parents." The treaty gives the children the right to benefit from these services and facilities. The treaty even obligates the government to ensure "standards" for child care institutions, services, and facilities.

The UN treaty grants the child the right to be protected against neglect or negligent treatment (Article 19). Could homeschoolers be charged with "neglect" for not sending their children to an institutional school? Or for not sending children to school until age seven or eight?

Since the treaty is a legal document that, if ratified, would become part of the "supreme law of the land," we could expect lawyers to bring test cases to see how far the courts would extend its provisions. The Convention would open up a Pandora's box of litigation, either in some international court or in US courts, or both. It's hard to say which venue would be worse.

Article 24 requires the government to "take all effective and appropriate measures with a view to abolishing traditional practices prejudicial to the health of children." The practice doesn't have to be harmful or even negligent, but merely "prejudicial," and this new "standard" would be defined by unelected judges, or the so-called experts.

What would it mean to enforce Article 28, which makes "primary education compulsory and available free to all"? Would that require us to ban private and religious schools or to modify their religious practices? Do we want United Nations courts to answer these questions?

The UN Convention on the Rights of the Child is vague, misleading, and contradictory on the fundamental issue of whether or not an unborn child is accorded any rights. Article 6 states that every child has a "right to life." However, Article 16 purports to establish the right to "privacy." Under US Supreme Court decisions, "privacy" is the operative word that created the right to abortion. We can be sure that feminist lawyers will argue that the treaty creates a right to "privacy" that can subsequently be used by the courts to include abortion. Article 24 grants the right to "family planning education and services," language that is generally used as a legal rationale for abortion services.

Of course, all these grandiose UN treaty goals would not be complete without the establishment of a new international bureaucracy and mechanism of control. Articles 43 and 44 would set up a Committee on the Rights of the Child, consisting of ten "experts" chosen by secret ballot from a list of nominees submitted by the governments that sign the treaty. There is no assurance that any American will be on this committee of experts, not even any assurance that even one "expert" will be friendly to American institutions and traditions.

The UN Convention on the Rights of the Child is a bad deal for Americans on every count. It should never be ratified by our Senate. It is a threat to our most precious freedoms, civil liberties, and respect for the nuclear family.

UN TREATY ON DISABILITIES

The UN Convention on the Rights of Persons with Disabilities (CRPD), another piece of global mischief, was signed by UN ambassador Susan Rice in 2009, but fortunately the US Senate has never ratified it. Since it was signed by 117 other countries, the CRPD claims it is part of what globalists euphemistically call international law.[69]

The notion that the United Nations can provide more benefits and protections for people with disabilities than the United States can is bizarre. The United States always treats individuals, able or disabled, better than any other nation. We don't need a committee of foreigners who call themselves "experts" to monitor what we do or to dictate our laws and customs. We already have protections and benefits for individuals with disabilities enshrined in US laws, regulations, and enforcement mechanisms. These include the Americans with Disabilities Act, the Individuals with Disabilities Education Act, the Fair Housing Act, the Rehabilitation Act of 1973, the Telecommunications Act of 1996, the Air Carrier Access Act of 1986, the Voting Accessibility for the Elderly and Handicapped Act of 1984, the Civil Rights of Institutionalized Persons Act, and the Architectural Barriers Act of 1968.

Under the CRPD, we would be required to make regular reports to a "committee of experts" to prove we are obeying the treaty (Article 34).[70] The "experts" would have the authority to review our reports and make "such suggestions and general recommendations on the report as it may consider appropriate" (Article 36). These demands are often outside the treaty's scope of subject matter. They override national sovereignty in pursuit of social engineering, feminist ideology, or merely busybody interference in parents' rights.[71]

Particularly offensive is the treaty's Article 7, which gives the UN committee the power to override every decision of the parent of a disabled child by using the caveat "the best interests of the child." This phrase is repeatedly abused by US family courts to substitute judges' decisions for parents' decisions, and giving use of that phrase to a UN committee is even more dangerous.[72]

The feminists saw to it that this treaty on disabilities includes language in Article 25 that requires signatory states to "provide persons with disabilities . . . free or affordable health care . . . including in the area of sexual and reproductive health and population-based health programmes." US secretary of state Hillary Clinton is on record as stating that the definition of "reproductive health" includes abortion. In testifying before the House Foreign Affairs Committee on April 22, 2009, she said: "Family planning is an important part of women's health, and reproductive health includes access to abortion."[73]

When the UN approved the CRPD, the United States made a statement that the phrase "reproductive health" does not include abortion, but that's just whistling in the wind, because international law does not recognize the validity of one nation's reservations to a treaty ratified by many other nations.

After ratification, treaties become part of the "supreme law" of the United States on a par with federal statutes. That gives US supremacist judges the power to invent their own interpretations, which some are eager to do. This treaty is a broadside attack on parents' rights to raise their children, and it's a particular threat to homeschooling families because of the known bureaucratic bias against homeschooling and against spanking. It is clear that the United States and people with disabilities are much better off relying on US law than on any UN treaty.

4

FAMILY COURTS CONTROL
THE FAMILY

I n 1997, New York ordered all its family courts to be open to the public. Anyone was then supposed to be allowed to witness the hundreds of thousands of cases of divorce settlements, child custody orders, domestic violence, foster care, and child neglect that are ruled on every year. But the family courts remained defiantly closed to the public. Court officials and security officers simply ignored the law and sometimes were even hostile about it.

The *New York Times* was more specific in describing the closed-door policy:

> Some courtrooms were locked, and many were marked with "stop" and "do not enter" signs. Court officers stationed at courtroom doors repeatedly barred a visitor, sometimes with sarcasm or ridicule, frequently demanding to know who he was and what he was doing. Armed court officers at times appeared so rattled by a visitor's efforts to enter courtrooms that, in several instances, a group of them nervously confronted the visitor, their holsters in easy reach.
>
> On the fifth floor of Family Court in Downtown Brooklyn, where people waited in bleak assembly areas for their cases to

be called, an officer was asked whether a member of the public could attend—as is permitted in other New York courts. "Not allowed, not in Family Court," he said flatly. . . .

During one week in particular, a reporter tried to enter 40 courtrooms in the city's five Family Courts as a member of the public or a civic group monitoring the courts. Entry was permitted to only five of the courtrooms, some where no case was under way—a closed rate of nearly 90%. In those cases, the reporter did not identify himself. In other instances, officials insisted that, even for reporters, free access to courtrooms was not permitted. . . .

But that's not what the law says. American legal principles have long favored open courts as a check on government, and New York law has specifically stated for more than a century that "the sittings of every court within the state shall be public."

By 1997, the Family Courts had been closed for decades, with rare exceptions. Critics said the chaos of the courts was amplified by their secrecy—a veil that had grown over the years with the support of judges, lawyers and social-agency representatives.[1]

Critics assert that closed courtrooms keep hidden the controversial ways the courts deal with those unlucky enough to have their lives ruled by family courts.

"The courtroom is pretty much closed," said Susan Jacobs, executive director of the Center for Family Representation, which has lawyers who handle cases in Manhattan and Queens. She said visitors would be shocked if they saw some of the routine proceedings in Family Court, like one in which, she said, the final decision to permanently strip a mother of her rights to her children took seven minutes.[2]

Are family courts incompetent or evil? Incompetent people make mistakes of fact and judgment, but their mistakes are not ideologically one-sided, and honest mistakes are corrected when pointed out. It is not possible to believe that family courts follow the rule of law as that term has been understood in American law for more than two centuries.

Major social trends of the past three decades, including unilateral divorce, illegitimate births, the feminist movement, the broad redefinition of domestic violence, aggressive enforcement of child support laws, and custody and property disputes, have vastly increased the number of Americans who come into family courts. Very few people have the funds to finance an appeal. Few decisions are ever reported in the law books. Since decisions are a matter of judicial discretion, the chances of overturning a family court judge are close to zero unless gross judicial abuse can be proved.

JUDGES' OPINIONS REPLACE PARENTAL RIGHTS

Family courts are considered to be lowest in the judicial hierarchy, but they are actually the most powerful, activist, and unaccountable of all courts. They control millions of families and vast amounts of private money and property.

The US Census Bureau reported that in 2002 judges had control over the private living arrangements and income of 48.3 million Americans, one-sixth of our population. The Census Bureau also reported that same year that $40 billion in transfer payments were made between households, money that is under the direction and control of family court judges. These figures prove that family courts have enormous power over the private lives and incomes of millions of Americans. The Libertarians, who want to get government out of the marriage business by taking away its authority to issue marriage licenses, are strangely silent about the vast control government exercises over the breakup of marriages and what happens to spouses, the custody of children, and the family home, income, and property.

These shocking statistics show that family courts are now an arm of government that routinely exercises virtually unlimited power to dictate the private lives and income of millions of American citizens who have committed no actionable offense. Family courts exercise the same power to dictate the private lives and income of parents who are self-supporting, law-abiding, and responsible in the care of their children as family courts exercise over parents who are none of those things.

The extraordinary power of family court judges is shown by this rule issued by the Pennsylvania Supreme Court on December 31, 2008: "Only judges may make decisions in child custody cases. . . . Courts shall not appoint any other individual to make decisions or recommendations or alter a custody order in child custody cases."[3]

It is clear that "any other individual" includes parents. A family court judge has full power to make and enforce his own decision, dissolving any agreement about child custody, even one made by the parents.

Barbara Kay reported in the *New York Daily News*:

> Divorce is initiated by women 70% of the time. From the day they make that decision, the system colludes with them in gaining control of the children. Women can falsely allege violence or sexual abuse of children without having to prove it (unscrupulous lawyers often advise their women clients to do this). When they do, the father is often removed from the home while trying to prove his innocence. The court will assign financial support obligations to the father. If the father fails to pay his support, even if he can't, the heavy hand of the law will punish him instantly. But if the mother arbitrarily denies rightful access to the father, the court is reluctant to penalize her. As one Canadian judge told a family lawyer arguing for his client's continually denied access rights, "It's not my job to punish mothers."[4]

"The best interests of the child" is universally accepted today as the standard for how family courts should handle child-related issues. That slogan is subjective, unworkable, contrary to the rule of law and due process, and a vast usurpation of parental rights and family autonomy.

The modern concept of the best interests of the child is relatively recent. Under English common law, as compiled by William Blackstone in 1765, parents were presumed to be responsible for their own children's interests. There was a presumption that courts should generally stay out of family decisions because, as the US Supreme Court wrote in 1979, "natural bonds of affection lead parents to act in the best interests of their children."[5] Some states say "best interests" and some say "best interest," but it means the same thing. Each is just a buzz phrase to conceal the transfer of parental rights to judges.

In the 1970s, when many states revised their family law statutes, the concept of the best interests of the child became disconnected from parents. This phrase is now used as an affirmative grant of power to family court judges to overrule parents on all child-related issues.

Three things are wrong with the current interpretation of "best interests of the child." First, it is contrary to the rule of law by giving judges extraordinary discretion to enforce their own prejudices and to micromanage lives. They punish parents for things that were never legislated as crimes or offenses. Second, the "best interests" standard undermines parental rights. Instead of saying that parents are the final authorities, as the family unit was understood for centuries, it allows judges to make routine child-rearing decisions. Third, courts have no competence to determine a child's best interests, so they rely on poorly trained evaluators who make unscientific recommendations about custody and visitation. There is rarely any evidence that a court-defined schedule is better than joint child custody.

The "best interests of the child" rule is totally subjective. Parents make thousands of decisions about their children, and they should have the right to make their decisions even if they contravene so-called experts. Whether the decision is big (such as where to go to church or school) or small (such as playing baseball or soccer), there is no objective way to say which is "best."

Since judges are supposed to base their decisions on evidence presented in open court, and there is no objective basis for deciding thousands of questions involved in raising a child, judges often call on the testimony of witnesses who are introduced as "experts." A big industry has grown up of psychologists, psychiatrists, social workers, custody evaluators, and counselors who are eager to collect fees for giving their opinions. Having opinions produced by individuals with academic degrees is a way to make subjective and arbitrary judgments appear objective. With the volume of cases coming through family courts, judges can evade responsibility for controversial decisions by rubber-stamping opinions of these court-appointed witnesses.

Not only is the best interest rule wrong and subjective; it is also bad policy because it pits the two parents as adversaries against each other, and that conflict is hurtful to the children. Sometimes the rulings are against women, but most decisions are against men, especially fathers. It's time to call a halt to the practice of letting the family court judges make decisions that are rightfully the parents' prerogative.

In recent years, liberals have popularized another slogan: "The village should raise the child." As I stated in chapter 2, to the liberal/progressive crowd *village* is a code word for government, that is, judges, bureaucrats, and public schools. The liberals are glad to give judges the power to decide the lifestyle of American families, the authority parents have over their own children, and the length of time each parent is permitted to spend with his or her own children.

The notion that the "village" rather than parents should make child-rearing decisions is manifested in the way public schools have taken over many responsibilities traditionally in the domain of parents, such as providing meals (even breakfast), health care, and prekindergarten supervision. Public schools notoriously assert their right to override parental decisions about the assignment of books that parents find immoral or profane, the use of privacy-invading questionnaires, teaching about sex and evolution, the provision of contraceptives and abortion referrals, the use of school counselors, and demands that children be injected with vaccines or given psychotropic drugs.

The growing power of the public schools to override parents' rights is evident in the 2005 Ninth Circuit outrage, *Fields v. Palmdale School District*. Three supremacist judges ruled, based on their "evolving understanding of the nature of our Constitution," that parents' fundamental right to control the upbringing of their children "does not extend beyond the threshold of the school door," and that a public school has the right to provide its students with "whatever information it wishes to provide, sexual or otherwise."[6] The Ninth Circuit subsequently retracted some of this wording against parental rights, but only after the House of Representatives voted 320 to 91 to affirm the Supreme Court precedent in favor of the rights of parents to control the education of their children. The Ninth Circuit did not retract its ruling against parents in the *Palmdale School* case.

Having family court judges determine the best interests of the child is fundamentally contrary to the rule of law, as law has been understood since Hammurabi in ancient Babylon. Plato advocated rule by a philosopher-king, but his student Aristotle convincingly explained the superiority of the rule of law. Western civilization is built on the concept that Aristotle was right.

All American courts are supposed to be based on the rule of law, but family courts cling to the idea that a judge can act as a philosopher-king and decide what is in the best interest of a child. This cannot be done without punishing parents and others for acts that are not contrary to any laws, rules, regulations, or policies that are written anywhere. The idea that a judge or psychologist can read some legal briefs or interview the parties and then objectively make child-rearing decisions is as outrageous as Plato's idea.

The main argument against Plato's approach is that necessary wisdom and objectivity are unattainable. Even if a judge of infinite wisdom could be found, there are at least two other reasons that such a judge would be unacceptable. First, if a judge is not ruling based on written rules, then there is necessarily an arbitrariness to his decisions, and we are not free people if we live under arbitrary decisions. Second, such judicial actions destroy incentives. For example, even if a judge could be found to assess taxes in a way that wisely and fairly collects and redistributes the wealth, incentives to earn money would be dampened because men could not reliably predict what they could keep.

These same objections apply to family court. Parents do not have the freedom and authority to be parents if they can always be second-guessed by a family court judge. And court interventions create bad incentives.

Suppose a judge orders grandparent visits if there has been a history of such visits and the judge's opinion is that the best interest of the child requires continuing such visits. Other parents may see this and decide that allowing grandparent visits is dangerous because it exposes the family to court intervention. Thus, one order in favor of grandparent visitation may result in other grandparents being refused visits. The best interest of the child is the core of the problem. If the law said that all grandparents have a right to visit their grandkids for two hours a week, then our arguments would not apply. The problem occurs when judges try to play God, a procedure that is beyond the power of judges and contrary to legal standards.

Most states make no attempt to define the best interests of the child. A couple of states (examples are Michigan and Florida) list a dozen factors to consider. But the judge has no guidance on how to evaluate or rank the factors. When it comes to a simple question like grandparent visits, the judge relies on his or her gut instincts.

Many states rely on psychologists or other so-called experts for recommendations. But even the psychology profession is largely of the opinion that these recommendations are unethical. Their expertise is in treating mental disorders, and they usually have no professional competence or basis for making a decision about grandparent visits.

Our Western civilization is based on the idea that parents should have the autonomy to rear their kids as they believe is best. This principle served us well for centuries. Maybe an exception should be made to require grandparent visits; we do not take a position on that. But such an exception should be carefully considered by the legislature and codified so it will be a predictable regulation. Relying on each judge's opinion is unpredictable, unworkable, and contrary to everything our justice system stands for.

The rule of law, sometimes called supremacy of the law, is a legal maxim that says governmental decisions should be made by applying known principles or laws with minimal discretion in their application. Rule of law is a great pillar of civilized societies, but it is routinely violated by US family courts. It does not decide child custody or visitation based on known principles or laws. It is entirely in the discretion of the individual judge. Is it too much to ask that the rule of law apply to family courts?

Here is a liberal opinion from Ruth Bettelheim in the *New York Times*:

> In divorced families, whose needs count for more: those of parents or those of children?
>
> When parents divorce, their child custody plans are supposed to place the "best interests of the child" first. We know children's needs change as they grow. Unfortunately, Family Courts ignore that when ordering and often make children feel helpless by denying them any influence over the arrangements that govern their lives.
>
> Today, most divorces involving children include a parenting plan that dictates where children will live and which days they will spend with each parent. The process of agreeing on a custody arrangement is often very difficult for parents, who naturally have little desire to revisit the divorce experience. As a result, the legal agreement they reach typically will govern the daily rhythm and schedule of children without change until they turn 18.
>
> In reality, a custody agreement that meets the needs of a toddler is unlikely to be right for a teenager. . . . Rendering children voiceless and powerless to meet their own changing needs, or burdening them with guilt if they try to do so, is in no one's best interest.[7]

A five-to-four Supreme Court majority ruled against a Cherokee dad who wanted to regain custody of his daughter, known as Baby Veronica. The family court had ordered an adoption by a non-Indian couple, which was arguably contrary to federal Indian adoption law.

The wife had a PhD in developmental psychology, and a judge ruled that giving them custody was in the best interest of the child. Only Justice Scalia made an argument based on parental rights in his dissent:

> The Court's opinion, it seems to me, needlessly demeans the rights of parenthood. It has been the constant practice of the common law to respect the entitlement of those who bring a child into the world to raise that child. We do not inquire whether leaving a child with his parents is "in the best interest of the child." It sometimes is not; he would be better off raised by someone else. But parents have their rights, no less than children do. This father wants to raise his daughter, and the statute amply protects his right to do so.[8]

There is no reason in law or policy to dilute that protection. As Scalia wrote, the court has become hostile to the rights of parents to raise their own children. The right to free speech is not just the right to express the most noble opinions. If families are to be free, parents must be free to make decisions that are contrary to what some judge thinks is best. Marriage must continue to be recognized as the essential unit of a stable society wherein husbands and wives provide a home and role models for the rearing of their children.

FAMILY COURTS VERSUS THE FIRST AMENDMENT

Family courts even deprive divorced fathers of many constitutional rights. For example, do you think judges should have the power to decide to which religion your children must belong and which churches they may be prohibited from attending? In December 2009 a Chicago judge made those rulings.

Cook County Circuit Judge Edward Jordan issued a restraining order to prohibit Joseph Reyes from taking his three-year-old daughter to any non-Jewish religious activities because his ex-wife argued that would contribute to "the emotional detriment of the child." Mrs. Rebecca Reyes wanted to raise her daughter in the

Jewish religion, and the judge sided with the mother. When Joseph Reyes's divorce attorney, Joel Brodsky, saw the judge's restraining order, he said, "I almost fell off my chair. I thought maybe we were in Afghanistan and this was the Taliban."

Mr. Reyes took his daughter to church anyway and let the Chicago media know about it. Soon he was back in court to be prosecuted for contempt in violating the family court order. The good news is that Reyes then drew another Cook County judge, Renee Goldfarb, who ruled on April 13, 2010, that Reyes can take his daughter to "church services during his visitation time if he so chooses." Judge Goldfarb said her decision to let Reyes take his daughter to church was based on "the best interest of the child," but then criticized Reyes for going public with his case.[9]

This case is a good illustration of the dictatorial power of family courts. Both judges purported to decide what church a child may attend based on the judge's personal opinion about what is "the best interest of the child." The choice of a church should be none of the government's business, even if the parents are divorced.

Not only did the family court try to take away a father's parental rights and his freedom of religion rights, but also his First Amendment free-speech rights. The second judge severely criticized Reyes for telling the media about his case. But publicity was the reason the family court backtracked from sending Reyes to jail for violating the restraining order. It's important to shine the light of publicity on the outrageous denial of parental rights by the family courts.

In another 2009 divorce case, a family court in New Hampshire (where the state motto is "Live Free or Die") ordered ten-year-old Amanda Kurowski to stop being homeschooled by her mother and instead to attend fifth grade in the local public school. Judge Lucinda V. Sadler approved the court-appointed expert's view that Amanda "appeared to reflect her mother's rigidity on questions of faith" and that Amanda "would be best served by exposure to multiple points of view."[10]

In March 2012, the Tennessee Court of Appeals said Lauren

Jarrell must face a criminal contempt hearing for violating a court order that major decisions regarding the religious upbringing of her two children should be made jointly with the children's father. Emmett Blake Jarrell, the father, is a member of the United Methodist Church, and she's a Presbyterian. Lauren is facing jail time for baptizing her two children, ages five and seven, without her ex-husband's knowledge or consent. The father thought the children should be baptized when they are older and better able to understand the significance of the baptismal ceremony.

Where did family court judges get the power to decide what church and what school the children of divorced parents must attend and at what age a child may be baptized? Family court judges have amassed this extraordinary power by co-opting and redefining "the best interest of the child."

CHILD PROTECTIVE SERVICES

The Child Abuse Prevention and Treatment Act was passed by Congress in 1974, and about forty-five states passed complementary state laws. Taxpayers' money began to flow big-time to the bureaucrats. The results of research into the outcome of these laws were reported in the October issue of the *Archives of Pediatrics & Adolescent Medicine*, accompanied by an editorial entitled "Child Protective Services Has Outlived Its Usefulness." It argued that Child Protective Services (CPS) should not be engaged in law enforcement. If it's a crime, call the police; if it's neglect, call a public health nurse; if it's an unsuitable living situation, call the appropriate social services.

Child Protective Services, which rushes into action based on anonymous tips, investigated more than 3 million cases of suspected child abuse in 2007. Researchers examined the records of 595 children nationwide alleged to be at similar high risk for abuse and tracked them from ages four to eight. The researchers concluded that CPS's intervention did little or nothing to improve the lives of the children, and there was no difference between children in the families CPS investigated or did not investigate. The social scientists looked at all the factors known to increase the risk for abuse or neglect: social support, family functioning, poverty, caregiver education and depressive symptoms, plus child anxiety, depression, and aggressive behavior.

Unfortunately, the researchers did not look at the harm caused by CPS bureaucrats who arrive unannounced with the police, interfere with a functioning family, and often take the children away from their parents and turn them over to foster care.

Two cases involving Child Protective Services reached the US Supreme Court. One case involved the interrogation of an elementary school child at school by a CPS caseworker and a deputy sheriff about possible sexual abuse at home.[11] Oregon investigators appealed a lower court ruling that they violated a nine-year-old girl's constitutional right to be free from unreasonable search and seizure when they interviewed her for two hours at school without a warrant, court order, parental consent, or exigent circumstances.

The other CPS case involved the constitutionality of the child abuse index, or list, maintained by Child Protective Services in California, where more than eight hundred thousand people are listed. These listings are very hurtful to individuals since employers consult the list before hiring employees to work with children.[12]

CPS puts people on this list from agency reports based on anonymous tips and suspicion, not proof. It's mighty easy for a malicious wife or ex-wife to allege child abuse as part of her game plan to get child custody or increased child support. There are no procedures, no standards, and no criteria for a wrongly accused ex-husband to get his name off the child abuse index. In 2006 Congress toyed with a plan to create a national child abuse registry, but the plan was abandoned because of unreliability of state lists and lack of due process.

THE "GAMESMANSHIP" OF DIVORCE

Family court judges issue restraining orders virtually for the asking, without any evidence of actual domestic violence or even threat of violence. In June 2005 the *Illinois Bar Journal* explained how mothers use court-issued restraining orders as a tool to get sole child custody and to bar the father from visitation. In big type, the *Journal* proclaimed: "Orders of protection are designed to prevent domestic violence, but they can also become part of the gamesmanship of divorce."[13]

The "game" is that mothers can assert falsehoods or trivial complaints against the father in order to get a restraining order based on feminist ideology that men are naturally abusers of women. Restraining orders are in reality a tactical legal maneuver familiar to all family court attorneys as a way to obtain an order of contempt and unfairly increase the leverage of one side (typically the woman's) in bargaining with the other (typically the man's).

The *Illinois Bar Journal* article stated that restraining orders, which courts "customarily" issue at an "ex parte hearing without testimony," actually "make the case ineligible for mediation," "limit settlement options," and mean that "joint parenting is not an option."

The *Final Report of the Child Custody and Visitation Focus Group* of the National Council of Juvenile and Family Court Judges admitted that "usually judges are not required to make a finding of domestic violence in civil protection order cases."[14] In other words, judges saddle fathers with restraining orders on the wife's say-so without investigation as to whether her claim is true or false, and without accountability if it is false. If a hearing is held, the woman merely needs to prove her claim by a "preponderance of the evidence." That means she doesn't have to prove the abuse happened, only that it is more likely than not to have happened.

Elaine Epstein, former president of the Massachusetts Women's Bar Association, admitted in 1993: "Everyone knows that restraining orders and orders to vacate are granted to virtually all who apply. . . .

In many [divorce] cases, allegations of abuse are now used for tactical advantage."[15]

The consequences of the issuance of restraining orders are profound: The mother gets a sole-custody order, and the father can be forbidden all contact with his children, be excluded from the family residence, and have his assets and future income put under control of the family court. A vast array of noncriminal behavior is suddenly criminalized with harsh penalties. The restraining order frequently precludes the father from possessing a firearm for any purpose, which means he loses his job if he is in the military service or law enforcement, or working for a company with so-called zero tolerance policies.

The Fourth Amendment guarantees US citizens the right to be "secure in their persons, house, papers, and effects." But each year, restraining orders are issued against men without proof or even evidence, forcing innocent men out of their own homes. In thirty-three states, fathers can be thrown in jail for even a technical violation of a restraining order, such as sending his child a birthday card or telephoning his child on an unapproved day. The application for restraining orders is usually not motivated by safety concerns but by an attempt to get child custody. It is long overdue for courts to blow the whistle on that game and restore the high standards of judicial procedure that apply in other areas of law.

Family courts have avoided facing up to whether restraining orders issued against fathers are constitutional. Accused criminals enjoy a long list of constitutional rights, but feminists have persuaded judges to issue orders that restrain noncriminal actions of husbands and fathers and punish them based on flimsy, unproved accusations. Most states do not require proof even by a "clear and convincing" standard of evidence. Even though restraining orders are issued without the due process required for criminal prosecutions, they carry the threat of a prison sentence for anyone who violates them.

The *New Jersey Law Journal* reported that an instructor taught judges to be merciless to husbands and fathers, saying, "Throw him out on the street, give him the clothes on his back, and tell him 'See ya around.'"[16]

Too often, the restraining order serves no legitimate purpose, but is just an easy way for one spouse to get revenge or the upper hand in a divorce or child custody dispute. Once a restraining order is issued, it becomes nearly impossible for a father to regain custody or even get to see his own children. That is the result even if alleged domestic violence (which doesn't have to be physical or proven) did not involve the children at all.

Probably two million restraining orders are issued each year in domestic relationships. These restraining orders often increase harm; studies show that the safest place for adults and children is in a home with two parents rather than one that is broken by a restraining order.[17] In 1999 there were 58,200 abductions of children by nonfamily members,[18] a crime often the direct result of inadequate adult supervision.

There is no evidence that the millions of restraining orders issued annually increase the overall safety of the applicants or children, and most likely the opposite is true. When an adult is ordered out of a home based on some allegation of domestic violence, the children in that home are no longer supervised as before and the danger of victimization by crime and accidents necessarily increases.

It is false to claim that because domestic violence often occurs behind closed doors, it is somehow difficult to prove. In fact, real domestic violence is easier to prove than most crimes. The medical record and forensic evidence provide clear and convincing evidence for real domestic violence. The time and place of the crime are easy to determine, and a restraining order may be appropriate. It is difficult to disprove false allegations of nonserious domestic violence, so a higher standard of proof should be required to sift fact from fiction.

It seems elementary that husbands and fathers who are accused of crimes by their wives or girlfriends should have the same constitutional rights accorded to criminals, but they do not in family courts. They are routinely denied equal treatment under law, the right to a fair trial, the presumption of innocence until proven guilty, the right to confront their accusers, and a court-appointed lawyer when they can't afford to hire an attorney. Imposing criminal-like sanctions of stigmatization and deprivation of access to one's family and home based on a mere "preponderance of evidence" is contrary to the basic presumption of innocence and is unconstitutional. The tens of thousands of restraining orders that separate fathers from their families probably cause more harm than they prevent.

It's time to restore basic constitutional rights to husbands and fathers and repudiate the feminist agenda that treats men as guilty unless proven innocent. State legislatures should pass laws specifying that a restraining order for domestic violence shall issue only on proof of "clear and convincing evidence" and that divorced parents shall have joint legal and physical custody of their children unless proof shows a parent to be unfit. The anti-father abuses by family courts are a national scandal.

The American Bar Association (ABA) is a special-interest group like any other association representing its members. A good example of a special-interest publication is "10 Custody Myths and How to Counter Them," which was produced "for use in litigation" by an ABA subgroup called the Commission on Domestic Violence.[19] This "one-page laminated tip sheet" is designed to teach lawyers how to win money verdicts against fathers by using misleading arguments masquerading as objective research. The same techniques can theoretically be used against mothers, but fathers are the chief targets because they usually have more financial resources than mothers. Litigation is often stimulated by the search for deep pockets.

An organization called Respecting Accuracy in Domestic Abuse Reporting (RADAR) published a detailed analysis of the ABA's "10 Myths." RADAR's report proves that "10 Myths" uses bogus statistics and is "profoundly and systematically biased . . . unworthy to be used as a foundation for legal practice or public policy."[20]

The ABA's "10 Myths" denies the big problems: that women frequently use false allegations of domestic violence to win child custody, and that children can be coached to betray their fathers. The publication also ignores the fact that family courts regularly deny custody and issue restraining orders against men based on a woman's unsubstantiated accusation and without giving the man fundamental due process rights.

DEBTORS' PRISONS

Debtors' prisons were common in colonial times, but they were abolished by the US government in 1833, one of the great improvements we made on English law. We also adopted bankruptcy laws to allow people a fresh start when they are overwhelmed by debt. But child-support debts are not permitted to be discharged in bankruptcy.

The federal Bradley Amendment takes us back to the cruel days of debtors' prisons. It forbids a child-support debt from being retroactively reduced or forgiven. The courts must enforce payment regardless of any change in a father's income, whether he is sent to war or locked up in prison, unemployed or hospitalized or even dead, even if DNA proves he is not the father, and even if he is never allowed to see his children.

Did you know that a family court can order a man to reimburse the government for the welfare money, falsely called "child support," that was paid to the mother of a child to whom he is not related? And that if he doesn't pay, a judge can sentence him to debtors' prison without letting him have a jury trial?

Are you aware that though our country abolished debtors' prisons (putting men in prison because they can't pay a debt) even before we abolished slavery, they exist today to punish men who are too poor to pay what is, again, deceptively labeled "child support"?

Did you know that when corporations can't pay their debts, they can file for bankruptcy and pay off their debts for pennies on the dollar, but a man can never get an alleged "child support" debt forgiven or reduced, even if he is out of a job, penniless, homeless, medically incapacitated, incarcerated (justly or unjustly), unable to afford a lawyer, serving in our Armed Forces overseas, not the child's father, or even if he never owed the money in the first place?

When a woman applying for welfare handouts lies about who is the father of her child, are you aware that she doesn't worry about being prosecuted for perjury? Or that judges can refuse to accept DNA evidence showing that the man she accuses is not the father? Did you know that alleged "child support" has nothing to do with supporting a child, because the mother has no obligation to spend even one dollar of it on a child, and in many cases none of the "support" money ever gets to a child because it instead goes to fatten the payroll of the child-support bureaucracy? These are among the injustices that feminists, and their docile liberal/progressive male allies, have inflicted on fathers.

Many of these family court injustices are caused by the Bradley Amendment, named for its sponsor, former Democratic senator and presidential candidate Bill Bradley. That 1986 federal law prohibits retroactive reduction of so-called child support even in the circumstances listed above. The Bradley law denies bankruptcy protections, overrides all statutes of limitation, and forbids judicial consideration of obvious inability to pay. Most Bradley-law victims never come to national attention because, as Bernard Goldberg wrote in his book *Bias*, mainstream media toe the feminist propaganda line of denigrating men, especially fathers, using the epithet "deadbeat dads."[21]

One egregious case did make news in 2009. Frank Hatley was in a Georgia jail for more than a year for failure to pay child support, even though a DNA test nine years earlier, plus a second one in 2009, proved that he is not the father. His ex-girlfriend had lied and claimed he was. The August 21, 2001, court order, signed by Judge Dane Perkins, acknowledged that Hatley is not the father, but nevertheless ordered him to continue paying and never told him he could have a court-appointed lawyer if he could not afford one.

Hatley subsequently paid the government (not the mom or child) thousands of dollars in "child support." Even after he was laid off from his job unloading charcoal grills from shipping containers and reduced to living in his car, he continued making payments out of his unemployment benefits.[22]

But he didn't pay enough to satisfy the avaricious child-support bureaucrats, so Judge Perkins ruled Hatley in contempt of court and sent him to jail without any jury trial. With the help of a Legal Services lawyer, he finally was released from jail and relieved from future assessments, but (because of the Bradley Amendment) the government demanded that Hatley continue paying at the rate of $250 a month until he paid off the $16,398 debt the government claimed he accumulated earlier (even though the court then knew he was not the father). He paid the debt down to $10,000 but was jailed for six months in 2006 for falling behind on payments during a period of unemployment. When he became unemployed and homeless in 2008, he was jailed again. Altogether, Hatley paid so-called child support for thirteen years and spent thirteen months in jail because of a woman's lie, the Bradley Amendment, the ruthless "child support" bureaucracy, and the family court bias against fathers.[23]

In 2009, the court relieved Hatley of any future child support payments (probably because of press publicity about this case) but did not restore his driver's license. This system is morally and constitutionally wrong, and the Bradley Amendment is particularly evil, yet authorities say all the court orders were lawful.

The New Jersey newspapers have run many articles on the sad plight of scores of unemployed men who have been thrown in jail because they've fallen behind on their child support payments. These men were even denied the services of public defenders to argue their cases.

Another type of feminist attack on marriage is the use of false allegations of child sexual abuse in order to gain child custody and the financial windfall that comes with it. Former Vancouver,

Washington, police officer Ray Spencer spent nearly twenty years in prison after being convicted of molesting his two children, who are now adults and who say it never happened. The son, who was nine years old at the time, was questioned, alone, for months until he said he had been abused in order to get the interrogator to leave him alone. The daughter, who was then five, said she talked to the interrogator after he gave her ice cream.

There were many other violations of due process in Spencer's trial, such as prosecutors withholding medical exams that showed no evidence of abuse and his court-appointed lawyer failing to prepare a defense, but the judge nevertheless sentenced Spencer to two life terms in prison, plus fourteen years. Spencer was five times denied parole because he refused to admit guilt, a customary parole practice that is designed to save face for prosecutors who prosecute innocent men.[24]

Judges routinely jail people to make them pay so-called child support even when they have no money to pay. As Ethan Bronner reported in the *New York Times,* minor offenders who cannot pay a fine or fee often find themselves in jail cells. Felony offenders who have completed their prison sentences are often sent back to jail when they cannot pay fees and fines they owe because they could not earn money while locked up. Often, these defendants are not told that they have a right to a court-appointed lawyer to challenge their detention.[25]

We read about debtors' prisons in Charles Dickens novels, but we assume they are unconstitutional in the United States today. Not so. Debtors' prisons are alive and well in one-third of the states in this country. The ACLU did an extensive investigation of debtors' prisons in 2013. Their published report documents how contemporary debtors' prisons work and profiles some of the real people in Ohio who have been impacted by this system.[26] The law requires that the court hold a hearing to determine whether the defendant is actually able to pay what he owes, but this rule is widely disregarded. The use of debtors' prisons wreaked havoc on the lives of those profiled in the ACLU report and relegated them to the outskirts of hope.

Most of the reservists called up to serve in the Iraq War paid a big price: a significant reduction of their wages as they transferred from civilian to military jobs, separation from their loved ones, and of course, the risk of battle wounds or death. Regrettably, on their return home, some divorced fathers faced other grievous penalties: loss of their children, financial ruin, prosecution as "deadbeat dads," and even jail.

Reservists' child-support orders are based on their civilian wages, and when they are called up to active duty, that burden doesn't decrease. Few can get court modification before they leave, modifications are seldom granted anyway, and even if a father applies for modification before deployment, the debt continues to grow until the case is decided much later.

These servicemen fathers cannot get relief when they return because federal law forbids a court to reduce the debt retroactively. Once the arrearage reaches five thousand dollars, the father becomes a felon subject to imprisonment plus the loss of his driver's and professional licenses and passport.

Likewise, there is no forgiving the interest and penalties on the child-support debt even though it is sometimes incurred because of human or computer errors. States have a financial incentive to refuse to reduce obligations because the federal government rewards the states with cash for the "deadbeat dad" dollars they collect.

Laws granting deployed service personnel protection against legal actions at home date back decades, but they are ignored in the family courts. Child kidnapping laws do not protect military personnel on active duty from their ex-wives relocating their children.

Congress and state legislatures should remedy this injustice to our troops serving overseas, before more fathers meet the fate of Bobby Sherrill, a father of two from North Carolina, who worked for Lockheed in Kuwait before being captured and held hostage by Iraq for five terrible months. The night he returned from the Persian Gulf, he was arrested for failing to pay $1,425 in child support while he was a captive.[27]

A Wilkes-Barre, Pennsylvania, judge sentenced twenty-eight fathers to jail for failure to pay small amounts of child support.[28] One of the most common punishments for falling behind in family court–ordered payments is to take away the father's driver's license, costing him his job, then demand that he make his child-support payments anyway, and throw him in jail when that proves impossible.

The *New York Times* exposed the ridiculous case of truck driver Donald Gardner, who was left penniless after a 1997 car accident cost him three years of hospitalization. When he tried to return to work, he found that the state had taken away his driver's license because he owed $119,846 in child support.

The *Times* further reported that, as of 2003, fathers allegedly owed $96 billion in child support. However, 70 percent is owed by men who earn less than $10,000 a year or have no wage earnings at all,[29] so the government bureaucracy is trying to get blood out of a turnip.

The most bizarre part of the system is that child-support payments are not required to be spent on the children and are not based on any estimate of their needs or expenses. The support orders come from court-created formulas based on the father's income, while the mother is allowed to treat the payments like any other cash entitlement, such as welfare.

As annoying as the Internal Revenue Service is, it follows accounting regulations and taxes only actual income. But a family court judge can ignore current income (or lack thereof) and instead calculate child support on past income or on imputed future income.

Although there are no official statistics, estimates are that more than a hundred thousand fathers are jailed each year for missing their child-support payments.[30] Another perverse feature of the current system is that child-support payments have nothing whatsoever to do with whether the father is allowed to see his children, and there is no enforcement of his visitation rights.

FAMILY COURT FATHERPHOBIA

Unsurprisingly, the media overlooked an impressive vote in November 2004. By 85 percent to 15 percent, a ballot initiative in Massachusetts approved equal legal and physical custody of children whose parents are divorced.[31] That ballot vote was nonbinding, but it is indicative of the will of the people and the growing recognition that children are best off under the care of both parents.

This initiative was sponsored by a fathers' rights group whose members believe that fathers are systematically discriminated against by family courts, which nearly always award physical custody to the mother even when the father has committed no fault. Family courts typically deny faultless fathers their equal parental rights even when state law appears to require equal custody.

Family court judges find unwelcome the task of rendering a judicial decision detached from the law and from any due process finding of fault, so they usually call on a court-appointed psychologist to provide his opinion of who should have custody. But the issue before the court is not psychological (except in rare cases of mental illness), and the psychologist's credentials no more qualify him to determine what is the best interest of the child than the father or mother.

We've been led to believe that the plight of fatherless children is caused by husbands walking out on their wives, fathers abandoning their children, and so-called deadbeat dads. No evidence supports the claim that large numbers of non-welfare fathers are voluntarily abandoning their own children. Thousands, perhaps millions, of middle-class children are growing up fatherless because family courts have deprived them of their fathers. Some 80 percent of divorces are involuntary, over the objections of one spouse.[32] Very few of these divorces involve fault, such as desertion, adultery, addictions, or abuse.

We urgently need a comprehensive study of how many family court decisions deprive fathers of their parental rights and deprive children of their fathers, when that awful punishment is not based on any finding of fault. Information is difficult to gather because most of what family courts do is not available to public scrutiny. How many children are separated by judicial fiat from involuntarily divorced fathers who have done nothing wrong? How many are separated from their fathers because of questionable child abuse accusations without any evidentiary hearing or due process?

Nebraska published a landmark study on child custody awards from 2002 to 2012. It revealed that mothers were awarded sole or primary custody in 72 percent of cases, but fathers in only 13.8 percent. Joint custody was awarded in only 12.3 percent. The average parenting time for noncustodial parents was only 5.5 days per month, and average summer parenting was 14 days.[33]

A major threat to children's rights to be raised in mother-father homes comes from the fatherphobia of family courts and from the psychologists and counselors hired by the judges. Under unilateral divorce, equality is the rule: either spouse can terminate a marriage without the other spouse's consent and without any fault committed by the cast-off spouse. But when it comes to determining child custody, sexism is the rule. By making allegations of fault (true or false, major or petty) against the male, the female can usually get the family court to grant her their children and his money.

It is supposed to be settled law in the United States that parents (note the plural) have a fundamental right to the care, custody, and control of the upbringing of their children. But feminists have persuaded the family courts, upon divorce, to acquiesce in their demands that the mother typically be given most of those fundamental rights that belonged equally to both parents before divorce.

What's behind this feminist reversal about child care? Freud famously asked, "What does a woman want?" The explanation appears to be the maxim "Follow the money." Beginning in the mid-1980s, the feminists used their political clout to get Congress to pass draconian postdivorce support-enforcement laws that use the full power of government to give the divorced mother cash income based on state-mandated formulas that are unrelated to what she spends for the children or to her willingness to allow the father to see his children.

Since the father typically has higher income than the mother, giving near-total custody to the mother enables the states to maximize transfer payments and thereby collect bigger cash bonuses from the federal government. When fathers appeal to family courts for equal time with their children, they are opposed by a big industry of lawyers, psychologists, custody evaluators, domestic-violence agitators, and government bureaucrats who make their living denying fathers their fundamental rights.

THE HOSTILITY OF FAMILY COURTS

A very public marital melodrama played out in 2012 in San Francisco and shows the extremism of the feminists and how they get government agencies to break up marriages. It started with the public release by a busybody neighbor of a picture of a bruise on the arm of the wife of the elected sheriff, Ross Mirkarimi. After six months of demeaning publicity, the city's Ethics Commission suspended him without pay and the local prosecutor charged him with the crimes of domestic violence and child endangerment. The domestic violence charge was based on Mirkarimi grabbing his wife's arm during a New Year's Eve argument which allegedly left a bruise, and the child endangerment charge was based solely on their toddler (who was not touched) being present when this argument took place.

Mirkarimi's wife, Eliana Lopez, never made any complaint and publicly defended her husband. She was a former Venezuelan telenovela star, well able to make her own decisions. At Mirkarimi's arraignment, Lopez declined to paint herself as a domestic violence victim. She told the judge, "This is unbelievable. I don't have any complaint against my husband. This country is trying to pull my family apart." She made a written statement saying that the episode was "completely taken out of context." Outside the court, Lopez told reporters that "this country has not allowed me to work on my marriage in a healthy way. I feel like ... this country is destroying my family."

Lopez did not request a restraining order but Judge Susan Breall issued one anyway, forbidding Mirkarimi to see his wife or son or to go into his own house. He didn't see them for many months. Faced with defending himself at a criminal trial, Mirkarimi agreed to a plea bargain. The prosecutor dropped the three original charges, but Mirkarimi was sentenced to three years' probation, 52 weeks of domestic violence classes, 100 hours of community service, a $400 fine, and required attendance at family counseling.

Why was this minor marital argument, in which no one filed a complaint, any of the government's business? The feminist lobby intimidated most public officials from speaking out, but former mayor Art Agnos said, "I know this man and this woman. They love each other. They love their child. It does not rise ... to anything close to domestic violence."

Despite an extended string of US Supreme Court decisions upholding the fundamental right of parents to the care, custody, and control of their children, and despite a very high standard that the government must supposedly meet in order to terminate parental legal rights, fathers are often denied due process when it comes to determining child custody after divorce.

Family courts often rely on court-appointed child-custody evaluators or psychotherapists. There is no requirement that they have any experience with raising children, and they are allowed to use their own personal prejudices to overrule the parents.

Family court judges routinely rubber-stamp child-custody evaluators who recommend mother custody, allowing the father so-called visitation only every other weekend. This is despite the mountain of social science research, such as that presented in Dr. Warren Farrell's book *Father and Child Reunion* (Tarcher, 2001), that proves that the best interest of the child of divorced parents is usually to give the child equally shared parent time.

Family courts rule as though fathers have no value except their money and routinely banish fathers (who have not been proven to have committed any misdeed) from their children's lives, except for every other weekend. Dr. Farrell describes this typical custody pattern as a loser for the child, causing intense feelings of deprivation and depressive behavior.

In his book *Twice Adopted*, Michael Reagan tells how, as the child of divorced parents, he was allowed to see his father, Ronald Reagan, only on alternating Saturdays. Michael wrote, "To an adult two weeks is just two weeks. But to a child, having to wait two weeks to see your father is like waiting forever."[34]

American courts are presumed to be based on an adversarial system, with each side arguing its best case, subject to standards of due process, evidence, and proof. Somehow, that doesn't function in family courts. Some divorce lawyers advise wives to manipulate the process by using a three-step technique: making domestic violence or child abuse allegations, demanding full custody, and demanding large amounts of child support and alimony.

In trying to defend himself against accusations, the father is denied the basic rights enjoyed by criminal defendants, such as the presumption of innocence and the necessity that the accuser provide proof beyond a reasonable doubt. Family courts force fathers to submit to interrogations and evaluations by court-chosen child-custody evaluators. Fathers are forced to pay the high fees of these private practitioners, whom they have not hired, whose services they do not want, and whose credentials and bias are suspect.

If the father objects to this process, the wife can make more accusations. The evaluators then call it a high-conflict divorce and give custody to the wife, declaring that shared parenting won't work. If the husband doesn't acquiesce, he is reprimanded by the court for "not buying into the process."

One of the most un-American aspects of family court procedure is the sentencing of fathers to attend reeducation classes and psychotherapy sessions to induce them to admit fault and to indoctrinate them in government-approved parenting behavior. The court-selected psychotherapists report back to the court on the father's supposed progress. His attendance at these Soviet-style reeducation sessions continues until he conforms.

A cozy relationship exists among the local lawyers and court-approved psychotherapists who recommend each other for this highly paid work of making evaluations, counseling, and conducting reeducation classes. The psychotherapists refuse to challenge each other's recommendations or question their competence, and the lawyers seldom cross-examine them, because they all want to continue the profitable practice of referring business to each other and collecting fees from fathers who are desperate to see their own children.

Many parents are subjected to what is called "supervised visitation." That means a parent can see his child only under carefully controlled circumstances with a court-appointed babysitter observing and reporting on everything that is said and done. These parents are not criminals and not guilty of any wrongdoing. The supervision can be ordered just because the judge has a suspicion that the parent may do or say something the judge does not approve of. This supervision can cost the parent up to one hundred dollars per hour and can continue until the child is eighteen.

The family court assumes the power to second-guess any decision a parent might make. For example, family court judges and the so-called experts they hire seldom approve of homeschooling. The latest trend is for judges to make rulings about food. One parent may complain that the other parent feeds the kid too much fast food and the kid might get fat. The judge is asked to decide how much fast food is too much.

Lurking behind the family courts' antagonistic behavior are the pretentious claims of the American Law Institute, or ALI. The ALI has presumed the authority to require broad changes to the legal definition of parenthood and the rights of parents. The ALI demands that traditional parental rights be replaced with government management of a child's interests. Under ALI proposals, parents could no longer take for granted that the government will defer to a mom and dad's decisions. The ALI wants to subject parents' wishes to the competing claims of adults not connected to the child in any way, with a judge rendering the final decision. Since the ALI rejects biology, marriage, and adoption as factors defining a parent's status, the state must decide who is and is not a parent, all at a judge's discretion. The ALI thus puts the government above the social institution of the family, and the decisions of non-related adults over the needs of children and the rights of parents. Theirs is truly a radical agenda.[35]

JAILED FOR CRITICIZING A JUDGE

Dan and Melissa Brewington were married in 2002 and had two kids in Indiana. Melissa filed for divorce in 2007, demanding sole custody, and the judge appointed psychologist Edward Connor to do a child-custody evaluation. His report recommended sole custody for Melissa, based on his argument that Dan has attention deficit disorder (ADD) and other defects, such as not handling criticism well. The only complaints about his parenting practices were things like taking the kids to an Austin Powers movie.

Dan vigorously contested the report in court before Judge James D. Humphrey and on his personal blog. He demanded that Connor substantiate his findings and accused him and Humphrey of being unethical and not following the law. Connor and Humphrey then complained about the exposure they were getting and said they felt threatened. Dan was charged with several felonies for intimidating them, convicted, and sentenced to five years in prison.

The core of the conviction was for threatening the judge. That sounds bad, but the court defined that to include exposing him to "hatred, contempt, disgrace, or ridicule."[36] The appeals court upheld the conviction in January 2013 and ruled that there was not any need to prove that Dan Brewington's criticisms were false. Dan had expressed the opinion on his blog that the judge's actions were morally tantamount to child abuse because he was forcing his kids to grow up without a father. The appeals court said that it is a felony in Indiana to criticize a judge in this way.

UCLA law professor Eugene Volokh, a leading expert on free

speech law, wrote, "This decision is wrong, and quite dangerous."[37] The First Amendment guarantees a right to criticize government officials, and often public criticism is the only way to hold corrupt officials accountable.

After Brewington completed his sentence, the Indiana Supreme Court upheld his conviction in May 2014. It conceded that Brewington had a constitutional right to criticize and ridicule judges and other court officials and that his jury was incorrectly instructed otherwise, but the court said Brewington's lawyer invited the error by vigorously asserting his free speech rights. This may be a case of judges trying to shelter other judges from criticism.

Used by permission of Chuck Asay and Creators Syndicate, Inc.

5

INCENTIVES UNDERMINE
THE FAMILY

America has changed dramatically over the last three decades in population growth and has radically changed ethnically, geographically, and culturally. The most costly of the many changes is the fact that having children has become increasingly detached from marriage. Illegitimate births for all Americans rose from 26 percent in 1990 to nearly 41 percent in 2010. Among Hispanics the rate of illegitimacy rose to 53 percent, among blacks to 73 percent, and among whites to 29 percent.[1]

This extraordinary change is the primary reason that government budgets, both federal and state, are so bloated. Without fathers to provide for these millions of children, their mothers turn to Big Brother. Economist Robert J. Samuelson summarized this by saying that "the welfare state is winning the budget war." The bipartisan budget deal, which slashed our military budget but kept welfare-state handouts off-limits, turned out to be "a triumph of the welfare state over the Pentagon."[2]

That was exactly what Barack Obama planned to do in 2008 when he told Joe the Plumber he wanted to redistribute the wealth and told Chicago's WBEZ-FM that his favorite Supreme Court chief justice, Earl Warren, wasn't radical enough because the Warren Court "never ventured into the issues of redistribution of wealth."[3] We are already spending nearly a trillion dollars a year in means-tested welfare payments and benefits.

The famous economist Arthur Laffer explained the powerful role of financial incentives:

> It is tempting to dismiss the role played by incentives in economics, but the persistence of poverty in the inner city and elsewhere is difficult to explain with any other view of human behavior. Poor people, like everyone else, respond to incentives. . . .
>
> The first step is to consider the role played by disincentives; disincentives do work because government benefits fall away as income rises. . . .
>
> A single mother of two in the Keystone State earning no wages will obtain welfare benefits—such as food stamps, child care and Medicaid services—worth more than $45,000 annually. If the woman begins earning wages, her total annual income, including the value of her welfare benefits, will rise as well—up to about $9,000 in wages. But the next $5,000 in wages will not increase her total income, because she will lose some Medicaid and other benefits. In short, she faces the equivalent of a 100% marginal tax.
>
> From about $14,000 to $29,000 of gross wages, she will also lose government benefits such that her total annual income will rise only about $5,000—an effective marginal tax rate of 67%. At $29,000 of wages, the woman will realize a little less than $57,000 in net income plus benefits. Once she earns more than $29,000 in wages her housing subsidies and food subsidies drop way down. With wages above $43,000, her child-care subsidies disappear, and once her wages top $57,000 her family will no longer qualify for the Children's Health Insurance Program.
>
> What this means is that her total income—welfare benefits plus wages, minus taxes—won't reach $57,000 until her gross wage income rises to $69,000. In other words, the money earned by her between $29,000 and $69,000 faces a marginal tax rate, on average, of 100%. She receives no net benefit from her labor.[4]

So the subsidies to women who have no husbands have promoted more and more children growing up without fathers. As long as the taxpayers pay the financial costs of supporting millions of illegitimate children, we cannot restore the limited government and balanced federal budgets that we say we want and respect. When we were a nation of nuclear families, with fathers as providers and protectors, we got along jolly well without government handouts. When the nuclear family disappears, the government steps in as provider and decider.

Therefore, the decline of marriage is not just a moral, social, or cultural issue. It is America's biggest fiscal issue. Spending problems begin with marriage absence and quickly move to massive deficit spending. Without marriage, single moms look to the government for handouts, and marriage absence has become a major cause of national deficits. Poverty is chiefly predicted by family structure. Married individuals are more in control of their lives, more productive, and more likely to work full time and make the extra effort to succeed regardless of their line of work. Without marriage, people lack the economic structure necessary for starting and running small businesses—the backbone of our economy.

In the 1998 *Survey of Consumer Finances*, researchers reported that, compared to cohabiting households, single male–headed households and single female–headed households, marriage-based households (1) have higher median incomes, (2) are more likely to own a business and real estate, (3) carry less debt relative to their assets, and (4) have greater net worth. The study also found that married-couple households enjoy greater levels of human capital as expressed in the number of their children.

W. Bradford Wilcox, director of the National Marriage Project at the University of Virginia and president of Demographic Intelligence, the premier provider of US fertility forecasts and fertility analytics for major companies, told *National Review Online* how marriage and fertility impact the economy:

Adults are more likely to behave responsibly from a financial perspective when they get and stay married. We also know that children in the U.S. are more likely to graduate from high school, attend college, and be gainfully employed when they are raised in an intact, married family.

Finally, men work harder, work smarter, and work longer hours after they get married. This translates into a marriage premium of about 19% for men in the United States. Thus, marriage seems to draw men into a higher level of engagement in the economy.

So, the fact that the marriage rate has fallen by about 50% since 1970, and that about half of all American children will now spend time outside of an intact, married family would seem to be of some consequence for the health of the American economy.

Insofar as the family is a major generator of human and social capital and a major engine of consumption, I think it's fair to make the case—as we do in *The Sustainable Demographic Dividend*—that strong families play a key role in sustaining long-term economic growth, the viability of the welfare state, the size and quality of the workforce, and the profitability of large sectors of the modern economy.[5]

The American people were first alerted to the effects of family breakup by a liberal in Lyndon Johnson's Labor Department, Daniel Patrick Moynihan, who wrote a report in 1965 called, "The Negro Family: The Case for National Action." The American people didn't want to believe his message, but time has proven him prophetic.

Moynihan didn't identify the cause of family breakup, but with the benefit of hindsight we can see that it wasn't poverty that produced broken families; the black family remained intact during the Great Depression. Government subsidies produced illegitimacy and poverty. Giving cash and benefits to single moms, beginning with Lyndon Johnson's War on Poverty, destroyed families by making fathers unnecessary. Fathers even became an impediment to the women receiving free money.

This analysis was confirmed by British commentator Melanie

Phillips, who described the 2012 London riots as the result of "the promotion of lone parenthood" and "the willed removal" of fathers from the family unit by the welfare state and the "ultra-feminist wreckers" of the traditional family with its male breadwinner. She called for removing "the incentives to girls and women to have babies outside marriage" and for dismantling "the concept of entitlement" from the welfare state.[6]

Financial incentives are powerful motivators built into tax credits, tax reductions, and tax bonuses. They significantly influence human behavior in home ownership, use of energy, choice of transportation, and even waste management. Sometimes the law contains incentives that produce unplanned, unexpected, or undesirable results. The Great Society welfare system is now recognized as a social disaster that promoted illegitimacy, women's dependency on the government, and fatherless children. Channeling taxpayer handouts only to mothers provided a powerful financial incentive for fathers to depart; they were not needed anymore.

Marriage absence is the biggest cause of poverty and a major cause of unbalanced budgets and our colossal national debt. The social issue of marriage and the fiscal cost of marriage are linked in a tight embrace and cannot be separated. Political campaign strategists are ridiculous when they advise candidates to avoid social issues. Social issues are where the taxpayers' money is spent. We must reverse the giving of taxpayer-financed incentives *from* anti-marriage and anti-father *to* pro-marriage and returning the provider role to husbands and fathers.

WELFARE REFORM

The Republican Congress elected in 1994 made welfare reform one of its major goals. It was part of the Contract with America. The Personal Responsibility and Work Opportunity Act of 1996,[7] which President Bill Clinton finally signed, was cheered as a stunning legislative achievement because it helped move millions of welfare recipients out of dependency and into productive jobs.

However, the work condition of this act, which required those receiving aid to get a job, or train to get a job, did not produce more marriages or a return of fathers to the home. Then, President Obama unilaterally and illegally abolished the "Work" requirement on July 12, 2012.

One of the purposes of the 1996 welfare reform was to reduce the budget deficit by recovering welfare costs from absentee fathers. The law incentivized the states to go after "noncustodial" fathers to recover child-support payments (usually through wage garnishment), thereby making sure that a large segment of Americans are under tight control of the welfare bureaucracy and the family courts. However, in the welfare class, most absentee fathers are unemployed or working for wages so low that little or no money can be squeezed out of them.

The federal government annually provides more than $4 billion in block grants to states to serve as collection agencies. This includes 80 percent of their costs for technology and 66 percent of their costs of DNA testing for paternity. The more cases the states can create and the more operational expenses that states incur, the more federal funding flows to the states to expand their welfare bureaucracy. No performance standards are required to get this money, and the feds even provide a bonus fund for which the states compete. Federal funding thus encourages states to maximize the number of single-parent households with high transfer payments.

These powerful financial incentives produced massive anti-marriage and anti-father unintended consequences. Without justification or any public debate, the law incentivized the bureaucracy to put many thousands of middle-class "never welfare" families under the control of the welfare bureaucracy and under supervision of the family courts. Here is how the bureaucracy did it.

When a couple with children is separated, the family court typically labels one parent "custodial" and the other "noncustodial." The more time with the children that is awarded to the custodial parent (usually the mother), the more money the noncustodial parent (usually the father) is ordered to pay, which can then be reported by the states as collections that qualify for the federal bonus competition. Federal funding thus produces incentives for states to maximize their number of single-parent households with high transfer payments, and to minimize equal mother-father child custody cases that don't require large transfer payments. Depriving or reducing children's access to one parent thus became a source of revenue for the states.

These incentives influence family court "discretion" and skew the opinions of the vast army of lawyers, psychologists, custody evaluators, and parenting counselors who rationalize the process. They hide their anti-father custody rulings under the caveat "the best interest of the child."

Put another way, forcibly depriving children of access to one parent, usually the father because he typically has a higher income than the mother, became a source of revenue to the state bureaucracies. The more support orders that are issued and the higher they are, and the more fathers who are threatened with jail and loss of their driver's and professional licenses for challenging the system, the more money a state receives from the feds.

This effect was accurately predicted by Leslie L. Frye, chief of Child Support for the California Department of Social Services. In testifying to the Human Resources Subcommittee of the House Ways and Means Committee on March 20, 1997, Frye said the new regulations "encouraged states to recruit middle class families, never dependent on public assistance and never likely to be so, into their programs in order to maximize federal child support incentives."[8]

Of the 43 percent of American children now growing up in homes without their own fathers, very few are victims of the stereotypical deadbeat dad.[9] Many are victims of the federal incentives to create female-headed households, first by the Democrats' welfare system and then by the Republicans' so-called welfare reform. Many consciences should be burdened with the realization that taxpayers' money provides financial incentives to deprive millions of children of their own fathers.

Back in 1993, pondering the sad plight of the 20 million

American children growing up without their fathers in the home, Charles Murray identified illegitimacy as "the single most important social problem of our time . . . because it drives everything else."[10] He was prophetic; by 2010 illegitimate births in the United States had increased to 41 percent,[11] and US taxpayers were spending more in cash and benefits on those dependent on government than on national security.

Prior to Lyndon Johnson's War on Poverty, most husbands and fathers provided for their families. Now, the unmarried moms and their out-of-wedlock babies look to Big Brother as their financial provider. The Left is content to let this problem persist because 70 percent of unmarried women voted for Barack Obama for president.[12]

The financial incentives that encourage non-marriage are one of the biggest reasons why federal spending is out of control. There is no way to make significant cuts in the federal deficit unless we address the marriage-absence problem. Poverty is massively greater for children living with a single, divorced, or cohabiting parent than with parents who are married to each other. The poverty rate for single parents with children is 36.5 percent, but is only 6.4 percent for married couples with children.[13]

At the same time that government becomes the financial provider and caregiver for millions of children, government's tax receipts to pay for the handouts are reduced. Income tax day now divides us into two almost equal classes: those who *work* for their income and those who *vote* for their income.

Obama's solution for the poverty problem is more redistribution of money from taxpayers to the poor. There's no evidence that more money is the remedy, because we've been increasing handouts every year, and the problem keeps getting worse. Contrary to a lot of chatter, this isn't just a teenage problem (only 7.7 percent of new single moms are minors[14]), it isn't a failure of birth control, and it isn't the accidents of unplanned pregnancies. Most of the single moms want their babies and confidently expect Big Brother to provide for them.

THE HIDDEN WELFARE STATE

Robert Rector's congressional testimony on April 17, 2012, summed up the fiscal costs of the means-tested welfare state: seventy-nine programs and $927 billion in annual spending:

> The hidden welfare state [is] a massive complex of 79 federal means-tested anti-poverty programs.
>
> The public is almost totally unaware of the size and scope of government spending on the poor. This is because Congress and the mainstream media always discuss welfare in a fragmented, piecemeal basis. Each of the 79 programs is debated in isolation as if it were the only program affecting the poor. This piecemeal approach to welfare spending perpetuates the myth that spending on the poor is meager . . .
>
> Sound policies to aid the poor must be developed holistically, with decision makers and the public fully aware of the magnitude of overall spending. . . .
>
> The size of the federal means-tested aid system is particularly large because it is funded not only with federal revenue but also with state funds contributed to federal programs. . . .
>
> The means-tested welfare system consists of 79 federal programs providing cash, food, housing, medical care, social services, training, and targeted education aid to poor and low income Americans. Means-tested welfare programs differ from general government programs in two ways. First, they provide aid exclusively to persons (or communities) with low incomes; second, individuals do not need to earn eligibility for benefits through prior fiscal contributions. Means-tested welfare therefore does not include Social Security, Medicare, unemployment insurance, or worker's compensation. . . .
>
> In FY2011, federal spending on means-tested welfare came to $717 billion. State contributions into federal programs added another $201 billion, and independent state programs contributed around $9 billion. Total spending from all sources reached $927 billion.
>
> About half of means-tested spending is for medical care. Roughly 40 percent goes to cash, food, and housing aid. The remaining 10 to 12 percent goes [to] what might be called

"enabling" programs, programs that are intended to help poor individuals become more self-sufficient. These programs include child development, job training, targeted federal education aid and a few other minor functions.

The total of $927 billion per year in means-tested aid is an enormous sum of money. One way to think about this figure is that $927 billion amounts to $19,082 for each American defined as "poor" by the Census. . . .

Despite the fact that welfare spending was already at record levels when he took office, President Obama has increased federal means-tested welfare spending by more than a third. . . .

The 79 means-tested programs operated by the federal government provide a wide variety of benefits. The federal welfare state includes: 12 programs providing food aid; 12 programs funding social services; 12 educational assistance programs; 11 housing assistance programs; 10 programs providing cash assistance; 9 vocational training programs; 7 medical assistance programs; 3 energy and utility assistance programs; and, 3 child care and child development programs. . . .

Since the beginning of the War on Poverty, government has spent $19.8 trillion (in inflation-adjusted 2011 dollars) on means-tested welfare. In comparison, the cost of all military wars in U.S. history from the Revolutionary War through the current war in Afghanistan has been $6.98 trillion (in inflation-adjusted 2011 dollars). The War on Poverty has cost three times as much as all other wars combined.[15]

Rector's solution to the poverty problem is marriage. He urges government policies to promote and strengthen the institution of marriage instead of providing disincentives to discourage it. Marriage drops the probability of child poverty by 82 percent. Marriage has just as dramatic an effect as adding five to six years to the parents' level of education. If single moms were to marry the fathers of their children, the children would be lifted out of poverty. Eight out of ten of these fathers were employed at the time of the births of their out-of-wedlock children.[16]

Government should reduce or eliminate the marriage penalties in welfare programs, in tax law, and even in Obamacare. Rector explains that marriage penalties occur in many means-tested welfare programs, such as food stamps, public housing, Medicaid, day care, and Temporary Assistance to Needy Families (TANF).

Interviews with low-income single moms show that they are not hostile to marriage as an institution or as a life goal. In fact, they dream of having a husband, children, a minivan, and a house in the suburbs "with a white picket fence,"[17] but nobody tells them they will probably always be poor if they have babies without getting married. What about the guidance we give kids in school? We tell them they will be poor if they become school dropouts and that it's self-destructive to use illegal drugs, but it's just as important to warn them about the life of poverty ahead of them if they produce babies without marriage.

What about the moral guidance we expect from the churches? Do they tell young people not to pretend they can form a "family" without marriage? Where is compassion for the children who need and want their own fathers to help raise and guide them? What about the conservatives who limit their concerns to fiscal priorities? Do they face up to what the taxpayers' money is spent on? Do they advocate cutting the taxpayer-paid incentives that encourage illegitimate births?

The temptation to cheat is ever present. The Census Bureau reported that one-quarter of single moms receiving generous tax-payer cash and benefits actually have a partner living in the house whom they don't marry because marriage would reduce their government handouts.

INCOME TAX POLICY

For more than sixty years, the federal income tax treated the family as an economic unit. A husband and wife had the benefit of pooling their income in a joint tax return that afforded larger deductions and lower rates. The joint income tax return for husband and wife was landmark legislation, passed by the Republican Congress in 1948 over President Harry Truman's veto.

As originally designed, the joint return recognized a husband and wife as two equal partners, even if the husband earned all the family's income. Each tax bracket, deduction, and exemption was equal to twice that of a single person. Single-earner married couples filed their income tax return as two people, which they certainly are.

The postwar baby boom happened during the twenty-year period when married couples were thus fairly valued in the federal income tax. That's not coincidence; incentives matter. America's marriage rate and birth rate plummeted after the value of the joint return was reduced.

Subsequent tax reform bills, especially the one signed by President Nixon in 1969 (which also introduced the hated Alternative Minimum Tax), reduced the value of a joint return to only about 1.6 persons, while increasing the tax benefit of an unmarried "head of household" to about 1.4 persons. Simple arithmetic (1.4 + 1 = 2.4 persons) shows that a single parent with an unmarried live-in "partner" gets more favorable tax treatment than respectable married couples struggling to support their own children.

The tax code severely undermines marriage when it gives unmarried households (mostly single women with children) better benefits than married couples with children. Having babies without marriage should be discouraged, not rewarded with tax breaks. Any low-income allowance or standard exemption should be reserved for families headed by a mother and father who are legally married to each other, living together, and raising their own natural or adopted children. Single-parent households with children should not be eligible for tax breaks (especially if they are cheating by not reporting the income of a live-in "partner").

The majority of Americans say they support traditional marriage: the union of a husband and a wife.[18] So we should not permit our fiscal policies to discriminate against traditional marriage and against the right and need of children to have a father and a mother married to each other. It's time to restore marriage preference in the income tax code.

Don't let anyone tell you that federal policy should be neutral about marriage, children, the family, or the tax rates that apply to them. There is no such thing as a neutral tax or a neutral deduction or a neutral credit. Every part of our income tax return is a manifestation of some social policy.

The whole concept of a progressive income tax is social policy. We as a nation adopted the social policy that those with more income must pay federal income taxes at higher *rates* than those with less income. It's a decision of social policy that we can deduct gifts to religious and charitable organizations and for some retirement savings. It's a decision of social policy to promote home ownership by being able to deduct mortgage interest payments.

Social policy honoring and benefiting the full-time homemaker has been an essential feature of the Social Security system since its creation in 1935. Under the Carter administration, the feminists pursued three alternative plans to deprive full-time homemakers of this benefit, but fortunately they were not successful.[19]

The clear recognition of the unique role that traditional marriage plays in society and of the duty of government to give it preference over other lifestyles was explained in a 2013 Canadian Supreme Court decision. In what became known as the Eric and Lola case, this decision upheld Quebec's laws that provide rights to married couples that do not apply to couples merely living together: "Those who choose to marry choose the protections, but also the responsibilities, associated with that status. Those who choose not to marry avoid these state-imposed responsibilities and protections."[20]

GLOBALISM VERSUS HOMEMAKERS

A major goal of the feminists from the beginning of their push for liberation from the patriarchy was and is to make full-time homemakers discontented with their lot and drive them into the paid labor force to enjoy the feminist promise of a more fulfilling life. This feminist strategy never had anything to do with a family's economic need. It was based on the premise that taking care of one's own children is a demeaning occupation for an educated woman and that she can achieve "identity" and fulfillment only by working a paid job in the labor force. Feminist political pressure demanded affirmative action jobs for women, so the majority of jobs Obama's stimulus created were for women, not men. Obama and the liberals engaged in a lot of idle talk about "shovel-ready jobs," but since those would have been mostly men's jobs, they didn't materialize. Gone were the days of arguments for a family wage and preferences for a man supporting his family, so homemakers flooded into the workplace.

Feminist dogma demands that husband and wife discard the different, complementary roles that centuries of experience indicate are most likely to produce stable marriages, enlivened by satisfying sexuality. Feminist Karen DeCrow (former president of the National Organization for Women, who was not married) summarized the feminist demand: "No man should allow himself to support his wife—no matter how much she favors the idea, no matter how many centuries this domestic pattern has existed, no matter how logical the economics of the arrangement may appear, no matter how good it makes him feel. . . . Love can flourish between adults only when everyone pays his or her own way."[21]

America's great economic growth in the first half of the twentieth century offered the realistic opportunity for a man from the wrong side of the tracks, and an immigrant just getting off the boat at Ellis Island, to start with a low-pay, entry-level job and, within a few years, rise into the middle class. America built a middle class that was the envy of the world. It was part and parcel of respect for the nuclear family, based on the complementary roles of husband and wife: a husband-provider, professional or blue-collar, earning a salary that paid enough to support his wife as a full-time homemaker, plus their children, and to buy or rent a dwelling for his family to live in. That's what we called the American Dream.

In the 1970s and '80s, that American Dream was chased away by two powerful pressure groups: the globalists and feminists. The one-world globalists and their lobbyists jimmied our laws to force Americans to compete with low-wage workers in poor countries all over the world. Their slogans of globalism and free trade turned out to be a tremendous aid to the feminists in helping them achieve their primary goal of killing the nuclear family.

Free trade transferred millions of good, middle-class jobs to low-wage countries, thereby reducing or even destroying the financial ability of millions of men to support a full-time homemaker. This facilitated the feminists' goal of driving full-time homemakers into the paid labor force.[22]

High US corporate taxes, the highest in the world, are one major factor in making American manufacturing noncompetitive and incentivizing corporations to outsource plants to foreign countries. Our policy that imposes high business taxes on profits from domestic manufacturing, while postponing taxes on overseas profits almost indefinitely, provides more incentives. The products made in foreign countries enter the United States with little or no US tax ever paid.

Over the past four decades, the United States has transferred millions of our high-paying manufacturing jobs overseas. We lost an average of fifty thousand manufacturing jobs every month between 2001 and 2011. Working-class earnings fell more than 20 percent from their high point in 1973. Husbands are no longer able to support their families, and demoralized workers have taken low-paying or part-time jobs, or have left the labor force.

Unemployment figures are not a good measure of the problem. The most important factor is that 20 percent of American men are not in the workforce, and those 20 percent are not all included in unemployment figures. Some have just dropped out of the count, no longer looking for a job, perhaps depending on the paychecks of their wives, girlfriends, or parents.

Since millions of good jobs have been outsourced to China and other low-wage countries, the husband is now lucky if he gets a low-paid or part-time job and can send his wife out to look for another minimum-wage job. NPR reports that taxpayers are now supporting fifty million Americans on food stamps.[23]

Free trade doesn't mean products moving freely from country to country. Free trade requires rules that nations are supposed to obey. What is marketed as free trade means a giant step toward global government. In 1994 in a lame-duck session, Congress surreptitiously added the fourteen-page charter for the World Trade Organization to a twenty-two-thousand-page treaty called the General Agreement on Tariffs and Trade. That locked us into a sort of global supreme court of trade, empowered to make unappealable rulings, monitor national responses, compel enforcement of its decisions, impose sanctions and fines, and authorize retaliation against disobedient nations. The goal of many supporters of this agreement is to force American workers to compete with the pitifully low wages paid in the rest of the world, both by sending US jobs overseas and by importing cheap labor.

"Free trade" is a dishonest slogan to describe our economic relations with other countries. In the words of the old adage, "it takes two to tango," but the United States abides by World Trade Organization (WTO) rules while other countries don't dance and remain highly protectionist.

With the Communist Party in the driver's seat, China cheats Americans coming and going. China violates international law and trade agreements, slaps taxes and regulations on US plants in China, forces US corporations to give our patents and manufacturing secrets to Chinese competitors, and uses regulations to reward China's friends and punish noncooperative countries. It produces illegal copies of our copyrighted music, movies, and software; makes illegal knockoffs of our patented designer apparel and medicines; subsidizes the export of goods made in Chinese-owned plants; and repeatedly sends us medicines, fish, and toys contaminated with poisonous substances.

Free trade with China is certainly not a two-way street. China has no plan to become a market for American products. China's principal imports are and will continue to be US jobs.

The elimination of jobs that enable a man to support a full-time homemaker caring for his own children turned out to be a tremendous victory for the feminists' antifamily, antimale ideology. Free trade became a major force responsible for the killing of the American nuclear family. The financial cost of free trade on families was underscored on April 22, 2014, when the front page of the *New York Times* announced that the United States no longer has the most prosperous middle class in the world. We rank only third.

MARRIAGE PENALTY IN HEALTH CARE

Even though all evidence shows that marriage is the best remedy for poverty, lack of health care, domestic violence, child abuse, school dropouts, and bloated welfare programs, government policies continue to discriminate against marriage and give taxpayer handouts to those who reject marriage. A huge marriage penalty is hidden in Obamacare. This isn't any accident; it is a central part of the Democrats' political strategy that resulted in 70 percent of unmarried women voting for Obama for president.[24]

Obama's health care law discriminates against marriage while financially favoring unmarried couples living together. Here is the cost in the House bill for an unmarried couple who each earn $25,000 a year (total: $50,000). When they each buy health insurance (which is mandatory), the combined premiums they pay will be capped at $3,076 a year. But if the couple gets married and has the combined income of $50,000, they will pay annual premiums up to a cap of $5,160 a year. That means they must fork over a marriage penalty of $2,084. The marriage penalty results from the fact that government subsidies for buying health insurance are pegged to the federal poverty guidelines. Couples who remain unmarried are rewarded with a separate health care subsidy for each income.

When a *Wall Street Journal* reporter quizzed the Democratic authors of Obamacare, they made it clear that this differential was deliberate. The staffer justified the discriminatory treatment because "you have to decide what your goals are." Indeed, the Democrats have decided what their goals are. They know that nearly three-quarters of unmarried women voted for Obama, and the Democrats want to reward this group with health insurance preferences.

The House staffer told the *Wall Street Journal* reporter that the Democrats can't make the subsidies neutral toward marriage because that would give a traditional one-breadwinner married couple a more generous subsidy than a single parent at the same income level. Horrors! The Democrats certainly are not going to allow traditional marriage to be preferred over couples who just cohabit!

Greenberg Quinlan Rosner, a liberal firm that consults for clients such as Bill Clinton and John Kerry, admitted: "Unmarried women represent one of the most reliable Democratic cohorts in the electorate . . . leading the charge for fundamental change in health care."[25]

Obamacare will thus ratchet up the federal welfare spending that already produces many financial incentives to remain single. These include the Earned Income Tax Credit (EITC), housing benefits, food stamps, child support enforcement, and the entire Great Society welfare apparatus.

Robert Rector summarized the marriage penalty in Obamacare in a Heritage Foundation report:

> One bizarre feature of the Senate-passed health care bill is its pervasive bias against marriage. Under the bill, couples would face massive financial penalties if they marry or remain married. Conversely, couples who cohabit without marriage are given highly preferential financial treatment. If the Senate bill becomes law, saying "I do" would cost some couples over $10,000 per year.
>
> Most people feel that marriage is a healthful institution that society should encourage and strengthen. Inexplicably, the Senate health care bill takes the opposite approach. At nearly all age and income levels, the bill profoundly discriminates against

married couples, providing far less support to a husband and wife than to a cohabiting couple with the same income. If the bill is enacted, married couples across America will be taxed to provide discriminatory benefits to couples who cohabit, divorce, or never marry. . . .

The stiff anti-marriage penalties and heavy "cohabitation bonuses" built into the Senate ObamaCare bill send a negative social message. In addition, the bill creates large incentives for couples to "game the system," allowing and encouraging them to reap large financial rewards by living together rather than marrying. For example, a young couple without children, age 20, each making $20,000, would receive $4,317 more in health benefits each year if they cohabit rather than marry. Slipping on the wedding ring would cut the couple's annual disposable income by more than 10%. Rather than pay this new wedding tax, the couple is likely to postpone marriage or forgo it entirely.

Under the bill, the anti-marriage penalties increase sharply as a couple ages. The discriminatory anti-marriage penalties are particularly severe on middle-class "empty nester" couples. Many of those couples would pay an effective tax of $5,000 to $10,000 per year for the right to remain married. For example, a 60-year-old couple, each earning $30,000 per year, would receive $10,425 per year less in benefits if they marry or remain married. Simply by divorcing and then living together, the couple can boost their post-tax, take-home income by nearly one-fourth. . . .

Annual penalties actually understate the depth of the anti-marriage bias in the Senate bill. The bill's wedding tax is perpetual. Penalties against married couples add up year after year as long as the couple remains married. Some couples who remained married throughout their adult lives would face cumulative penalties of over $200,000 during the course of their marriage. . . .

The Senate health care bill sends a clear message: Married couples are second-class citizens. On the other hand, the bill establishes cohabiters as a privileged special interest, quietly channeling tens of thousands of dollars to them in preferential government bonuses. Offering couples massive financial rewards on the condition they jettison their wedding vows, or decline to make them in the first place, is absurd social policy.[26]

"The way this bill is structured, there are disincentives for women to marry and disincentives for women to work," said Diana Furchtgott-Roth, a senior fellow at the Manhattan Institute for Policy Research, in testimony before the House Subcommittee on Health Care. "And for a bill that's supposed to make Americans healthier, these disincentives are truly startling."[27] Fox News commented on her testimony, explaining the disincentive:

> Critics say that beginning in 2014, Americans will find it more advantageous to stay single than marry because it will be easier to afford health coverage. Why? The new law provides generous subsidies for those without insurance so they can buy it on the new exchanges, but the subsidies are tied to one's income level and there's the rub. Two singles would each be able to earn $43,000 and still receive help to purchase health insurance, but if they got married and combined their earnings to $86,000, they would be far above the limit.[28]

Economist Robert J. Samuelson explains in the *Washington Post* how our economic policies are a major cause of the decline in marriage:

> In a paper for Third Way, a liberal think tank, economists David Autor and Melanie Wasserman of the Massachusetts Institute of Technology attribute the decline of marriage—which, like Murray, they say is concentrated among the poorly educated—to the eroding economic heft of men compared with women. Women are more independent economically; men are weaker. Marriage has lost much of its pecuniary pull.[29]

COLLEGE LOANS, DISINCENTIVES TO MARRIAGE

The huge debt when students come out of college is a powerful deterrent to marriage and also to having children. Young adults don't want to take on the additional expenses of marriage and children when they can't see any closure to their huge college debt. The *New York*

Times reported the experience of a college girl who thought she had met the man of her dreams. But the music stopped when he suddenly asked a very unromantic question: "What's your credit score?" He told her she was the perfect girl for him, but "a low credit score was his deal-breaker." Another woman explained, "Credit scores are like the dating equivalent of a sexually transmitted disease test."[30]

An Associated Press analysis in 2012 of college graduates ages twenty-five and younger reported that more than 50 percent are either unemployed or in jobs that don't require a college degree.[31] Yet some of them are carrying college debt of $100,000.[32] A study by Fidelity Investments found that 70 percent of the class of 2013 graduated with a college debt averaging $35,200.[33] Here is the practical attitude of one student, as reported in the *New York Times*: "The entire college loan system is a racket. The taxpayers don't owe anyone a college education. There are not enough jobs to make it worthwhile for everyone to go to college. The debt skyrocketed when students and colleges both saw the chance to get free money. It now looks like we'll end up with the taxpayers picking up the major part of the financial loss."

The effect of incentives was explained further by Glenn Harlan Reynolds, law professor at the University of Tennessee:

> Here's where the real immorality kicks in. The skyrocketing cost of a college education is a classic unintended consequence of government intervention. Colleges have responded to the availability of easy federal money by doing what subsidized industries generally do: Raising prices to capture the subsidy. Sold as a tool to help students cope with rising college costs, student loans have instead been a major contributor to the problem.[34]

Freakonomics radio podcast provides a lesson on incentives called the "cobra effect": This "refers to a scheme in colonial India where the British governor, or whoever [was] in charge in Delhi, wanted to rid Delhi of cobras. Apparently . . . there were too many cobras in Delhi, so he" placed a bounty on cobras, expecting that to "solve the problem." But some of the population in Delhi "responded by farming cobras. And all of a sudden the administration was getting too many cobra skins. And they decided the scheme wasn't as smart as it appeared initially and they rescinded it." The cobra farmers were left with a population of cobras and no market to get rid of them. So they just released them, which significantly worsened the cobra menace in Delhi. India learned a good lesson on the power of incentives.[35]

In 2012 I wrote an article about facing the reality of social issues. An anonymous commenter posted:

> I am a Physician Assistant who works in a pediatric office. I am repeatedly appalled at the morality of the parents of the young children that I treat. Most are not married but have chosen to have many children. The father has a good job with health insurance and the mother and child are on Medicaid. They ask that child's Medicaid be charged for their child's healthcare so that they do not have to pay father's insurance co-pays. They see this as a benefit to staying unmarried. Children see that the value placed on money takes precedence over the institute of marriage. This is so sad. When I discuss this with others, many laugh and say that they are glad the little guy has found a way to cheat the system like our government cheats us. How can we ever restore this broken system?[36]

FALLOUT FROM THE 2012 ELECTION

The 2012 election exit polls showed that the future of the Democratic Party depends on destroying the traditional family. Mitt Romney decisively won the votes of citizens in nuclear families. Barack Obama received his winning votes from unmarried voters, non-Christians, and other groups that reject American familialism.

On his syndicated radio program, Rush Limbaugh argued that Obama was reelected president because he now symbolizes the "low-information voter." Richard Stengel, the editor of *Time* magazine, explained that *Time* chose Obama for "Person of the Year" because he is "a symbol, the champion, of the new low-information American." Rush Limbaugh played Stengel's explanation:

> Our Person of the Year for 2012 is . . . President Barack Obama. . . . He won reelection despite a higher unemployment rate than anybody's had to face in 70 years. He's the first Democrat to actually win two consecutive terms with over 50% of the vote. That's something we haven't seen since Franklin Delano Roosevelt. And he's basically the beneficiary and the author of a kind of new America, a new demographic, a new cultural America.
>
> Our story by Michael Scherer, our White House correspondent, really probes deeply into the "data folks" at the White House who really help make it happen. And one of the things they found out is there's about 15% of voters who actually don't care about politics. These are the people we didn't know who are gonna show up at the polls who actually like Barack Obama, in the sense they feel like he's outside of politics.[37]

This 15 percent voter bloc cannot be reached with debates and rational political argument. They don't know enough about what is going on, and they vote like zombies.

New York Times columnist Maureen Dowd, whose book *Are Men Necessary?* talks about the difficult time feminists have finding a husband, wrote that in the 2012 election, voters were demagogued into voting tribally by Democrats who spread anti-Republican hatred. Here is her liberal gloating:

> The Mayans were right, as it turns out, when they predicted the world would end in 2012. It was just a select world: the G.O.P. universe of arrogant, uptight, entitled, bossy, retrogressive white guys. Just another vanishing tribe that fought the cultural and demographic tides of history. . . .
>
> Instead of smallpox, plagues, drought and Conquistadors, the Republican decline will be traced to a stubborn refusal to adapt to a world where poor people and sick people and black people and brown people and female people and gay people count.[38]

Dowd and other progressives are counting on the tribal and low-information voters and are convinced that Democrats now have enough of those voters to control the political future of America.

The Democratic Party base consists of people who are dependent on government benefits and liberals playing victims of supposed Republican policies.[39] The real trick was getting all those people to vote. The Obama campaign machine did this successfully with negative ads, early voting, absentee voting, hate campaigns, social media, clever spam, press manipulators, and nagging the base.

Since the 2012 election, Democrats have been bragging that trends are making them the majority party. They say they have won women, immigrants, and young people, and therefore have a lock on the White House. The truth requires a deeper look. Ann Coulter wrote:

> On closer examination, it turns out that young voters, aged 18–29, overwhelmingly supported Romney. But only the white ones. According to Pew Research, 54% of white voters under 30 voted for Romney and only 41% voted for Obama. That's the same percentage Reagan got from the entire white population in 1980. Even the Lena Dunham demographic—white women under 30—slightly favored Romney.
>
> Reagan got just 43% of young voters in 1980—and that was when whites were 88% of the electorate. Only 58% of today's under-30 vote is white and it's shrinking daily.[40]

So young people and women didn't suddenly start drinking the Kool-Aid. Young white voters went for Romney, and so did married women. The trends that are so favorable to the Democrats are the dramatic rise of Third World immigration and our high unemployment rate that has made the nuclear family unable to support itself. Coulter continued:

Eighty-five percent of legal immigrants since 1968 have come from the Third World. A majority of them are in need of government assistance. . . . More than half of all babies born to Hispanic women today are illegitimate. As Heather MacDonald has shown, the birthrate of Hispanic women is twice that of the rest of the population, and their unwed birthrate is one and a half times that of blacks.

That's a lot of government dependents coming down the pike. No amount of "reaching out" to the Hispanic community, effective "messaging" or Reagan's "optimism" is going to turn Mexico's underclass into Republicans.[41]

You can be sure that Democrats are analyzing these same demographics and concluding that they can guarantee future elections by continuing high Third World immigration, granting amnesty to illegal aliens, and destroying the nuclear family.

Jonathan V. Last elaborated with "A Nation of Singles" in the *Weekly Standard*:

President Barack Obama's victory over Mitt Romney pointed to two ineluctable demographic truths. The first was expected: that the growth of the Hispanic-American cohort is irresistible and will radically transform our country's ethnic future. The second caught people by surprise: that the proportion of unmarried Americans was suddenly at an all-time high. . . .

Properly understood, there is far less of a "gender" gap in American politics than people think. Yes, President Obama won "women" by 11 points (55% to 44%). But Mitt Romney won married women by the exact same margin. To get a sense of how powerful the marriage effect is, not just for women but for men, too, look at the exit polls by marital status. Among nonmarried voters—people who are single and have never married, are living with a partner, or are divorced—Obama beat Romney 62-35. Among married voters Romney won the vote handily, 56-42.

Far more significant than the gender gap is the marriage gap. . . . Singles broke decisively for Obama. Though his margins with them were lower than they were in 2008, he still won them handily: Obama was +16 among single men and +36 with single women. But the real news wasn't how singles broke—it was that their share of the total vote increased by a whopping 6 percentage points. To put this in some perspective, the wave of Hispanic voters we've heard so much about increased its share of the total vote from 2008 to 2012 by a single point, roughly 1.27 million voters. Meanwhile, that 6 percentage point increase meant 7.6 million more single voters than in 2008. They provided Obama with a margin of 2.9 million votes, about two-thirds of his margin of victory.[42]

Yes, Obama got the votes of various ethnic groups, but the real election story is that Mitt Romney got the nuclear family vote and Obama got the single voters. Obama's typical voter was Sandra Fluke, who publicly demanded her sexual freedom be financed by government-mandated benefits but had no obvious interest in marriage or family.

Laura Wood added an extreme suggestion: "Preaching hasn't worked for the black family and it won't work for the white family either (except for those at the top). As long as our government sustains single mothers, as long as family courts continue to strip spouses of their assets and children when they have done no wrong, preaching is an exercise in fatuous denial."[43]

Unmarried voters are essential to the future of the Democratic Party, and Democrats will surely continue to support antifamily policies.

As more data become available from the exit polling after the 2012 election, the extent of the marriage gap—the differences in candidate choice between married and unmarried women— becomes more obvious and undeniable. A chart constructed by a Democratic group trying to get more single women to show up to vote makes this clear. The marriage gap transcends all racial, age, income, education, and other distinctions. Young or old, rich or poor, white, black, or Hispanic, unmarried women voted overwhelmingly in 2012 to reelect President Obama.

Steve Sailer has analyzed the data and proposes a metric that explains the red/blue state difference, i.e., states with married women voted Republican: "This metric: average years married among white women ages 18 to 44 on the 2000 Census (what I'll call "Years Married" for short). "Years Married" had its best won-loss record yet in 2012. Mitt Romney carried 23 of the 24 highest-ranked states. Barack Obama won 25 of the 26 lowest-ranked states."[44]

The Obama campaign turned out its base by whipping up feelings of resentment toward core Americans—those people whose great-great-grandparents built our country, who largely keep it running today, who own their homes, and who have successfully kept their families together. Obama did a spectacular job of taking people from the fringe and telling them they should resent white married people, and that there's something shameful, unfair, or at least uncool about coming from the core of America.

It was a brilliant strategy. Obama ran a really ugly 2012 campaign full of subliminal hatred. The Democrats managed to keep the stew of ill will they were brewing under wraps until after the votes were counted. But in the days following the election, out poured the noisy exultation, the mindless fury against the male bogeyman for being old and white.

Expanding certain demographic groups is critical to the success of the Democrat Party. Republicans are more likely to get the voter who is married, stays married, has children, owns a home, is employed, and has a future-time orientation. Democrats gain by making those people a declining share of the population.

Democrats will continue to promote the policies that get them votes. That means espousing antifamily incentives, such as those for divorce, out-of-wedlock births, dependency on welfare benefits, and immigration from countries that don't value the traditional American nuclear family.

6

EXPERTS REDEFINE
THE FAMILY

The decline of the American family has been pushed and cheered by an assortment of so-called experts who appear to have the backing of academic, science, psychology, and progressive spokespeople. However, their advice is often directly contrary to published scientific evidence. These experts show up in psychology offices, on TV talk shows, and in schools, colleges, courts, and government agencies, such as Child Protective Services. They pretend to give professional advice on all sorts of marital and child-care disputes, but there is nothing scientific about their advice. You would be better off listening to your grandparents.

The evidence is overwhelmingly in favor of the nuclear family structure. Our civilization is based on the family unit, with moms and dads rearing kids according to traditional values that have been passed down for generations. No modern research shows that anything else is any better. Yet we are bombarded with advice from experts who try to tell us something different.

American divorces are subject to family court decisions on child custody. The process is based on the premise that a judge, possibly with the help of a court-appointed psychologist, can decide who is the better parent. All evidence indicates that judges do not have superior wisdom. Judge William Kelsay of Santa Cruz, California, presided over such trials for years, and acknowledges that most of them turned out badly.

Child custody trials turn out badly because kids are better off with both parents, even if they are divorced. As previously discussed, studies show that joint custody with the natural parents works best. So-called experts are willing to take large fees to present alternate plans, but those plans usually make things worse.

Scientific American Mind published a paper by psychologists Robert E. Emery, Randy K. Otto, and William O'Donohue, entitled "Custody Disputed," which states:

> Our own thorough evaluation of tests that purport to pick the "best parent," the "best interests of the child" or the "best custody arrangement" reveals that they are wholly inadequate. No studies examining their effectiveness have ever been published in a peer-reviewed journal. Because there is simply no psychological science to support them, the tests should not be used. . . . Court tests that expert evaluators use to gauge the supposed best interests of a child should be abandoned. . . . The coupling of the vague "best interest of the child" standards with the American adversarial justice system puts judges in the position of trying to perform an impossible test: making decisions that are best for children using a procedure that is not. . . . We believe it is legally, morally and scientifically wrong to make custody evaluators de facto decision makers. . . .
>
> We are simply urging the same rigor that is applied to expert testimony in all other legal proceedings.[1]

The *Wall Street Journal* published a comment on experts, appropriately titled "How Psychiatry Went Crazy":

> The Diagnostic and Statistical Manual of Mental Disorders is often called the "Bible" of psychiatric diagnosis, and the term is apt. The DSM consists of instructions from on high; readers

usually disagree in their interpretations of the text; and believing it is an act of faith.

At least the Bible lists only 10 Commandments; the DSM grows by leaps and bounds with every revision. The first edition, published by the American Psychiatric Association in 1952, was a spiral-bound pamphlet that described 11 categories of mental disorder.... The new DSM-5 ... is 947 pages. It contains, along with serious mental illnesses, "binge-eating disorder" (whose symptoms include "eating when not feeling physically hungry"), "caffeine intoxication," "parent-child relational problem" and ... "antidepressant discontinuation syndrome." ...

The DSM has grown too powerful to ignore; it is the linchpin of the pharmaceutical-medical complex. Adding more disorders allows doctors to be compensated for treating any kind of problem, from garden-variety sorrow to incapacitating depression. Drug companies encourage new disorders so that they can create medications or repackage old ones.[2]

Dr. Allen Frances, whom the *New York Times* describes as "the most powerful psychiatrist in America,"[3] has pointed out that anyone living a full life experiences stresses, sorrows, and setbacks, all of which are normal and should not be treated as psychiatric disease. Yet millions of people are receiving unnecessary treatment. Dr. Frances warns that stigmatizing a healthy person as mentally ill leads to unnecessary, harmful medications and the draining of family and government budgets.

According to Dr. Frances, the new edition of the so-called bible of psychiatry will convert millions of normal people into "mental patients." Dr. Frances, former chairman of the DSM-4 Task Force, wrote: "This is the saddest moment in my 45-year career of studying, practicing, and teaching psychiatry. The Board of Trustees of the American Psychiatric Association has given its final approval to a deeply flawed DSM-5 containing many changes that seem clearly unsafe."[4]

Here is a summary, from that same posting, of DSM-5's ten most potentially harmful changes:

1. Disruptive Mood Dysregulation Disorder: DSM-5 will turn temper tantrums into a mental disorder. . . .

2. Normal grief will become Major Depressive Disorder. . . .

3. The everyday forgetting characteristic of old age will now be misdiagnosed as Minor Neurocognitive Disorder. . . .

4. DSM-5 will likely trigger a fad of Adult Attention Deficit Disorder leading to widespread misuse of stimulant drugs. . . .

5. Excessive eating 12 times in 3 months is no longer just a manifestation of gluttony and the easy availability of really great tasting food. . . .

6. The changes in the DSM-5 definitions of autism will result in lowered rates—10% according to estimates by the DSM-5 work group, perhaps 50% according to outside research groups. . . .

7. First time substance abusers will be lumped in definitionally with hard core addicts despite their very different treatment needs and prognosis and the stigma this will cause.

8. DSM-5 has created a slippery slope by introducing the concept of Behavioral Addictions. . . .

9. DSM-5 obscures the already fuzzy boundary between Generalized Anxiety Disorder and the worries of everyday life. . . .

10. DSM-5 has opened the gate even further to the already existing problem of misdiagnosis of PTSD in forensic settings.

Most of these DSM-5 changes "loosen diagnosis and threaten to turn our current diagnostic inflation into diagnostic hyperinflation," Dr. Frances stated, concluding, "DSM-5 violates the most sacred . . . tenet in medicine: First, Do No Harm!"[5]

Most or all of these changes can be explained as serving the convenience of the profession. For example, psychiatrists want to be able to prescribe antidepressants to those experiencing the normal grief of a death in the family. Natural News tried to explain how modern psychiatry really works:

> The new, upcoming DSM-5 "psychiatry bible," expected to be released in a few months, has transformed itself from a medical reference manual to a testament to the insanity of the industry itself.
>
> "Mental disorders" named in the DSM-5 include "General Anxiety Disorder" or GAD for short. GAD can be diagnosed in a person who feels a little anxious doing something like, say, talking to a psychiatrist. Thus, the mere act of a psychiatrist engaging in the possibility of making a diagnosis causes the "symptoms" of that diagnosis to magically appear.
>
> This is quack science and circular reasoning, yet it's indicative of the psychiatry industry which has become a laughing stock among scientific circles, and even science skeptics are starting to turn their backs in disgust. Psychiatry is no more "scientific" than astrology or palm reading, yet its practitioners call themselves "doctors" of psychiatry in order to try to make quackery sound credible.[6]

Most people have some sorrows in their lives. Psychiatry historically has refrained from calling normal grief a mental disorder. The previous DSM stated that when symptoms of sadness, distress, insomnia, trouble concentrating, and lack of appetite begin within two months of a loved one's death, for example, but do not persist, psychiatrists should not label this a "major depressive disorder."

DSM-5 narrowed the window from two months to two weeks. A person who has five of nine symptoms that define depression could now be diagnosed as mentally ill and be medicated. Some see this shrinking window as a windfall to manufacturers of psychotropic drugs.

This inflation of diagnosis makes the industry subject to fraud. The Florida Department of Justice announced on March 15, 2013, that Florida psychiatrist Gary Kushner was sentenced to twelve years in prison for submitting more than $50 million in false and fraudulent claims to Medicare. His examinations of patients often lasted only minutes before he authorized fraudulent billings.

Sarah Hrdy is an advocate of "alloparenting," where individuals other than actual parents act in a parental role. She is a big advocate of government day care for kids, based on her study of monkeys and other primates.

It is interesting that anthropologists study African apes and New Guinea tribes, but it's hard to see how this relates to American society. Western civilization became great in part because it rejected alternate family models and adopted the Judeo-Christian nuclear family. The more anthropologists discover that primitive societies have other social structures, the more we should make sure that our American society does not imitate anything resembling those primitive societies.

Sociology experts' analyses of problems are based on three prejudices:

1. They are teaching sociology students the liberal line that "merit is irrelevant," that people do not succeed on the basis of their own merits. As Barack Obama said, if you succeed, somebody did it for you.

2. Ethnocentrism is unacceptable. Sociologists teach that it is wrong to judge others by the standards of our own culture.

3. Punishment is ineffective.

Townhall columnist Mike Adams described the experts' attitude toward widespread student cheating on exams: "Liberals would prefer to ignore evidence of cheating in order to preserve a vision of what 'society' ought to be and could be if only they were given the means [read: more of our money] to re-engineer it. But evidence of student cheating has become too widespread to ignore." Adams concluded by advising students, "[when you go to college,] don't cheat yourself by choosing a major populated by hypocrites who cannot abide by the consequences of their own ideas."[7]

Forensic psychologist Stephen Diamond believes that psychotherapy has been feminized. As evidence, he cited a *New York Times* article titled "Need Therapy? A Good Man Is Hard to Find." According to that article's writer, Benedict Carey, men have been abandoning the psychotherapy field in droves for decades, so much so that the profession has now become almost totally dominated by female practitioners. "Less than 20% of Master's degrees in psychology, clinical social work or counseling are being sought by men today," Dr. Diamond reported, citing Carey. "Women outnumber men in doctoral psychology programs by a ratio of at least 3 to 1.

"But this has not always been so," Diamond continued. "Certainly not when I was a graduate student back in the mid-1970s. What's happening to the psychotherapy profession? Why have men gradually deserted the field? And does gender really matter in psychotherapists?

"I personally witnessed this insidious shift to a predominantly female demographic during my twenty years of teaching psychotherapy to graduate students," he concluded.[8]

If psychotherapy were a real profession with established standards and procedures, like orthopedic surgery, maybe it would not matter if they were all female, gay, or neurotic. But it does matter. Psychotherapists cannot relate to a masculine man. They cannot empathize with him, and they have no evidence-based methodologies for advising him.

Judith S. Wallerstein was a controversial Berkeley feminist psychologist. Her *New York Times* obituary gave the impression that she was controversial because she said that divorce is bad for kids. But that has been conventional wisdom for millennia. No one has any studies saying that divorce is good for kids.

The *Times* obit failed to mention her notorious role in the California move-away cases, *Burgess* and *LaMusga*. She argued that social science research favors letting custodial moms move to other states because kids do not need dads and noncustodial dads just cause trouble. Her work was not just sloppy psychology research; it was worse. She used her academic credentials to force her feminist view on California, depriving kids of their dads. She claimed that research backed her up, but it does the opposite. Other experts criticized her briefs as wrong and irresponsible: "We are united in our judgment that the Wallerstein et al. Brief offers a skewed and misleading account of the social science evidence relevant to this case. Although it purports to be an objective summary of knowledge, the brief runs counter to the prevailing opinions of the majority of experts who conduct divorce research and of those who apply this research to their clinical and forensic practices."[9]

The *Burgess* opinion adopted the claim of Wallerstein et al. that most children's well-being is tied to continuity of their care by a "primary" parent. "*Burgess* goes on to assume that when a parent is chosen to play the larger caretaking role in early childhood, that allocation of parental responsibilities will continue to meet the needs of an older child. Neither of those views is a majority view within the community of professionals who study the impact of divorce on children."[10]

The *New York Times* understated why Wallerstein was so controversial. She was a psychologist with her own personal daddy issues:

Judith Hannah Saretsky was born in New York City on Dec. 27, 1921. Her interest in children and loss grew from her own early life. Her father, a director of Jewish community centers, died of cancer when she was 8. She had not known he was ill, little was explained, and it took her a long time to believe he had died. The painful memories heightened her awareness of the bonds between parents and children, and she later saw herself in some of her research subjects.[11]

PSYCHOLOGICAL DISORDERS

The universities have produced a lot of self-appointed experts who want to take over authority for child rearing. One part of their plan is to convince parents that their normal child is actually suffering from some sort of disorder that must be treated by an expert. *Slate* has reported about American Academy of Pediatrics guidelines that urge parents and doctors to be on the lookout for signs of Attention Deficit Hyperactivity Disorder (ADHD) in children as young as four. Previous guidelines set the minimum age at six. How can you tell if a child has ADHD?

> He would fidget, interrupt, and not play well with others. ADHD is two disorders combined into one. Some children suffer from the "predominantly inattentive" form of the disease, which means they can't focus on schoolwork, don't follow basic instructions, and lose things all the time. Four-year-olds, however, are more likely to be diagnosed with the "predominantly hyperactive, impulsive" variety. These kids are extra squirmy, and act "as if driven by a motor." They also climb things at inappropriate times and answer questions before the interrogator is finished asking. They're lousy play mates because they have trouble sharing and waiting their turn. The disorder can present a safety risk—young children with ADHD sometimes bolt out into traffic.[12]

Parents know that nearly all four-year-olds, especially boys, exhibit some of these symptoms. Yes, a four-year-old might bolt out into traffic. That is not a disorder. Responsible adults watch a four-year-old near a busy street until he learns he could get hit by a car.

There is no objective test for ADHD or ADD. There is no blood test, genetic marker, or brain scan. There is no agreed-upon definition of ADHD. All pediatricians have is questionnaires asking the parents whether the kid talks too much or is more fidgety than his classmates. Some kids get diagnosed with ADHD just because they are a little younger than their classmates. Drugs like Ritalin are given to toddlers to improve their behavior. The goal of these experts is to zero in on younger and younger kids, label them as mentally ill, and subject them to drug and other therapy.

The medical profession is starting to have second thoughts about ADHD, its diagnosis, and its treatment. See *ADHD Does Not Exist* by Richard Saul, MD (HarperCollins, 2014). Dr. Richard Saul discusses his years of worry about the overdiagnosis and misdiagnosis of "ADHD" symptoms in children and adults. He claims to have found dozens of conditions that are frequently misdiagnosed as ADHD. He says "raising a generation of children – and now adults – who can't live without stimulants is no solution. ... It's time to rethink our understanding of this condition."

Dads are frequently blamed for personality characteristics, even though there is no consensus that the personality is disordered or harmful or has any relevance to the issues tackled in the family court. For example, someone might be introverted or extroverted. Extroverts often think that introverts are abnormal, and introverts think that extroverts are abnormal. The truth is that they are just personality types, and neither is known to be better suited to be a parent.

Likewise, there is a contrast between social and analytical thinking. While it may seem to some that empathetic thinking is superior, it is not. It comes at the expense of analytic thinking. Psychologists should know that the published papers do not say one personality type is better than the other.

Jodi Arias was convicted of first-degree murder after a twenty-week trial in Arizona in 2013 that was carried live on television. A couple of forensic psychotherapists testified on her behalf.

Jodi drove hundreds of miles to see her ex-boyfriend, seduced him, took naked pictures with his new camera, shot him in the head, stabbed him twenty-nine times, slashed his throat, attempted to destroy the evidence, and discarded her gun in the desert. When police found her, she told a wild story about what happened and bragged on national TV that no jury would convict her.

At her trial, psychologist Richard Samuels testified that he gave her a computer-scored personality test and diagnosed her with Post-Traumatic Stress Disorder (PTSD). Apparently the anxiety of shooting her boyfriend caused her to forget why she stabbed him twenty-nine times and slashed his throat, and where she dumped the gun. Samuels concluded that she probably shot in self-defense, because a premeditated murder would be less likely to cause PTSD.

Even more ridiculous testimony came from a well-known domestic violence expert, Alyce LaViolette. She testified that the dead ex-boyfriend was the jealous domestic violence perpetrator, not Jodi Arias. Drawing on anecdotes from twenty-five years of California court-ordered domestic violence classes, LaViolette testi-fied that emotional abuse is worse than physical abuse, and that the worst emotional abuse is so subtle that only an expert like herself can detect it. Her evidence was mostly e-mails and text messages with name-calling, such as Arias being called a "sociopath." She concluded that Arias's boyfriend's messages were worse than they sound because of the common saying that "90% of all communica-tion is nonverbal."[13]

The problem with these experts is not just that they are hired guns who are biased toward the source of the money, or that they say things contrary to common sense. The deeper problem is that their whole testimony is directly contrary to American rules of evidence and procedure. An ideal expert witness serves to inform the judge and jury on generally accepted published knowledge that is not easily accessible to the layman. For example, a DNA expert might explain how DNA tests work and the significance of a DNA match, but leave it to the jury to decide the defendant's guilt or innocence. The expert testimony should be objectively verifiable by consulting textbooks.

Samuels said that as a psychologist he can speak only in prob-abilities and not certainties, but he never gave any probabilities for anything. He had no generally accepted knowledge on murderers having PTSD.

LaViolette never cited any published knowledge, except her own chart showing how all human relationships lie on a "continuum of aggression and abuse."[14] Most of her testimony consisted of arguing that she had sifted through volumes of hearsay and had determined who was telling the truth and who was lying. Lie detector tests and FBI profilers are not allowed in court, and for good reason. They are speculative. They can be manipulated. They are unreliable. If the perfect lie detector gets invented someday, maybe we won't need judges and juries anymore. That day has not arrived.

Samuels and LaViolette had no actual expertise with issues bearing on the guilt of Arias. Samuels could recite the symptoms of PTSD, but had no explanation as to why some particular definition of PTSD would be relevant. LaViolette could not even recite a definition of domestic violence or abuse.

The emptiness of their testimony was revealed by their inability to answer hypothetical questions. Ordinary (nonexpert) witnesses testify only about facts, but experts testify about how scientific knowledge can be applied to the facts of the case, and the jury is empowered to decide the facts. Ideally, experts should not express any conclusions about whether the defendant is telling the truth, but leave that to the jury in the light of scientific knowledge.

Arias's expert witnesses spent most of their time giving opinions and conclusions on subjects on which they had no expertise at all. For example, LaViolette testified about the importance of Mormon baptism and whether various people were faithful to Mormon teachings. Part of LaViolette's claimed expertise was in conducting California child custody evaluations and in testifying for family court child custody disputes.

CHILD SUPPORT FICTIONS

The basic fallacy that underlies many academic analyses is that a father who is head of the household and living with his wife and their own children will pay just as much financial support to an ex-wife living with another man and a child he never sees. That makes no sense. It is as if someone decided there is no social benefit for fathers to be involved with their kids, so the law should create monetary incentives against it.

Do you ever wonder what sort of economic analysis goes into child support guidelines? Most of the states use something called the Betson-Rothbarth estimator. If you think child support is based on some expert economic analysis of child expenses, read this explanation:

> In the early 1990s, PSI asked David Betson of the University of Notre Dame to revise the Income Shares methodology. He also used an income equivalence approach, borrowing a technique from Erwin Rothbarth. The Rothbarth methodology compares changes in levels of household spending on purely adult goods to determine child costs. The idea is that looking at purely adult goods reduces the problem of shifts between adult and shared goods after having a child or an additional child. For measuring child costs, Betson specifically uses a particular bundle of adult goods to measure a household's level of well-being—this bundle consists of adult clothing, alcohol, and tobacco. In other words, he replaced the food-only indirect measure with spending in three adult-only areas and switched from shares of consumption to levels of consumption. Because the cost tables are based on a Betson version of Rothbarth's earlier research, they are sometimes referred to as Betson-Rothbarth tables.[15]

Apparently the analysis isn't based on child expense data at all. The idea seems to be that if a couple with no kids spends twice as much on adult clothing, alcohol, and tobacco as a couple with one kid, then a couple with one kid should spend half its money on the kid. There are so many things wrong with this approach.

Here is a summary of what is wrong with the US child support system: It is not related to kids' actual needs or expenses. There is no requirement or obligation to spend the money on the kids. The formulas give each parent a huge financial incentive to deny the other parent access to the kids. Payments are required even if the custodial parent is rich. The formulas presume that a parent who never sees his kid should spend just as much on him as one who sees his kid every day. The formulas are supposed to be based on income, but do not use actual income, such as IRS tax returns. The system has turned middle-class single and remarried parents into welfare cases. Debts are treated as criminal offenses, and a man can be jailed for nonpayment even though he is unemployed and broke. A man can be forced to pay so-called child support even if a DNA test proves he is not the father. Parents have no financial privacy, and a bitter ex-spouse can use the system for many years of harassment. Judges can ignore the formulas with impunity, and there is rarely any appeal.

We can no longer ignore how taxpayers' money is incentivizing divorce and creating fatherless children. Nor can we ignore the government's complicity in the predictable social costs that result from 24 million children growing up in homes without their biological fathers.[16] Fatherless boys are more likely to run away and to abuse drugs, and fatherless girls are more likely to get pregnant and to commit suicide. Fatherless boys and girls are more likely to drop out of school and end up in jail.

CHILD CUSTODY EVALUATORS

As we discussed in chapter 4, family courts have assumed the responsibility of restructuring families according to the "best interest of the child." When they need justification for imposing arbitrary rules on families, they turn to the new billion-dollar industry of professional quacks, including child custody evaluators.

The evaluators are often psychologists, but also can be counselors or social workers who have specialized in forensic work. Usually they have some sort of therapist license, but there is no requirement to actually know anything about child rearing. In California, the main requirement is to take a seminar on domestic violence. But even with a license and a record of seminar attendance, they still have no actual training in making evidence-based custody evaluations.

When a divorcing couple heads to court with lawyers, the judge figures that if they have enough money for lawyers, then they have enough money for psychologists and counselors. The judge then sends the couple to an evaluator to interview the couple and the kids and to make a recommendation. The evaluator is not required to follow any legal or scientific standards and may simply give an opinion based on his or her own prejudices. If this sounds crazy, it is. These evaluations are even controversial within the psychology profession, as many psychologists believe it is unethical to do them. According to the article in *Scientific American Mind* quoted earlier in this chapter, the guidelines judges and psychologists use to decide child custody cases have little basis in science.

Courts are overwhelmed with couples who are splitting up and disputing custody of their children. If parents cannot agree on their children's fates, a judge will decide who gets custody. Psychologists are increasingly involved as expert evaluators during legal wranglings. But do any of these professionals have proof that the basis for their life-determining decisions is empirically sound? It seems not, and it is the children who suffer.

Some people seem to think that judges possess some special wisdom that allows them to determine a custody arrangement that is somehow better than what parents can devise themselves. They don't. Although details vary, every state's law indicates that custody decisions are to be made according to the "best interest of the child." That rule of thumb is so vague that the outcome of every case is unpredictable. The possibility of "winning" in court, paired with the emotional dynamics of divorce, encourages parents to engage in custody disputes, which only increases conflict between them—and conflict is a major cause of lasting psychological damage to children of separating spouses.

Custody evaluators often administer to parents and children an array of tests to assess which custody arrangement might be best. Given the frequency, high cost, and social importance of custody evaluations, we might expect to find a large body of research on the tests' scientific validity.

Only a few studies have been completed, and more are needed, but the few that exist show that the tests are deeply flawed. Other, more general psychological tests that evaluators sometimes use, such as IQ tests, have little or no relevance to custody decisions and should also be dropped.

While openness is usually considered a necessity in a fair judicial system, the work of these evaluators in shrouded in mystery. Their reports are not made public, and it is often impossible for even the parents to read them. A new law in California says that an inappropriate disclosure of a report is subject to a fine that the statute does not limit. The law says that the judge can make the fine large enough to deter the conduct, even if that is millions of dollars.

One reason evaluators cannot effectively compare parents is that there is very little scientific evidence that any parenting method or style is better than any other. For example, many child psychologists recommend against spanking kids for discipline, but researchers have been unable to show that it is inferior to any other discipline method. They can show that kids do worse if they are beaten regularly by abusive parents, but studies about moderate spanking are inconclusive.

The one thing that parenting studies consistently show is that kids do best when reared by their biological mom and dad. Even when the parents are divorced, kids do better under joint custody than sole custody on all available measures. The research is explained in the 2000 book *Father and Child Reunion* by Dr. Warren Farrell.

One might think that joint custody works only when the parents have very similar personalities, beliefs, parenting styles, and values, and when they agree on relevant issues. The research shows the opposite. Kids benefit when dads act like dads and moms act like moms. The more that divorced parents disagree, the more important it is that they share fifty-fifty joint custody so the kids will benefit from what each parent has to offer.

Some recent examples of work by prominent evaluators show

how bad the process is. In a Southern California case, for example, the parties fundamentally disagreed on how best to raise their highly intelligent son, J., who was diagnosed at a young age with what used to be called Asperger's syndrome, a form of high-functioning autism. The parents care deeply for their son, but they hold diametrically opposed views on the extent of his disabilities and on the efficacy of certain types of autism treatment. Mother has written a published book on autism, gives lectures on the subject, helps other families obtain services for their autistic children, and plans to write several more books about autism. Father is a special education attorney and has a master's degree in psychology.[17]

In 2008, when the parents divorced, they agreed, in a stipulated judgment pursuant to Code of Civil Procedure section 664.6, to submit future disputes about matters involving J. (such as custody and education) to a special master selected in accordance with the judgment. The judgment provided that: (1) the special master would be a licensed mental health professional; (2) if a party disagreed with the special master's decision, the party could seek the court's intervention; and (3) the special master would report any unresolved conflicts to the court. Under the judgment, the parties shared joint legal custody of J. and divided their physical custody of him based on a designated schedule.

In January 2009, Mother discontinued any direct communication with Father and advised him that she had asked her fiancé to be "an intermediary, whenever possible, for ALL communications with you." The mom then remarried and tried to cut the dad out of their boy's life. They went to court, and the judge appointed psychologist David J. Jimenez as a child custody evaluator. His website advertises:

Family Law Child Custody Evaluations: Full & Solution-Focused Evaluations, Relocation & "Move Away" Evaluations, Domestic & International, Attachment & Bonding Evaluations, Parental Alienation, Visitation & Parenting Plans, Collaborative Divorce Expert Witness[18]

Psychological Consultation, Evaluation, Treatment, and Expert Court Testimony in Family Law, Criminal, & Dependency California Superior Court matters since 1991.

Privately Retained by Both the Prosecution and Defense.

Provided Thousands of Court Evaluations under Court E.C. 730 Appointment (PC:1368, 288, Etc.)

Provided Expert Testimony in over one hundred Family Law, Juvenile & Adult matters[19]

SPECIAL EXPERTISE:
'Full' Child Custody Evaluation (sliding fee scale)[20]

Jimenez told another psychologist that his clients had "deep pockets." He sided with the mom and billed forty-two thousand dollars, which the court observed "is exceptionally high" but nevertheless ordered the mom and dad to pay.

It is common for parents to have more expertise in parenting their kids than court evaluators and special masters. This case was unusual in that the parents had the credentials to prove it. These parents had some minor disputes about schooling and other matters, but they had a settlement agreement with a mechanism to resolve disputes. That is what should have happened. Instead the court found it was in J.'s best interest for Mother to have sole legal custody. As to Father, the court stated: "None of [father's] positive and constructive involvement with [J.] will be adversely affected by [mother] having sole legal custody. He can continue to provide beneficial and very helpful assistance in doing homework, particularly math . . . [and] can continue to try and involve his son in quality activities such as boating and even if they share a common interest in pocket knives."[21]

This devalues fatherhood to just someone who pays money to the mom, helps with homework, and takes the boy boating, but is stripped of any authority or responsibility for the boy.

We know about this case only because it was appealed to a higher court, which reversed the decisions of the family court. The appellate court laid out the facts recited above in a thirty-six-page opinion that castigated Jimenez for his misconduct and bias.[21] The California Board of Psychology filed a complaint seeking to revoke Jimenez's license for his misconduct in the J. case, but no action was taken and Jimenez was allowed to renew his license number 10629 for another two years.

By some estimates, 25 percent of Americans have some diagnosable mental disorder at some point in their lives. Many also have physical disabilities, illnesses, and other problems. It is supposed to be our public policy not to take kids away from parents just because the parent has some disability or shortcoming.

The New Yorker magazine carried a nine-page article about the sad case of a mother having her child taken away from her and given out for adoption only because she left a three-year-old alone in the house while she went to work. There were no other charges against her, and she wasn't given any chance to reform her ways (such as by taking a parenting class, as even drug addicts are allowed to do). The mom was a well-educated Egyptian-American who fought vigorously to reclaim her child, including filing two lawsuits, but she was unsuccessful. The government "gestapo" was so eager to take her child away that an undercover policeman was used to try to trick her into advocating something illegal, but the recording showed that she never advocated anything illegal. The government prosecuted her for attempted kidnapping anyway, even though the government's own tape exonerated her. The jury acquitted her, but she never got her child back.[22]

ADVICE FROM NEWSPAPERS

A newspaper advice column said:

DEAR MARGO: I don't know what to do. Last December, my boy-friend proposed to me. We planned a small, simple wedding to take place in the early fall. . . . We still want to go through with the ceremony—but not tell people about the non-legal aspect. . . . Are we wrong?—Faux Bride

DEAR FAUX: These days, there is no "wrong" when it comes to tying the knot and having babies. There are shotgun weddings, babies without weddings, weddings that are really parties, parties that are really weddings, and white bridal gowns that accommodate a pregnant belly.[23]

Margo is the daughter of the woman who wrote the Ann Landers column. Margo's answer reflected popular wisdom. She said there is no right or wrong on the subject of marriage and having babies, and no one thinks that there is anything unusual about this advice. The next marriage you attend may be a fake.

It used to be considered shameful for a married woman to commit adultery, destroy two marriages, and walk out on a husband who has forgiven her. But here is Margo's current newspaper advice:

DEAR MARGO: I'm the oldest of three . . . [married] 15 years. My husband and I were struggling in our marriage. There were plenty of issues, but the catalyst was when I had an affair. Finally, my husband decided he wanted to fix our marriage, but by this time I was emotionally done. We divorced, and . . . are co-parenting our kids and doing fine. We're each dating someone else. I am seeing the man I had the affair with, who also divorced. My brothers stopped talking to me upon learning of my infidelity. Since then, one of them eased up a bit at Christmas, but refused to allow me in his home at Easter. . . .

DEAR R: Are your bothers [*sic*] Puritans, or Afghans? You really have done nothing to harm them, and their self-righteousness is deplorable. There is nothing for you to do except be a lady. . . . I see no reason for you to wear the scarlet "A" in this day and age, and I think the brothers sound odd.[24]

Even this advice was too retro for some newspapers, as they edited out the words "Afghans" and "lady."[25] These women have attitudes that are increasingly common among twenty-first-century women, and anyone who objects is called some name, like "Puritan" or "Afghan." If the writer were really a lady, none of this would have happened. Her brothers probably do not want her attitude to infect their own families. Someone should say that such behavior is wrong. Not inviting her over for Easter is a reasonable way to express disapproval.

Hardly any of the popular psychotherapists, counselors, and other advice-givers still believe in traditional marriage. Here is typical newspaper column advice to a bored wife:

It is possible to find someone more exciting, but that tends to be temporary. It's also possible to find passionate love, and that might free up your husband to find someone who truly loves him, as well. Or you could discover that this marriage is more worthwhile than you think. If you are looking for a man to fulfill your fantasies, the odds are against you. You need to ask yourself that Ann Landers question: "Are you better off with or without him?" And only you can supply the answer.[26]

Conspicuously absent from this advice is any suggestion that the wife has an obligation to stick to her marital commitment. She is told to make a decision based on her current needs and desires, as if the marriage had never taken place.

EMPATHY

Empathy has become a huge buzzword, as if it were a cure-all for society's ills. *New York Times* columnist David Brooks wrote:

> As Steven Pinker writes in his mind-altering new book, *The Better Angels of Our Nature,* the problem comes when we try to turn feeling into action. Empathy makes you more aware of other people's suffering, but it's not clear it actually motivates you to take moral action or prevents you from taking immoral action. . . .
>
> There have been piles of studies investigating the link between empathy and moral action. Different scholars come to different conclusions, but, in a recent paper, Jesse Prinz, a philosopher at City University of New York, summarized the research this way: "These studies suggest that empathy is not a major player when it comes to moral motivation. Its contribution is negligible in children, modest in adults, and nonexistent when costs are significant." . . .
>
> Moreover, Prinz argues, empathy often leads people astray. It influences people to care more about cute victims than ugly victims. It leads to nepotism. It subverts justice; juries give lighter sentences to defendants that show sadness.[27]

Psychologists like the empathy concept because that is how they make their income. A client comes into the shrink's office and tells a sob story, the shrink shows some empathy and bills for the service, and the client walks away as if she has benefited. So empathy is gold. But it is not necessarily a good psychological treatment technique. It is mostly a method for feel-good shrinks to manipulate patients.

Some schools already teach empathy. Progressive intellectuals have declared that teaching empathy is the best way to advance their leftist goals. Empathetic and analytic thinking are opposites. A reader sent this story:

> When the brain fires up the network of neurons that allows us to empathize, it suppresses the network used for analysis, a pivotal study led by a Case Western Reserve University researcher shows. . . .

At rest, our brains cycle between the social and analytical networks. But when presented with a task, healthy adults engage the appropriate neural pathway, the researchers found. The study shows for the first time that we have a built-in neural constraint on our ability to be both empathetic and analytic at the same time. . . .

"This is the cognitive structure we've evolved," said Anthony Jack, an assistant professor of cognitive science at Case Western Reserve and lead author of the new study. "Empathetic and analytic thinking are, at least to some extent, mutually exclusive in the brain."[28]

The *Wikipedia* article on empathy lists seventeen different experts who have seventeen different definitions of *empathy*. If empathy were really so significant, it would be possible to measure it and to do studies to show that it is effective in benefiting someone in some tangible way. As Brooks says, the studies fail to show the benefits.

The empathy deceit affects other important decisions. Here is then senator Barack Obama's statement explaining his decision to vote against John Roberts's nomination to be chief justice of the United States:

[W]hile adherence to legal precedent and rules of statutory or constitutional construction will dispose of 95 percent of the cases that come before a court . . . what matters on the Supreme Court is those 5 percent of cases that are truly difficult. In those cases, adherence to precedent and rules of construction and interpretation will only get you through the 25th mile of the marathon. That last mile can only be determined on the basis of one's deepest values, one's core concerns, one's broader perspectives on how the world works, and the depth and breadth of one's empathy.[29]

SELF-ESTEEM

The education establishment falls for a lot of fads, and in the 1990s the big fad was the self-esteem movement. Textbooks and curricula were rewritten to enhance self-esteem. In the elementary grades, whole courses were taught on it.

Researchers who examined the results found that too much self-esteem actually makes you less successful in life. They surveyed about nine million young people, each filling out a questionnaire called the American Freshman Survey. It asked students to rate how they measure up to their peers in several basic skills. The researchers discovered that there has been a dramatic rise in the number of students who describe themselves as being "above average" in academic ability, mathematical skills, self-confidence, and drive to achieve. The students labeled themselves as gifted in writing ability.

But test scores indicated that their actual abilities had gone down. The weaker students performed worse if they had people telling them positive things that boosted their self-worth. Teacher interventions that tell students to feel good about themselves actually remove the reason to work hard.

Author Joanne Lipman offered a common-sense analysis in a *Wall Street Journal* report called "Why Tough Teachers Get Good Results." She listed useful rules for training youngsters, including:

- A little pain is good for you;

- Drill, baby, drill (to emphasize memorization);

- Failure is an option;

- Strict is better than nice; and

- Stress makes you strong.[30]

Parents who give their children a constant diet of telling them they are "special" and talented tend to make them narcissistic. They begin to believe they are better than everyone else.

THERAPISM

Marriage and family experts are dominated by the concept of therapism, which means a culture or ideal of mental therapy. Authors Christina Hoff Sommers and Sally Satel exposed the evils of therapism in a 2005 book, *One Nation Under Therapy—How the Helping Culture Is Eroding Self-Reliance.* They debunk the myth that families need counseling and possibly medication to cope with the stresses of everyday life.[31]

Research studies do not support therapism. Cancer patients do not live any longer by discussing their ordeal in therapy sessions. Grief counseling does not help people get over tragedy. It may seem that counseling will usually help and could not hurt, but that is not true. Counseling can be depressing by focusing on problems better forgotten, and can encourage dependence and helplessness.

Sommers and Satel's brilliant book concludes: "The American Creed that has sustained the nation is now under powerful assault by the apostles of therapism. The fateful question is: Will Americans actively defend the traditional creed of stoicism and the ideology of achievement or will they continue to allow the nation to slide into therapeutic self-absorption and moral debility? Our very future depends on our answer."[32]

The word *therapism* does not appear in major dictionaries, but is found only in an obscure dictionary: "therapism (n.) a culture or ideal of mental therapy, empathy, or sharing of feelings, especially as a cure."[33] Sommers and Satel defined it like this:

> Therapism valorizes openness, emotional self-absorption and the sharing of feelings. It encompasses several additional assumptions: that vulnerability, rather than strength, characterizes the American psyche; and that a diffident, anguished, and emotionally apprehensive public requires a vast array [of] therapists, self-esteem educators, grief counselors, workshoppers, healers, and traumatologists to lead it through the trials of everyday life. Children, more than any group, are targeted for the therapeutic improvement. We reject these assumptions.[34]

One Nation Under Therapy documents the rise of therapism, the harm it is doing, and why it should be rejected. Therapism is a direct attack on the American family. The American ideals of determination, ingenuity, courage, endurance, heroism, achievement, and success are learned in the nuclear family. From the days of the thirteen colonies to the settling of the West, America has been about building a great country, with autonomous patriarchal families as the basic units of our society.

Now an army of psychiatrists, psychologists, counselors, social workers, teachers, and others are out to destroy that. They want to obliterate parental authority and give shrinks authority over child rearing because parents are not competent to solve their problems and rear their kids.

Feminists, especially, hate the self-made man. They want everyone dependent on public health insurance, food stamps, public schools, counselors, and social workers. They want their husbands to get counseling in order to demasculinize them. When they claim to have an intellectual position, it is really an ideological attack on traditional American values.

People often say they are helped by counseling. Bill and Hillary Clinton credit marriage counseling for helping save their marriage, but there is very little empirical evidence of any such benefits. More importantly, therapism undermines American values of self-reliance and fortitude. It enfeebles those it seeks to help.

Today thousands of American kids are required to play sports like soccer and basketball where no one keeps score. The idea is that if there are no winners or losers, adults will be free to promote the self-esteem of all kids equally. Parents and teachers worry that their kids' psyches are so fragile that they will be scarred by losing a soccer game. But there is no scientific evidence that such self-esteem–promoting tactics do anything to help success later in life.

Here is an exchange of letters from the *Straight Dope* column:

DEAR CECIL: Is it true that, as a class, psychotherapists and other mental health professionals are crazier than average? And that despite their training and experience, they can recognize their own issues less readily than the average nutcase?—Paul

CECIL ADAMS REPLIES: A widely noted study from 1980 found 73% of psychiatrists had experienced moderate to incapacitating anxiety early in their careers, and 58% had suffered from moderate to incapacitating depression. . . .

One British study found psychiatrists had nearly five times the suicide rate of general practitioners, and U.S. research indicates psychiatrists commit suicide at two to three times the rate of the general population. Similarly, depression, stress, and burnout are high among physicians but higher among psychiatrists; the same is true of alcohol and drug abuse. Psychiatrists have a divorce rate 2.7 times that of other physicians and as much as five times that of the general public. From a quarter to a half of psychiatrists say they're suffering from burnout at any given time.

A study of more than 8,000 Finnish hospital employees found the psychiatric staff was 81% more likely to suffer from a current or past mental illness and 61% more likely to miss work due to depression. Psychiatric staff were twice as likely to smoke as other hospital staff and had much higher rates of alcohol use. A 30-year study of 20,000 UK medical workers found psychiatrists were 46% more likely than their peers to die from injuries and poisoning, and at 12% greater risk of dying overall. . . .

Does the mental health field attract people with mental problems? Research is thin, but some studies have found mental health workers are more likely than average to have experienced early abuse and trauma. A much-cited 1963 study reported that 24 out of 25 psychiatrists had entered the field because of a wish to explore some personal conflict.

That gives one pause. Sure, there's value in consulting a health professional who's been down the same road as we have. But who wants their therapist thinking, "Maybe after I get this head case straightened out, I'll figure out what's wrong with me"?[35]

An article in *Psychology Today* explains "Why Shrinks Have Problems":

> In 1899 Sigmund Freud got a new telephone number: 14362. He was 43 at the time, and he was profoundly disturbed by the digits in the new number. He believed they signified that he would die at age 61 (note the one and six surrounding the 43) or, at best, at age 62 (the last two digits in the number). He clung, painfully, to this bizarre belief for many years. Presumably he was forced to revise his estimate on his 63rd birthday, but he was haunted by other superstitions until the day he died—by assisted suicide, no less—at the ripe old age of 83.
>
> That's just for starters. Freud also had frequent blackouts. He refused to quit smoking even after 30 operations to correct the extensive damage he suffered from cancer of the jaw. He was a self-proclaimed neurotic. He suffered from a mild form of agoraphobia. And, for a time, he had a serious cocaine problem.[36]

If your child has been exposed to some sort of psychological trauma, you might be tempted to take him to an expert for treatment of grief or depression, but your child will be better off if you don't. *Scientific American* reports on a new megastudy:

> In the aftermath of traumatic events like the Newtown massacre, Superstorm Sandy and Hurricane Katrina, children need to heal just like adults do. . . .
>
> Among the 20 treatments included in those trials were various psychotherapies focusing on trauma or grief, school-based programs, group therapy and three medication trials: imipramine (Tofranil), fluoxetine (Prozac) and sertraline (Zoloft). The results are sobering: researchers don't know if any medications help, don't know if anything works long-term, and don't know much about possible harms from interventions. . . .
>
> A growing body of research points to the importance of "protective factors" in helping children cope with trauma and to develop resilience.[37]

Scientific American lists several examples of "protective factors." The last one is "how attached they are to a caregiver." Is "caregiver" a new synonym for parents? The rise of therapism is an attempt to replace parents and support from family members with supposed experts, but their methods and prescriptions are not grounded in scientific research.

OVERMEDICATING CHILDREN

Nearly one in five children in the United States suffers from a mental disorder such as attention deficit/hyperactivity disorder (ADHD), anxiety, depression, or autism, according to a study conducted by the Centers for Disease Control and Prevention. This extraordinary percentage of up to 20 percent of American kids suffering from mental disorders is costing us $247 billion a year in medical bills and drugs. We need some studies to compare the effectiveness of high-priced psychiatrists and the drugs they prescribe to that of tender, loving care by mothers and fathers. The *New York Times* reported:

> Foster children are being prescribed cocktails of powerful anti-psychosis drugs just as frequently as some of the most mentally disabled youngsters on Medicaid, a new study suggests. The report, published Monday in the journal *Pediatrics*, is the first to investigate how often youngsters in foster care are given two antipsychotic drugs at once, the authors said. The drugs include Risperdal, Seroquel and Zyprexa—among other so-called major tranquilizers—which were developed for schizophrenia but are now used as all-purpose drugs for almost any psychiatric symptoms.
>
> "The kids in foster care may come from bad homes, but they do not have the sort of complex medical issues that those in the disabled population do," said Susan dosReis, an associate professor in the University of Maryland School of Pharmacy and the lead author.
>
> The implication, Dr. dosReis and other experts said: Doctors are treating foster children's behavioral problems with the same powerful drugs given to people with schizophrenia and severe

bipolar disorder. "We simply don't have evidence to support this kind of use, especially in young children," Dr. dosReis said.[38]

Drugging foster kids does not do them any good. It is just a way for government authorities to label them as damaged, treat them as subhuman, and pretend they are being helped. Today the $4 billion ADHD drug industry is about ten times its 1996 size, and Adderall is the reigning market leader.[39]

More and more, there is a systematic effort in our society to break down the family. To accomplish this, kids can be put under the control of judges, psychiatrists, social workers, and drugs. It used to be that when a mom had a ten-year-old boy who was "a bundle of uncontained energy," the dad would teach him to play football or work on the farm to burn up that energy and make a man out of him. But now our society has convinced this mom to kick out her husband, drug the boy, and let him get fat and lazy.

ABC-TV's *20/20* aired a show on the medicating of foster children. ABC said it spent a year investigating this story.[40] Across America, doctors are putting foster children on powerful, mind-altering drugs at rates up to thirteen times that of children in the general population. What's more, doctors are prescribing foster children drugs at doses beyond what the Food and Drug Administration has approved, sometimes in potentially dangerous combinations, according to a new report by the Government Accountability Office.

The research papers used to get FDA approval for some of these drugs show that the evidence for their effectiveness is very thin. The whole practice of courts or social service agencies forcing these drugs on kids is truly offensive.

The *New York Times* had a long article on diagnosing a misbehaving nine-year-old kid as a psychopath:

Over the last six years, Michael's parents have taken him to eight different therapists and received a proliferating number of diagnoses. "We've had so many people tell us so many different things," Anne said. "Oh, it's A.D.D.—oh, it's not. It's depression—or it's not. You could open the DSM and point to a random thing, and chances are he has elements of it. He's got characteristics of O.C.D. He's got characteristics of sensory-integration disorder. Nobody knows what the predominant feature is, in terms of treating him. Which is the frustrating part."[41]

Scientific American writer John Horgan discussed ugly experiments:

Are the days of ugly research over? If only. In the past two decades, American psychiatrists have been carrying out what is in effect an enormous clinical trial involving millions of children. Physicians are medicating children with stimulants such as Ritalin, antidepressants such as Prozac, anti-anxiety drugs such as Xanax, bipolar drugs such as lithium and antipsychotics such as Risperdal. "It's really to some extent an experiment, trying medications in these children of this age," child psychiatrist Patrick Bacon told producers of the 2008 PBS documentary "The Medicated Child." "It's a gamble. And I tell parents there's no way to know what's going to work." As of 2009, more than 500,000 American adolescents and children, including toddlers younger than two, were taking antipsychotics, which "may pose grave risks to development of both their fast-growing brains and their bodies," according to The *New York Times*. In *Anatomy of an Epidemic* (Crown, 2010), which I have written about previously, journalist Robert Whitaker presents evidence that psychiatric drugs may be hurting more children than they help. Since 1987, he reports, while prescriptions for children have soared, the number of patients under 18 receiving federal disability payments for mental illness has multiplied by a factor of 35. By this measure, the experiment does not seem to be working.[42]

Twenty years ago, a dozen child psychiatrists received $11 million from the National Institute of Mental Health to study ADHD and to answer the question, is the best long-term treatment medication, behavioral therapy, or both? The widely publicized answer to that question was that drugs (such as Ritalin or Adderall) trumped therapy, that they are "superior to behavioral treatment" by a considerable margin, and that behavioral therapy does little beyond what the drugs can do alone.[43]

That diagnosis started the heavy marketing of ADHD drugs, and insurance companies and schools relied on it as an excuse to abandon behavioral therapies (which are time-consuming and more expensive than pills). Today, more than one in seven US kids are diagnosed as having ADHD by the time they turn eighteen, according to the Centers for Disease Control, and 70 percent of those are prescribed ADHD drugs that quickly reduce the symptoms.

A lengthy *New York Times* report on December 30, 2013, was cautiously written to protect reputations, but it's clear that the experts are now rethinking and backtracking from their earlier diagnoses, analysis methods, and recommendations. When we read that the original study spent time measuring symptoms such as "fidgeting," the average parent may conclude that the study was biased against boys, who are simply unable to sit still at a desk as long as girls of the same age.

In chapter 4 you were introduced to some of the follies of the Child Abuse Prevention and Treatment Act, or CAPTA. Though a bill has been proposed to amend the act, a homeschooling group, Home School Legal Defense Association, opposes the bill:

> S.1877 will amend the Child Abuse Prevention and Treatment Act (CAPTA) to require—for the first time ever—every single state that receives federal funding under CAPTA to force every single adult to be a mandatory reporter of child abuse or neglect. Currently, most states only require certain people (*e.g.,* doctors and teachers) to be mandatory reporters. HSLDA opposes this for the following reasons:. . .
> Forcing the states to make every single adult a mandatory reporter with no exceptions will lead to a police-state environment, where every adult is forced to act as an informer against

friends, family, and neighbors, or face possible charges. There are grave threats to liberty and personal privacy that could result from this. . . .

S.1877 will lead to a massive increase in child abuse and neglect investigations upon families. The stated purpose of S. 1877's mandatory reporting expansion, along with the education campaign and training program, is to *"improve reporting"* of child abuse and neglect. The bill will give states new federal grants to set up *"experimental, model, and demonstration programs for testing innovative approaches and techniques that may improve reporting of and response to suspected and known incidents of child abuse or neglect by adults to the State child protective service agencies or to law enforcement agencies."* . . .

HSLDA has seen firsthand how malicious or ignorant child abuse and neglect allegations have destroyed innocent families.[44]

Two more reasons this proposed law is particularly bad is that it requires reporting *suspected* abuse, and it permits the report to be *anonymous*. The reporting of an actual crime is one thing, but it is much more insidious to require everybody to report every suspicion he or she has. It is a license for troublemakers to make false accusations anonymously.

All fifty states have mandated report laws already. Homeschoolers are sensitive to this because they routinely face false CPS reports from those who disapprove of homeschooling. But they aren't the only ones threatened. This is an attempt to expand the jurisdiction of the federal government and the state social service agencies, and to reduce the autonomy of the American family by forcing them to regularly defend themselves against anonymous accusations and explain their parenting practices to government social workers.

BEWARE OF WOMEN'S STUDIES

The most doctrinaire and intolerant antifamily teaching is in the colleges and universities, especially women's studies courses, and spilling over into the psychology, sociology, and anthropology departments. Radical feminism is the cornerstone of the political correctness that dominates campus culture.

The first commandment of feminism is: thou shalt overthrow the patriarchy, because women are its victims. The second commandment is: thou shalt support gender interchangeability; any deviation from gender sameness is a social construct. Today's professors will not tolerate theories that women and men have different capabilities and often choose different roles. The Communists used to severely punish as "deviationists" all those who strayed from the party line, but feminist professors have taken to new heights their demand that everyone kowtow to feminist orthodoxy. No one is too high-ranking to escape feminist dogma.

Look what the feminists did to the president of Harvard University. They lassoed and dragged him groveling through the ivy until they wrung from him all they wanted and more. It didn't save President Lawrence Summers that he had been Bill Clinton's secretary of the Treasury. Summers thought he was chatting off the record with intellectuals who had the maturity to engage in a little light banter about suggestions for academic research or new PhD dissertations. He was wrong. To the liberals, some subjects are not only undebatable, they are unresearchable, because they don't want the public to know the facts that research might uncover.

President Summers said that he had tried gender-neutral upbringing on his daughter by giving her toy trucks to play with. She immediately pretended they were dolls and named them "daddy truck" and "baby truck." Just as John Stossel explained on his ABC documentary, fathers quickly discover that "boys and girls are different." The rest of us can smile at such revelations, but to the feminists this is no laughing matter.

In his January 14, 2005, speech, Lawrence Summers calmly presented three rational hypotheses to explain why there are fewer women than men in science and engineering academia: (1) "the high-powered job hypothesis" (the concept that women voluntarily reject the eighty-hour workweek and the job intensity that top careers require); (2) "different availability of aptitude at the high end"; and (3) "different socialization and patterns of discrimination"[45] (that's the favorite feminist explanation for *all* sex differences).

Contrary to media reports, Summers did not assert that there are "innate" differences between men and women. His hypothesis #2 merely pointed out that the distribution of math ability may be different. In other words, there may be more smarter men at the high end and more dumber men at the low end. Then Summers suggested that academic studies be undertaken to explain why fewer women than men have succeeded in science and math careers in academia.

Abandoning all dignity, MIT professor Nancy Hopkins slammed down her laptop and stormed out of the room because, she said, "I would've either blacked out or thrown up." She said her "heart was pounding" and her "breath was shallow."[46] She reminded us of Miss Pittipat Hamilton in *Gone with the Wind*, calling for smelling salts before she swooned. We expect more willingness to discuss unpopular views from female professors who want to be taken seriously. Ms. Hopkins's behavior confirmed the stereotype that feminists are too emotional to handle intellectual or scientific debate. She made clear that feminists seek to forbid any research that might produce facts they don't want the public to know.

Summers didn't say anything that hasn't been said by scholars many times before. For example, University of Virginia professor Steven Rhoads's book *Taking Sex Differences Seriously* (New York: Encounter) is copiously documented. But the feminists ran to their friends in the media to ignite a firestorm of indignation and personal attacks on Larry Summers. As the dean at the very feminist Radcliffe Institute for Advanced Studies said, "we took our opportunity to see that the changes at Harvard get made." (Changes equals reverse discrimination to hire women on the Harvard faculty.)

The feminists demanded that Summers admit his guilt and submit to a week of "intense discussions." After two weeks of flagellation by the liberal media plus those "intense discussions"

(Soviet-style reeducation, really) to force Summers to accept feminist indoctrination, a contrite Summers apologized almost daily for two months. Summers appointed not one but two task forces: one on women in the Harvard faculty and another on women in science and engineering, to recruit, support, and promote women. The task forces were made up of twenty-two feminists and five men (the feminist mathematicians' version of gender equality). Summers also appointed a commissar of faculty diversity (or should we say, a commissarina?). The announcement didn't include any caveat that new female hires be as qualified as the men who would be passed over, since Summers was already on record as endorsing affirmative action.

Unconditional surrender and redundant apologies profited Summers nothing. The feminists had no mercy. On March 15, the Harvard faculty of Arts and Sciences voted 218 to 185 to censure him and express a lack of confidence in his leadership. When will American men learn to stand up to the nagging by the intolerant, uncivil feminists whose sport is to humiliate men? Men should stop treating feminists like ladies, and instead treat them like the men they say they want to be.

EXPEL THE EXPERTS

It's time to expel the "experts" from family life, according to Frank Furedi writing on a UK site:

> In repackaging parenting as a superbly complex, almost scientific task, a gaggle of experts hopes to colonise our personal lives. Parents are told time and again that their authority rests on outdated assumptions and that they lack the real expertise that one needs to socialise young people. And conscious of the fact that it is difficult to act authoritatively today, parents feel very insecure about rejecting expert advice. The explosion of various child-rearing and pedagogic fads is symptomatic of society's loss of faith in parental authority; it represents a futile attempt to bypass the question of finding some convincing alternative to old forms of pre-political authority. . . .

It is worth noting that the record of the "science" in areas such as child-rearing, education and relationships is a dubious one. It has consisted largely of ever-recurring fads that rarely achieve any positive durable results. Nevertheless, at a time when adult authority is on the defensive, the scientific expert has gained an ever-increasing influence over intergenerational relations. . . .

The philosopher John Stuart Mill, author of *On Liberty*, linked his call for the compulsory schooling of children to his distrust of parental competence. He believed that state-sponsored formal education might free children from the "uncultivated" influence of their parents. He asserted that since "the uncultivated cannot be competent judges of cultivation," they needed the support of enlightened educators to socialise their children.[47]

Mill is usually portrayed as a libertarian hero. But he demonstrated his elitist attitude when he advocated government control over schooling without respect for parental rights. Maybe that's the way it is with do-gooders. They think they know more than everyone else, so they want to coerce others into accepting their views.

Ironically, "not only are psychologists overwhelmingly leftist, but they have some of the lowest intelligence test scores of any discipline. On the GRE tests for grad school, only Physical Education majors have significantly lower scores." They're also bigoted. Bob Unruh reported:

A recent study by Tilburg University is gaining attention for its stunning conclusion that among psychologists, conservatives have reason to fear negative consequences should their political beliefs be revealed.

"In decisions ranging from paper reviews to hiring, many social and personality psychologists admit that they would discriminate against openly conservative colleagues," the authors, Yoel Inbar and Joris Lammers, wrote. "The more liberal respondents are, the more willing they are to discriminate."[48]

The study was done by the two members of the Department of Social Psychology at Tilburg University in the Netherlands. They warned specifically that conservatives who fear harm if their colleagues discover their leanings "are right to do so."

7

CULTURE MOCKS THE FAMILY

G overnment is the most powerful influence on our culture today because the federal government spends about $3.5 trillion a year. Every dollar carries the power to affect our culture and behavior through laws, regulations, grants, entitlements, court decisions, taxes, and tax credits. Supremacist judges have presumed to make dozens of major decisions on social and cultural policies.

THE INFLUENCE OF PUBLIC SCHOOLS

More influential in directing our culture—even more influential than the media—are the public schools. Often, parents who send their kids to private schools are unconcerned about the curriculum and other problems with the public schools. That is shortsighted, because it is public schools that guide the morals, attitudes, knowledge, and decision making of 89 percent of American children. The policies and prejudices taught in public schools profoundly affect us all, even those who have figured out how to avoid their most direct effects. Public schools are financed by $500 billion a year of our money, taken from us in federal, state, and local taxes, which the public school establishment spends under a thin veneer of account-ability to school boards.[1]

Before the 1960s, public schools and teachers accepted a respected role in defining the culture of the youngsters under their supervision. The schools, using a McGuffey Reader–style curriculum, were the mechanism through which American kids learned not only the basics, but also values such as honesty, respect for parents, and patriotism. Immigrant kids assimilated by learning our language, laws, and customs.

The American Citizens Handbook, published for teachers by the National Education Association in 1941 and republished in 1951, proclaimed: "It is important that people who are to live and work together shall have a common mind—a like heritage of purpose, religious ideals, love of country, beauty, and wisdom to guide and inspire them."

This message was fortified in this *NEA Handbook* by selections suitable for memorization, such as Old and New Testament passages, the Ten Commandments, the Lord's Prayer, the golden rule, the Boy Scout oath, and patriotic songs.

Public schools and teachers unions have dramatically changed! The turning point in public schools came with the immense influence of the *Humanist's* John Dewey and his Columbia Teachers College acolytes, who argued against objective truth, authoritative notions of good and evil, religion, and tradition. The *Humanist's* goal was spelled out in this quote from John Dunphy's prize-winning essay: "The battle for mankind's future must be waged and won in the public school classroom. The classroom must and will become the arena of conflict between . . . the rotting corpse of Christianity and the new faith of humanism."[2]

Sidney Simon's 1972 book *Values Clarification*, which sold nearly a million copies, was widely used to teach students to "clarify" their values—in other words, cast off their parents' values and make their own choices (moral or immoral). Then the public schools welcomed the Kinsey-trained sexperts to change the sexual mores of our society *from* limiting sex to marriage *to* anything goes. Concepts of right and wrong were banished, and children were taught about varieties of sex behavior without reference to what is moral, good, or even legal.

Alfred C. Kinsey published his *Sexual Behavior in the Human Male* in 1948, followed by *Sexual Behavior in the Human Female* in 1953. He is credited with starting the sexual revolution by pretending to offer as a fact that marital infidelity and homosexual behavior were epidemic. It was many years before the fraud in his data collection and analysis became known. The text of his gospel of the sexual revolution was that "anything is permissible between consenting adults."

Meanwhile, elementary and secondary school curriculum suffered a vast dumbing-down. Phonics and traditional arithmetic were censored out. Students were allowed to graduate without learning to read, write, or calculate. While tolerating massive illiteracy, the public schools are now powerfully impacting our culture by inculcating the values of situation ethics, diversity, political correctness, and the casual acceptance of sex outside of marriage. American history and literature courses now teach the doctrines of US guilt, multiculturalism, and globalism instead of the greatness of our heroes and our successes. Children are invited to be citizens of the world instead of American patriots.

High school math teacher Victor Dorff wrote in the *Los Angeles Times* that "cheating needs to be addressed as part of a cultural problem." Students of the older generation never considered that their grades on exams would be in competition with fellow classmates who cheated, but today cheating is the new normal. It's done by plagiarism, copying answers from smarter students, and programming smartphones. Once upon a time, Dorff said, "integrity was a crucial element in establishing a good reputation." But today, cheating is considered an "an accepted part of success."[3]

JUDGES AGAINST PARENTS

Our United States Constitution created a government of only delegated powers, and certainly one of the powers *not* delegated to government, but retained by the people under the Ninth and Tenth Amendments, is the right of parents to control the care and upbringing of their own children.

In the 1920s, the Supreme Court fully recognized this right of parents in what became known as the *Meyer-Pierce* doctrine, based on two Supreme Court decisions. In *Meyer v. Nebraska* in 1923, the Supreme Court recognized that the liberty guaranteed by the Fourteenth Amendment to the Constitution encompasses "the power of parents to control the education of their [children]."[4] In *Pierce v. Society of Sisters* in 1925, the court emphasized that "the child is not the mere creature of the state; those who nurture him and direct his destiny have the right, coupled with the high duty, to recognize and prepare him for additional obligations."[5]

Then again, in *Wisconsin v. Yoder* in 1972, the Supreme Court acknowledged that "this primary role of the parents in the upbringing of their children is now established beyond debate as an enduring American tradition."[6] Even as late as the year 2000, in *Troxel v. Granville*, a Supreme Court plurality stated, "It cannot now be doubted that the Due Process Clause of the Fourteenth Amendment protects the fundamental right of parents to make decisions concerning the care, custody, and control of their children."[7]

Everyone thought the so-called *Meyer-Pierce* doctrine was settled American law, widely understood and supported by our citizens and our courts. But in recent years, the lower federal courts have ruled in a very different direction. The federal courts are no friends of parents. When parents file suit to assert their right over the upbringing of their own children, federal courts nearly always rule against parents.

Five federal circuits have handed down anti-parent, pro–public school decisions, and not one of them even offered parents an "opt out" option to the school courses or materials that parents found offensive.

The Ninth Circuit ruled that parents' right to control the upbringing of their children "does not extend beyond the threshold of the school door." After heavy criticism in the US House, the court softened the "threshold" sentence but reaffirmed its decision. This case, *Fields v. Palmdale School District*, was brought by parents who discovered that their seven- to ten-year-old children had been required to fill out a nosy questionnaire about such matters as "thinking about having sex," "thinking about touching other people's private parts," and "wanting to kill myself." The parents were shocked and looked to the court for a remedy. No such luck. Three judges unanimously ruled against the parents. One judge was appointed by Jimmy Carter, one by Bill Clinton, and one by Lyndon B. Johnson. This *Fields* decision also stated that a public school can teach students "whatever information it wishes to provide, sexual or otherwise."[8]

"Whatever" was spelled out in anti-parent, pro–public school decisions handed down in five circuits in the following years.

In Kentucky, a federal court put its stamp of approval on a public school forcing students and teachers to watch a one-hour video that included dogmatic claims that homosexuality is immutable and that it is wrong to object to the gay lifestyle.[9]

A federal court in Massachusetts ruled against a father, David Parker, who had the audacity to demand that he be notified before his kindergarten son was given a "Diversity Book Bag" containing a book illustrating and describing same-sex couples.[10]

Diversity has become the code word not only for favorable teaching about homosexuality, but also for silencing anyone who criticizes it. Two cases, one in California and one in New Jersey, involved privacy-invading, self-incriminating, nosy questionnaires about teenage sex and use of illegal drugs, which the schools required students to answer. The parents were not accorded any right to opt out or even to be informed in advance about the objectionable survey.[11]

In Massachusetts, a federal judge ruled that a public school could require students to attend a ninety-minute program advocating homosexual conduct that used minors in sexually suggestive skits.[12]

In Dover, Pennsylvania, in 2005, a federal judge stuck a knife in the backs of parents in an Intelligent Design case and permanently banned the school from even notifying students that they could read other explanations of the origin of life in the school library.[13]

In California in 2003, a federal court ruled that the public schools had the right to teach seventh graders a course in Islamic history, culture, and religion, in which the students are taught how to act like Muslims.[14] They were given Muslim names, told to recite Muslim prayers from the Koran, encouraged to wear Arab clothing, and told to pretend they are making a pilgrimage to Mecca. They earned points for using Muslim religious phrases. The parents filed suit, but they lost in court, the Supreme Court refused to hear the parents' appeal, and the school continued to teach the course.

To sum up, federal courts in five circuits have handed down anti-parent decisions, and the US Supreme Court declined to hear any of these recent cases. The power in the hands of public schools and judges over children is awesome, and it is changing our culture every day by depriving parents of their fundamental rights over the upbringing of their own children.

Sex education for children as young as five is another attempt of the radical left to rob children of their innocence, modesty, and self-respect. Boys can quickly become susceptible to the seductive teachings that disarm any natural moral sense. Exposing them to graphic pictures and illustrations years before their readiness is emotional child abuse.

The North American Man/Boy Love Association (NAMBLA) is a pederast advocacy society that wants to abolish age-of-consent laws that criminalize adult sexual involvement with minors. Its deviant philosophy is consistent with the ideas of Alfred Kinsey, the reputed creator of American sexual mores.

Kevin D. Williamson gives an example of indoctrination in the public schools in *National Review Online*:

Fourth-grade students at Penn Valley Elementary School in the gilded Philadelphia suburb of Lower Merion will spend part of their school day watching and discussing a very clever piece of cinematic propaganda courtesy of organized homosexuality. The film is called *That's a Family!* and it is endorsed by the Human Rights Campaign along with other homosexual activist groups. . . .

That's a Family! is not about tolerance or treating people decently. It is about indoctrination, a fact that its enthusiasts make little attempt to hide. It lists among its endorsers such Democratic worthies as Senator Barbara Boxer, who declares that the film can be used to "break down" attitudes she finds disagreeable. Loret Peterson, a fourth-grade teacher in San Francisco, wrote that the film provides "a gentle starting point to reach elementary age children with a message of respect for all differences before biases become entrenched and the pressures of middle school set in. . . . We have the opportunity to take an active, moral approach to deflating the power of stereotypes by addressing them in the classroom." . . .

That the gay-rights movement is allowed to co-opt the government schools in its crusade—that it is in fact encouraged to do so—ought to be of concern even to those of us who are broadly in favor of helping gays to go about their business in society much the same as anybody else. . . .

There are no cease-fires in the culture wars, because the Left simply will not stop until it has achieved total conformity, which it pursues under the banners of "tolerance" and "diversity," *i.e.,* a virtue the Left does not possess and a condition the Left will not abide.[15]

A newspaper ad protested what the Toronto schools are teaching:

The K–12 schools have taught sex education for a long time, but now they teach sexual identity and orientation, including role-playing exercises. Parents have no say about this, as the Toronto Equity Inclusive Curriculum says:

Should Schools Send Notes Or Permission Slips Home Before Starting any Classroom Work On LGBTQ Issues? No. Can A Parent Have Their Child Accommodated Out Of Human Rights Education Based On Religious Grounds? No. Can

Teachers Seek Accommodation From Teaching Materials That May Contradict Their Religious Beliefs? No. The TDSB is part of the secular public education system. Can Schools/Teachers Choose Not To Address Controversial Issues For Fear Of Negative Parent Response? No.[16]

The *Dilbert* cartoonist wrote:

Sometimes it feels as if our school system is at war with parents, and winning. The kids are just the ammunition. Take homework, for example. Most schools load up the kids with hours of homework, which ruins a family's quality of life after school, putting parents in the position of being bad cops from the time school is out until bedtime. The kids are stressed, overworked, and tired. . . .

Now suppose your kid joins a sports team, or band, or competitive cheerleading, or just about anything. You'll find yourself spending weekends out of town for tournaments and competitions. You might be booking hotels for overnight stays, and generally building your life around these occasions. . . .

It is not that homework and competitive sports are bad. The complaint is that schools are increasingly saying that they know what is good for kids much better than parents, and schools are expanding their control beyond school hours.[17]

DECONSTRUCTION BY COMMUNISTS

Much of twentieth-century anthropology is dedicated to studying primitive tribes in the hope that we can learn from them. The modern writers' premise is that all people are the same, and that our social customs are not necessarily better than anyone else's. Their research is a big encouragement to feminists, Marxists, and others who are unhappy with Western social structures.

Any notion that Communism could promote better treatment of women is dispelled by looking at the private life of Karl Marx. He kept his wife and their children destitute while he disdained work.

He denied his daughters an education because he thought women were suitable only to be clerical assistants. He kept a female slave from the age of eight, never paid her a wage, used her as his mistress, and refused to acknowledge their child. She was the only member of the working class Marx ever knew; his alleged research about the so-called proletariat was a fabrication.

An Italian Communist, Antonio Gramsci, developed the Communist strategy in the early 1900s to focus on the culture war and thereby destroy Western social structure and overthrow the West from within. Gramsci attacked our values, morals, ethics, and social structure that held our society together, creating a cohesive people. These Western social structures include authority, morality, sexual restraint, monogamous marriage, personal responsibility, patriotism, national unity, community, tradition, education, conservatism, language, Christianity, law, and truth. His theory called for media and communications to slowly co-opt the people with a propaganda message.

Through a systematic attack on these institutions, which he allegedly called the "slow march through the culture," Gramsci theorized that when these institutions are sufficiently damaged, the people will allow totalitarian control of the Western world. Many of the Gramscian Marxist Communist ideas have been implemented in our government, education, and law. Feminists aided this goal by their constant attacks on men, marriage, and the traditional family.

Careful study shows that much of feminism is grounded in Gramscian Marxist Communism. Feminism's goals are to use women to undermine and destroy the culture by abandoning marriage and by not carrying on the critical task of "transmitting" the culture to the next generation. Today's feminists use women to advance the destruction of the family while convincing women they are victims of the patriarchy. "Patriarchy" is Orwellian Newspeak for the social structures and institutions that kept Western civilization together for decades prior to the social decay we see today.

America's Socialists and Communists make no pretense about their goal to promote the destruction of our free society by advancing a welfare state and the complete breakdown of the family. In the 1970s, it became conventional wisdom in the United States to admire Swedish Socialism, calling it the "middle way." A British journalist who returned from Sweden cautioned us:

> I have seen the Future and it doesn't work. Despite many evidences of the truth of that observation, many Americans—especially those in sociology and related disciplines—help maintain belief in the myth that Sweden's Welfare State is still a model for us and others to emulate. The family has become the target because it is the solidifying and most effective element for perpetuating those traditional values that often are the only defense posts against the totalitarianizition of our society. . . .
>
> In Sweden, the state now arrogates to itself the power to be the primary protector of the child. The child must be subjected to compulsory programs in sex education, socialization, and religion which are consciously and with ideological bias intended to counteract the child's values derived from parents within the family.[18]

JUDGES CHANGE PORNOGRAPHY LAW

One of the major changes in our culture is the immense amount of pornography that greets us from our television screens and movie theaters, and the even grosser stuff available on the Internet. This dramatic change from the 1950s is the work of supremacist judges on the US Supreme Court. From 1966 to 1970, the Earl Warren Court handed down a revolutionary series of thirty-four decisions that turned the previous US law of obscenity upside down. These decisions gave extraordinary victories to pornographers, reversing all the judges, juries, appellate courts, and law enforcement officials connected with those cases. Those thirty-four reversals made laws against obscenity almost impossible to enforce, thereby drastically lowering community decency standards throughout America.[19]

WHAT HAPPENED TO MARRIAGE?

For centuries, the purpose of marriage was for a man and a woman to voluntarily and jointly contract to assume the moral and legal responsibility for their offspring. Changes to marriage law have chipped away to the point where parental responsibilities under the law have very little to do with marriage.

After marriage law was decoupled from parenthood, gays were able to argue that any two people who love each other ought to be able to adopt children. Same-sex marriage is often promoted as a civil rights issue, or as a way to promote respect for gays. But it also changes the meaning of marriage in a way that is contrary to its traditional purpose.

Did you know that being pro-family is now considered a controversial, even outmoded ideology? Let's review *Wikipedia's* definition of *familialism*, introduced in part in chapter 1:

> Familialism is an ideology that promotes the family of the Western tradition as an institution. Familialism views the nuclear family of one father, one mother, and their child or children as the central and primary social unit of human ordering and the principal unit of a functioning society and civilization. . . .
> Familialism is usually considered conservative or reactionary by its critics who argue that it is limited, outmoded and unproductive in modern Western society.[20]

Conservatives usually consider the merits of the nuclear family to be self-evident and are probably not aware that many academic scholars now look on the American nuclear family as a counterproductive relic of the 1950s. Here is another *Wikipedia* definition: "Complementarianism is a theological view held by some in Christianity and other world religions, such as Islam, that men and women have different but complementary roles and responsibilities in marriage, family life, religious leadership, and elsewhere."[21]

Really? Is that just a theological view of a few Christians and

Muslims? Every civilization has been dominated by citizens who believe that men and women have different but complementary roles and responsibilities. And that includes societies that are not religious, such as Japan.

The past half-century has seen many trends contributing to the destruction of the American family: Feminism. Unilateral divorce. Cheap contraceptives. Welfare queens. Fatherphobia in family courts. Social acceptance of adultery and illegitimacy. Lobbying for free contraceptives for law students, with encouragement from President Obama. Hundreds of studies on society's ills point to family breakdowns or single-parent families as the problems.

The trends toward non-marriage and toward same-sex marriage are a direct attack on fathers. The bond between a child and his mother is an obvious fact of nature, but marriage establishes a direct link between a child and his father.

Alas, marriage rates in the United States have hit an all-time low as economic forces and social changes have pushed couples to delay or avoid matrimony, according to an analysis of census data by the Pew Research Center. Only 51 percent of people over age eighteen are married today, compared to 72 percent in 1960.[22] Trends are pointing toward married couples soon becoming a social minority. Yet most people who have never married say they would like to be married someday.

Outsourcing manufacturing jobs plus automation have contributed to the decline of marriages, especially among those without a college degree. Declining job security has also made marriage less appealing. University-educated people are still getting married, but usually not until they have finished college and built their careers. The age of first marriage has risen higher than ever to an average of 26.5 years for women and 28.7 for men.[23]

Within a few years, if current trends persist, less than half of the US adult population will be married. This steep decline isn't just a social problem; it's also an economic problem. The steadily dropping marriage rate contributes to income inequality and further entrenches it. Family structure is the new economic dividing line in American society.[24]

Since two-earner married couples have higher incomes and more education than struggling singles, the question is asked, does lack of financial stability encourage the decision not to marry, or does the decision not to marry cause financial instability? Either way, the trend is self-reinforcing and shows its effect on the next generation. Being raised in a stable, two-parent household is a strong determinant of educational achievement.

For those who are not college-educated, cohabitation is becoming the alternative to the marriage track. They are more likely than college-educated cohabiters to have children and lower household incomes. Cohabitation is certainly not the equivalent of marriage in terms of family stability. Demographers Sheela Kennedy and Larry Bumpass found that after twelve years, about two-thirds of cohabiting parents will have split up, compared to only a quarter of married couples with children.[25]

What is the role of government in defining our culture? Are we allowing our culture, and even our definition of marriage, to be redefined by legislators, judges, public schools, and the media? Should we demand that our elected representatives pass laws to address these issues? Should we permit nonelected judges to make policy decisions for us?

Another way our legal system has attacked the American family is in the decline of the marital privilege. In 1958, the US Supreme Court unanimously ruled in *Hawkins v. United States*:

> The common law rule, accepted at an early date as controlling in this country, was that husband and wife were incompetent as witnesses for or against each other. The rule rested mainly on a desire to foster peace in the family and on a general unwillingness to use testimony of witnesses tempted by strong self-interest to testify falsely. Since a defendant was barred as a witness in his own behalf because of interest, it was quite natural to bar his spouse in view of the prevailing legal fiction that husband and

wife were one person. . . . The rule yielded to exceptions. . . . But the Court emphasized that no exception left spouses free to testify for or against each other merely because they so desired.[26]

It's evident that the pressure to break the rule was to assist prosecutions, as one justice admitted:

> The rule of evidence we are here asked to reexamine has been called a "sentimental relic." . . . It was born of two concepts long since rejected: that a criminal defendant was incompetent to testify in his own case, and that, in law, husband and wife were one. . . . Any rule that impedes the discovery of truth in a court of law impedes as well the doing of justice. When such a rule is the product of a conceptualism long ago discarded, is universally criticized by scholars, and has been qualified or abandoned in many jurisdictions, it should receive the most careful scrutiny.[27]

The marital privilege was reversed in *Trammel v. United States*, which ruled that "the existing rule . . . be modified so that the witness-spouse alone has a privilege to refuse to testify adversely; the witness may be neither compelled to testify nor foreclosed from testifying."[28]

We don't know how many marriages have been destroyed by the abolition of this privilege. Sometimes the destruction is deliberate, if the authorities decide to bust up a couple with a history of domestic violence. Thus, one of the advantages of traditional marriage was abolished—without significant public debate—by lawyers who believe that the marriage bond is a "sentimental relic." After the privilege was abolished, it became easier for prosecutors to pit husbands and wives against each other.

THE HOOKUP SOCIETY

Many college women say they see building their résumés, not finding boyfriends (never mind husbands), as their main job. They envision their twenties as a period of unencumbered striving, when they might work at a bank in Hong Kong one year, then go to business school, then move to a corporate job in New York. The idea of lugging a relationship through all those transitions is hard for many to imagine. Almost universally, the women say they do not plan to marry until their late twenties or early thirties.

In this context, some women welcome the opportunity to have sex without relationships, preferring "hookup buddies" (regular sexual partners with little emotional commitment) to boyfriends. Some women say it is rare to find a relationship worth investing time in, so they avoid commitment altogether, assuming that someone better will always come along. These women enjoy casual sex on their terms—often late at night, after a few drinks.

According to the *New York Times*, "Elizabeth A. Armstrong, a sociologist at the University of Michigan who studies young women's sexuality, said that women at elite universities choose hookups because they see relationships as too demanding and too distracting from their career goals."[29]

LET'S BLUR THE GENDER LINES—OR NIX THEM

The feminists' determination to promote gender interchangeability extends to efforts to change our vocabulary. Using the website Salon.com to instruct Barack Obama to feminize his vocabulary, Tracy Clark-Flory complained: "[The] 'our wives, mothers, and daughters," phrase is one he routinely employs, but it is counterproductive to women's equality. . . . Defining women by their relationships to other people is reductive, misogynist, and alienating to women."[30]

It's obviously very easy to offend feminists. Suzi Parker complained in the *Washington Post*: "Have conservatives so corrupted the word 'feminist' that it is now tainted like the word . . . 'liberal' or 'environmentalist'? The fact that this is even in the realm of discussion in 2013 makes my head ache terribly—and makes me angry."[31]

Feminists try vigorously to force gender interchangeability on

American society, but they find it a hard sell when it comes to kids. A *New York Times* op-ed by Peggy Orenstein commented:

> Among the "10 characteristics for Lego" described in 1963 by a son of the founder was that it was "for girls and for boys." But the new Friends collection, Lego says, was based on months of anthropological research revealing that—gasp!—the sexes play differently.
>
> Toddlers interact similarly with the company's Duplo blocks, but by preschool girls prefer playthings that are pretty, exude "harmony" and allow them to tell a story. They may enjoy building, but they favor role play. So it's bye-bye Bionicles, hello princesses. In order to be gender-fair, today's executives insist, toys must be gender-specific.[32]

California sociology grad student Elizabeth Sweet complained in the *New York Times*: "Every day, people encounter toy departments that are rigidly segregated—not by race, but by gender. There are pink aisles, where toys revolve around beauty and domesticity, and blue aisles filled with toys related to building, action and aggression."[33]

WHY NOT MATRIARCHY?

The famous 1965 Daniel Patrick Moynihan report, *The Negro Family: The Case for National Action*, warned that the rise in single-mother families was not a harmless lifestyle choice, but was unraveling "the basic socializing unit" and causing high rates of delinquency, joblessness, school failure, and male alienation. Moynihan was bitterly attacked for speaking what is now universally recognized as the awful truth. Kay S. Hymowitz wrote in the Manhattan Institute's *City Journal* that Moynihan's critics romanticized female-headed families as a good thing. She described how the feminists, who were fixated on notions of patriarchal oppression, claimed that criticism of mother-headed households was really an effort to deny women their independence, their sexuality, or both.[34]

But like it or not, women need men—and not just as playthings, but as husbands. Unfortunately, American women face an increasingly tough marriage market, as Kate Bolick demonstrated in her 2011 *Atlantic* article "All the Single Ladies." Women continue to outpace men in educational attainment, employment rates, and earnings; thus, many men are seen as unmarriageable, while the shrinking population of desirable men is increasingly promiscuous. What is a single lady to do about it? Bolick's answer is female companionship.[35]

Only monogamous marriage, in which the heterosexual couple (rather than either gender) wields power and constitutes the basic unit of society, enables equality and true companionship between the sexes.

Suzanne Venker in *National Review Online* asked, is the fifty-fifty marriage the ideal?

> Does my mother's life, or mine, seem oppressive to you? That's what feminists and the women they've enlisted in their cause believe—and what they want you to believe. Consider this shocking statement by Sheryl Sandberg, COO of Facebook:
>
> We still haven't achieved the goal of real equality for women in the workplace and men in the home. Women continue to need protection not only globally where many women lack basic civil and human rights, but also here where the most dangerous place for an American woman is still shockingly in her home.
>
> The most dangerous place for an American woman is in her home! Wow! With this belief firmly planted in their brains, feminists tout a new model for marriage—one in which each spouse is expected to do the exact same thing. Sandberg explains that she and her husband share everything right down the middle: care of their two small children, full-time careers, cooking, cleaning, etc. What she doesn't mention (as most high-profile feminists don't) is that somewhere in the background of these two-earner couples is a full-time nanny who's doing the hard work—some might say the real work—for them.
>
> Paradoxically, most women don't want to give up precious years at home rearing their children so they can pursue demanding careers that place them at the mercy of bosses at

work and hired help at home. Much to the dismay of feminists such as Sandberg, most women—despite all their so-called career gains—still prefer to work part time, if at all, once they have children, giving women a type of freedom most men don't have. [36]

Weren't things supposed to be different? Wasn't the rise of women in the workplace supposed to usher in a new era where two-career couples would flourish side by side, sharing household and family duties and a balanced life? People used to say that men needed a wife at home and a wife at the office—the traditional secretary. Feminists now demand an assistant at work and a stay-at-home husband, or at least a husband who's very flexible and supportive.

But one thing that hasn't changed is the all-out commitment to work and career that is needed from men and women who want to reach the top. That is why so many women bail out. It's not the life they want.

THE INFLUENCE OF TELEVISION

Man Up! on ABC is one of several sitcoms that make fun of men. The word *man* is treated as a joke. ABC's other antiman comedy, *Last Man Standing*, stars Tim Allen, the onetime star of *Home Improvement*, as the marketing director of an outdoorsman's catalog who has to stay home to tend his three daughters. Mr. Allen is at war with male extinction, and that's why he may be the last man standing.

Man Up! is about men who are treated like children. *Last Man Standing* is more of a backlash against all the man-bashing. Like so many other men on television these days, the put-upon heroes of *Man Up!* and *Last Man Standing* are victims of a changed economy and a new social order in which men are the new women.

But men get on their wives' and girlfriends' nerves by not being manly enough. In *Man Up!* Will's wife, Theresa (Teri Polo), taunts him for drinking his coffee with hazelnut nondairy creamer. "Your grandfather fought in World War II, your father fought in Vietnam, but you play video games and use a pomegranate body wash," Theresa says acidly. "Are you saying I'm not a man?" Will asks. "You are man-ish," she replies.

The focus on men's failings partly reflects the fact that female TV viewers outnumber men; network executives, it seems, know what women want. The demeaning of men has been a topic of talk shows, pop psychology, and literature for years. Books, articles, and blogs about the changed status of men abound.

New York Times columnist David Brooks explained some reasons why men fail:

> Over the years, many of us have embraced a certain theory to explain men's economic decline. It is that the information-age economy rewards traits that, for neurological and cultural reasons, women are more likely to possess. To succeed today, you have to be able to sit still and focus attention in school at an early age. You have to be emotionally sensitive and aware of context. You have to communicate smoothly. For genetic and cultural reasons, many men stink at these tasks.[37]

In his article, Brooks mentioned the Jewish feminist Hanna Rosin. Here's her take on men and marriage, from her article titled "The End of Men":

> What if the economics of the new era are better suited to women? Once you open your eyes to this possibility, the evidence is all around you. It can be found, most immediately, in the wreckage of the Great Recession, in which three-quarters of the 8 million jobs lost were lost by men. It may be happening slowly and unevenly, but it's unmistakably happening; in the long view, the modern economy is becoming a place where women hold the cards.
>
> And so, a new matriarchy is emerging, run by young, ambitious, capable women who—faced with men who can't or won't be full partners—are taking matters into their own hands. Someday girls will be asking why their feminist grandmothers destroyed marriage as it had been known for generations.[38]

While yuppies are postponing childbirth so that they can get promotions or bigger mortgages, US population growth is coming from welfare queens and anchor babies. The fertility clinics used to be for forty-year-old yuppie couples looking for a first child, but now they cater to single women and lesbians.

More and more women are finding themselves either unable or uninterested in finding a partner with whom to raise a child. Single mothers by choice can obtain a child by adoption or by donor sperm insemination. Women can choose any anonymous donor sperm purchased from a sperm bank. The clinics are not allowed to discriminate based on marital status anymore. One single mom-to-be wrote:

> I thought it over, and made the decision to half and half: freeze some eggs, and freeze some embryos. This meant that I would need to choose a donor. While I have a good number of male friends, I didn't want any of them to be the donor, for various reasons. My doctor recommended a great clinic they often work with, and I went through the process of looking for a donor pretty quickly (all the donor information was online). This was a very interesting process: at times, I would think it was great—I could choose a donor of a certain height, weight, eye color, and, most importantly, I could see their family's medical history.[39]

What is lost in all of this is the recognition that the child needs a father as well as a mother. The *New York Times* reported:

> It used to be called illegitimacy. Now it is the new normal. After steadily rising for five decades, the share of children born to unmarried women has crossed a threshold: more than half of births to American women under 30 occur outside marriage.
>
> Once largely limited to poor women and minorities, motherhood without marriage has settled deeply into middle America. The fastest growth in the last two decades has occurred among white women in their 20s who have some college education but no four-year degree, according to Child Trends, a Washington research group that analyzed government data.[40]

What was once taboo and thought of as wrong for society is now being celebrated. Well before Murphy Brown, television was portraying single motherhood as an acceptable alternative to a two-parent family. The influence of television has had a big impact on the stability of our society.

CHILDREN'S RIGHTS

The fashionable crusade of children's rights is bound to be antifamily. The movement declares itself to be more interested in the welfare of children than their own parents are. It promises to give children legal sanctions against their parents, and in so doing, pits the interests of children against Mom and Dad. The inescapable implication is that children are not in safe hands with their own parents and that a whole movement must be called into being in order to protect them. Antifamily propaganda teaches that mothers and fathers are, at best, inadequate and, at worst, hostile to the needs of their children.

The loaded message of the term "children's rights" attempts to pack the punch of an appeal to both parental feeling and the nobility of action implied by the word "rights." But it is bogus! A "right" is classically defined as the freedom to act without interference, according to one's conscience. It means nothing unless the individual has the capacity to act upon his or her right. Children, because of their immaturity and inexperience, do not have that capacity.

Marriage is the best child-abuse prevention program in history. Children in married families benefit from maximum financial and parental resources, while parents are happier and have the time to raise them the way they know it should be done. Kids raised in intact families are the most likely to do well in school and become moral and productive adults. They arrive at school ready to learn. The best way to improve schools is by rebuilding marriage—so teachers can spend all their time teaching, not being surrogate parents to hundreds of troubled kids.

Since the lack of marriage is the primary predictor of poverty, marriage is the best economic justice program in history. We must get government out of the business of destroying marriage and replacing it with government programs. When marriage is absent, government control and manipulation take its place. Strong marriages defend themselves from government intrusion.

Demanding that husbands take on equal duties in child care, the National Organization for Women passed resolutions in the 1970s stating, "The father has equal responsibility with the mother for the child care role." In 1972, *Ms.* magazine featured premarriage contracts declaring housewives independent from essential housework and baby care, and obliging the husband to do half of the dishes and diaper changes. As a model, *Ms.* published the Shulmans' marriage agreement, which divided child-care duties as follows: "Husband does Tuesday, Thursday and Sunday. Wife does Monday, Wednesday and Saturday. Friday is split according to who has done extra work. All usual child care, plus special activities, is split equally. Husband is free all day Saturday, wife is free all Sunday."

As divorces became easy to get, the feminists did a total about-face in their demand that fathers share equally in child care. Upon divorce many mothers demand total legal and physical custody and control of their children. Gone are the demands that the father change diapers or tend to a sick child. The ex-husband is targeted as good for nothing except a paycheck, and the ex-wife is eager to proclaim her financial dependency. Feminists assert that, after divorce, child care should be almost solely the mother's job, and a father's only function is to send money. Feminists want the father out of sight, except maybe for a few hours a month of visitation at her discretion.

THE WAR ON BOYS

Feminists have been whining for years that girls don't get treated as well as boys in school. That's a big lie; there is gender discrimination in American schools, but it's the boys who are disadvantaged. Schools and colleges are increasingly anti-boys, antimale, and anti-masculine. Girls are excelling; boys are underachieving. Boys are more likely than girls to get poor grades, be held back a grade, have a learning disability, form a negative attitude about school, be put on antidepressants, get suspended or expelled, or drop out. The longer students are in school, the wider the gap.

The feminist battalions are even on the warpath against the right to *be* a boy. In elementary schools across America, recess is being eliminated; shocking numbers of little boys are drugged with psychosomatic drugs to force them to behave like little girls; boys are punished for playing the games of normal boyhood, such as tag and cops and robbers; and zero-tolerance idiocies that are particularly hurtful to boys are being enforced. Anyone who has raised children of both genders knows that boys cannot sit still at a desk as long as girls can. They must have the opportunity to run around outside so they can come back in the classroom and learn.

The American Association of University Women (AAUW) continues to spread the falsehood that public schools are unfair to girls and that this gender bias is damaging girls' self-esteem and academic achievement. The reality is that feminists are trying to make boys act like girls, and when they don't, they are considered to be unruly girls. Christina Hoff Sommers described some of this bias against boys in her book *The War Against Boys*:

> In their zero sum game of expectations, feminist educators believe that the only way for girls to prosper is for boys to decline. Feminists are trying to make schools into a unisex society, but it is difficult to take the boy out of the little boys. The feminists want to turn boys into passive men who will be ruled by females.
>
> Kay Hymowitz, in her 2011 book *Manning Up: How the Rise of Women Has Turned Men Into Boys*, describes how feminists have turned men in their 20s and early 30s into child-men. They are in a state of perpetual adolescence because the feminists have stacked the deck against males. Schools have a hard time getting boys to read books. The problem is the books have been feminized and books are selected for their appeal to girls. Though they cannot articulate it, boys can usually see right through the

modern psychobabble. In fact, say what you will about the Harry Potter books (and plenty has been said), they at least betray a consciousness of the old adventure ideal, and are light on the psychological reflexiveness—at least in the early books in the series.

Christina Hoff Sommers explained the hitherto unreported reason why boys graduate from high school with lower scores than girls—and it isn't because boys are not as smart as girls. She wrote on a *New York Times* blog:

> Boys score as well as or better than girls on most standardized tests, yet they are far less likely to get good grades, take advanced classes or attend college. Why? A study in *The Journal of Human Resources* gives an important answer. Teachers of classes as early as kindergarten factor good behavior into grades—and girls, as a rule, comport themselves far better than boys. The study's authors analyzed data from more than 5,800 students from kindergarten through fifth grade and found that boys across all racial groups and in all major subject areas received lower grades than their test scores would have predicted.
>
> The scholars attributed this "misalignment" to differences in "noncognitive skills": attentiveness, persistence, eagerness to learn, the ability to sit still and work independently. As most parents know, girls tend to develop these skills earlier and more naturally than boys.[41]

A study made by professors at the University of Georgia and Columbia University published in the *Journal of Human Resources* analyzed data on fifty-eight hundred students from kindergarten through fifth grade, linking test scores to teacher's assessments. The data showed that teachers uniformly favored girls, and in every subject area boys were scored below where their test scores would indicate. The study pointed out that these teacher assessments affect how fast kids move through school and get various academic opportunities and college admissions. Do feminist teachers expect elementary school boys to behave like girls, and then grade them down when they don't?

THE WAR ON COLLEGE MEN

In college, women now outnumber men by four to three.[42] Forty years ago, the opposite was true. The problem is not that more women are attending college; the problem is that men aren't keeping pace. The disparity is even greater among minorities. African-American women outnumber African-American men in college by two to one. Not only are men less likely than women to go to college; they're also less likely to graduate once they are there.

It turns out that when the gender ratio at a college tips decidedly toward women, both men and women become less attracted to that campus. Men don't want to enroll in what is perceived as a women's college, and women want men around to date. This presents a big problem for college admissions officials because the average female applicant has a higher GPA, participates in more extracurricular activities, and writes a better essay than the average male applicant. Admissions directors are faced with a dilemma. If they don't keep a gender balance in admissions, they will lose both good men and good women. What decisions would you make if you were a college admissions official?

The feminists' goal is to remake us into a gender-neutral society, not only by mandating identical treatment for males and females from toys to jobs, not only by forcing interchangeability of the genders, but also by eradicating from our culture everything that is masculine. Feminists despise macho men, like the brave male firefighters who charged up the World Trade Towers on 9/11 and our Special Forces who dared to enter the caves in Afghanistan. Justice Ruth Bader Ginsburg's Supreme Court ruling to sex-integrate Virginia Military Institute, and her demand for the sex integration of the Boy Scouts and Girl Scouts in her book *Sex Bias in the U.S. Code*, were not to achieve sex equality but to achieve gender interchangeability and diminish the machismo in men.

We see manifestations of this feminist goal in colleges and high schools with the implementation of Title IX, which feminists use as a vehicle to abolish wrestling and other very masculine sports. We see this in forbidding boys to play cops and robbers, and we see it in the overprescribing of Ritalin. We see the feminists' handiwork in textbook revision and in haranguing by the language gestapo to persuade us to use such gender-neutral idiocies as *he/she*.

Title IX of the Education Amendments of 1972 requires that colleges and schools receiving federal funds not discriminate "on the basis of sex." The law says nothing about equal numbers of men and women, sex integration, "proportionality," quotas, affirmative action, remedies for underrepresentation or past discrimination, or even sports. Title IX's author, US representative Edith Green, stated at the time that the law is "exceedingly explicit so that the establishment of quotas would be prohibited."[43]

Despite Representative Green's promise, gender quotas were created by the radical feminists in the Carter administration and have been enforced ever since. They invented a regulation called the "proportionality test," which means that the male-to-female ratio on competitive sports teams must equal the male-to-female ratio of total college enrollment. *Proportionality* became a feminist code word for "quota."

About 60 percent of college students today are women, yet only a fraction seek to compete in intercollegiate sports. It is an incontrovertible fact that men are more interested in competitive sports than women, and colleges usually have difficulty finding women to meet their quota targets.

The senseless bean-counting numbers game called proportionality has resulted in the elimination of hundreds of male teams. Howard University athletic director Sondra Norrell-Thomas announced her elimination of both wrestling and baseball teams on the same day. The promising baseball players at Howard University lost their chance to develop their skills and become stars. It should surprise no one that Howard University's male enrollment dropped to only 34 percent compared to 66 percent female.

The abolition of wrestling teams proves that Title IX enforcement has nothing to do with equalizing funding, since wrestling is one of the least expensive of all competitive sports. Title IX quotas forced the elimination of nearly five hundred college wrestling teams, a particular target of feminist anti-masculine ideology. Other victims of Title IX include men's track and field and swimming. Title IX caused the elimination of all but nineteen men's college gymnastics teams.

The anti-masculine feminists even require colleges to count "walk-ons" in figuring their proportionality quotas. A walk-on is a student who tries out for a sport even though he wasn't recruited and is not subsidized, hoping that someday luck will strike and he will get to play on the team. There are many times more male walk-ons than female because more men than women are eager to try out for sports, and are far more willing to sit on the bench day after day with little chance of starting in a game. Colleges have been forced to count walk-ons in figuring their proportionality totals even though most walk-ons never play on the teams.

On June 2, 1997, the feminist National Women's Law Center announced that it would file a complaint against Boston University, the fourth-largest private school in the nation, over its sports programs. Within months, BU terminated its football team, which had been in existence for ninety-one years. It is no surprise that male enrollment at Boston University dropped to 40 percent.

It's refreshing that a few college men understand feminist ideology and keep their sense of humor. In ridiculing the senselessness of sports quotas, the University of Kansas college newspaper published this ironic comment: "College sports for women should be compulsory. Granted, many women may insist they don't want to play sports, but after generations of patriarchal oppression, it isn't realistic to think women really know what they want. The goal of perfectly equal gender ratios is more important than what anybody 'wants.'"

College football produces social conservatives such as Steve Largent, J. C. Watts, and the late Jack Kemp and Supreme Court justice Byron White. College wrestling programs brought us conservative stalwarts defense secretary Donald Rumsfeld, speaker Dennis Hastert, representative Jim Jordan, and Kansas attorney general Phill Kline. Track and field yielded congressman Jim Ryun, one of the greatest mile-runners of all time. When the Duke of Wellington was asked how he won the Battle of Waterloo in 1814, he said it had been won on the playing fields of Eton.

Reducing opportunities for college sports is a powerful disincentive to men and is a major cause of the dramatic drop in male attendance. Why should men bother attending college if they can't play the sports they love?

But Title IX harms women too. The numbers game has caused the elimination of traditional girls' teams such as gymnastics (one hundred teams have been abolished) in favor of large-squad-size sports, such as rowing or horseback riding. Young women are ultimately hurt by this irrational feminist agenda. A 1999 study found that girls' softball had double the rate of serious head injuries of boy's baseball, despite a baseball's greater hardness and speed. Feminism is pushing girls into higher risks of injury and hormone-changing drugs. Studies show that female competitors, especially in soccer and basketball, have a higher incidence of knee and head injuries compared to men. Torn anterior cruciate ligaments (ACL) are crippling women athletes at an alarming rate. A study reported in *Arthritis & Rheumatism* states that more than half of the 103 soccer players included in the study, who were ages fourteen to twenty-eight at the time of an ACL injury, suffered osteoarthritis of the knee twelve years later.

The Obama feminists are now trying to apply this same mindless regulation to math and science departments, which are predominantly male because men are more interested in those fields than women and score significantly higher on math and science aptitude tests. Math and science departments have traditionally been based on merit and have produced technology essential to winning wars and preserving our freedoms. There isn't a shred of evidence that women are discriminated against in math and science. There are no separate tracks for men's math and women's math. There simply is a higher proportion of men than women who voluntarily choose math and engineering just as more men choose competitive sports. Why should we accept anything less than the best in our classrooms?

Feminists want a quota-imposed unisex society regardless of the facts of life, voluntary choice, human nature, common sense, or documented merit. And they use the power of government to achieve their goal. Feminists expect their whining and outbursts about alleged discrimination to intimidate men into giving them preferential treatment. They want to rig the system so they will not have to compete against men, but only against other women, for scholarships, resources, and professorships.

Subservience to feminist orthodoxy on campuses is not only mandatory; it is undebatable. Women's studies courses and many sociology courses are tools to indoctrinate college women in feminist ideology and to lay a guilt trip on all men, collectively and individually.

Why are men dropping out of college, leaving the workforce, and avoiding marriage at such alarming rates? Are they correct in believing that American society has become antimale and that they are not needed anymore? Do men want to escape from the matriarchy that the feminists have created? Have they gone "on strike" from a society that appears to be stacked against them, as author Helen Smith proclaims in her book *Men on Strike*? She claims that men are behaving rationally in response to the lack of incentives society offers them to be responsible fathers, husbands, and providers.

WHY ARE WOMEN UNHAPPY?

Some economists are trying to figure out the difference between men and women.

In a *Freakonomics* radio podcast called "Women Are Not Men," Stephen Dubner explained: "Equality of the sexes has long been a goal, and in many ways that goal is being met. But, as you'll hear on this program, the variance between men and women on some dimensions is still large." Later in the show, he asked economist Betsey Stevenson:

So how do you explain it, Betsey? I mean, women were given a larger choice set, which economists tell us larger choice sets to a degree are really good. Women were given and accomplished in a lot of other areas that we would associate with, you know, benefits of different kinds: financial benefits, psychic benefits, and so on. How do you account for the decline? How do you account for the paradox? What are the mechanisms by which that paradox exists?[44]

The best explanation came from this comment, which was hidden because it was so heavily disliked:

Women are designed to seek out men whom they deem above themselves in status. So by elevating the status of women you are shrinking the number of partners they consider suitable. As a result, this has created a lot of lonely and unhappy women. They either drop out of the dating market because they cannot get commitment from the men they desire or they settle for someone who isn't really above them in status (hence why they initiate 70% of divorce proceedings). It shows in statistics that when a woman contributes 50% or more to household income, the marriage is very shaky. When there is a huge disparity in contribution to household income in the man's favour, both sexes are happier and the marriages have lower divorce rates.[45]

Here is some of the new academic research:

Among adults age 25 to 39, marriage rates have declined from about 81% in 1970 to 51% in 2010. The authors calculate that as much as 29% of that decline may be linked to aversion to a wife earning more than her husband.

A married woman earning more increases the probability of unhappiness in her union. Using data from 4,000 married couples surveyed as part of the US National Survey of Families and

Households, the researchers show that the percentage of people who report being "very happy" with their marriage declines when a woman earns more money than her husband.[46]

Women seem to be happiest when they have lasting marriages to men they can look up to. Feminism has taught them that they will have more choices in life if patriarchal marriage is destroyed, but someday they will realize that feminism has made them unhappy.

The recently discovered phenomenon of hypergamy (women wanting to marry men who earn more than they do) is a deterrent to marriage. Research by Marianne Bertrand and Emir Kamenica of the University of Chicago and Jessica Pan from the National University of Singapore showed that the odds of a couple marrying are significantly reduced if the woman earns more than the man.[47] Feminist dogma to the contrary notwithstanding, women really want the gender gap in pay. Their commitment to hypergamy is not just a lingering 1950s prejudice; it's a very practical belief that the husband needs to earn a larger salary so the wife can quit her job at any time for any reason, such as caring for her babies.

Ponderous discussions about the changing attitudes of and toward women appear in print everywhere: Maria Shriver's report "A Woman's Nation Changes Everything," a *Time* magazine cover story headlined "The State of the American Woman," Gail Collins's book *When Everything Changed*, and articles from all the feminist columnists. One sentence in all those feminist articles confronted the fundamental reason today's women are not as happy as women were in 1972. *Time* magazine admitted: "Among the most dramatic changes in the past generation is the detachment of marriage and motherhood."[48]

All this self-psychoanalyzing of women's attitudes appears to have been triggered by a National Bureau of Economic Research study published in the *American Economic Journal*, called "The Paradox of Declining Female Happiness." This report concluded that women's happiness has measurably declined since 1970. Since this study covers the same time period as the rise of the so-called women's liberation movement, feminists recognized it as a challenge to the goals and alleged achievements of their movement.

The authors, University of Pennsylvania economists Betsey Stevenson and Justin Wolfers, advanced a theory that the women's liberation movement "raised women's expectations"[49] (sold them a bill of goods), making them feel inadequate when they fail to have it all. The authors also presented a second theory that the demands on women who are both mothers and jobholders in the labor force are overwhelming.

A more realistic explanation is that the feminist movement taught women to see themselves as victims of an oppressive patriarchy in which their true worth will never be recognized and any success is beyond their reach. Feminist organizations such as the National Organization for Women hold consciousness-raising sessions where they exchange tales of how badly some man had treated them. Grievances are like flowers; if you water them, they will grow. Self-imposed victimhood is not a recipe for happiness. If you believe you can never succeed because you are a helpless victim of mean men, you are probably correct.

Alice Walker was a trail-blazing feminist who looked upon motherhood as a form of servitude. Her daughter Rebecca Walker didn't buy into that nonsense but wrote eloquently:

> My mum taught me that children enslave women. I grew up believing that children are millstones around your neck. . . .
>
> In fact, having a child has been the most rewarding experience of my life . . . three-and-a-half-year-old Tenzin has opened my world. . . .
>
> I meet women in their 40s who are devastated because they spent two decades working on a PhD or becoming a partner in a law firm, and they missed out on having a family. Thanks to the feminist movement, they discounted their biological clocks. They've missed the opportunity and they're bereft.

Feminism has betrayed an entire generation of women into childlessness. It is devastating. . . .

The leaders of the women's movement close ranks against anyone who dares to question them—as I have learned to my cost. . . .

I am my own woman and I have discovered what really matters—a happy family.[50]

WHAT FEMINISM IS COSTING MEN

Feminists have rigged the social system, the educational system, and the workforce against men, and nobody likes it. They write articles and books filled with phrases such as "the end of men," "females are the breadwinners," and "men are not necessary," and women want a seat at the table—at the head of the table. They have made gender relationships a zero-sum game, and men have reacted by letting them have it.

Women graduate with more college degrees. Men have lost their ambition to work hard and achieve success to build a life to support home, wife, and children. Feminists have kicked men out of their family provider role.

In commenting on how old ways are broken, social historian Stephanie Coontz told the *Atlantic* that we are having "a historical revolution every bit as wrenching, far-reaching and irreversible as the Industrial Revolution."[51] While there are many factors producing this change, she believes they all trace back to one thing: the decline of the male breadwinner. So long as a man believes that when he grows up he should fulfill the role of provider for a woman and the children of his own flesh and blood, he looks for a career track that will meet the challenge.

That motivation has been substantially eliminated. Women want to be self-supporting; feminism has even taught that it's demeaning to a woman to be financially supported by a man. Premarital sex and two-income families have become the new normal.

As women have blossomed in the workforce, men get the message that they are not needed. Men no longer feel compelled to be the family breadwinners. They don't want to compete with women. With no incentive to work long hours, or take a moonlighting job to increase their families' comfort, some men turn to worthless or even dangerous time-wasters. The average American boy spends thirteen hours a week playing video games. Some are realistic games that teach them to become killers, sadists, mutilators, and monsters who murder, torture, dismember, and rape. Pornography, which is now so easily available, has also become pervasive. The average high school boy watches porn two hours a week, filling his mind and often substituting these mediums for healthy face-to-face interactions with people.

These factors are crushing manhood and masculinity. Men are getting false and confusing messages from society, the media, and women about what is a man's role and what makes a man.

WHAT FEMINISM HAS COST WOMEN

It's sad to read the self-psychoanalyzing and regrets of the feminists. In their college women's studies courses, they learned to plan a career in the workplace without any space for marriage or babies, at least until they are forty, and then their window of opportunity has closed. So they don't have the companionship of a husband in their senior years or grandchildren to provide a reach into the future.

In the pre-1970 era, when surveys showed women with higher levels of happiness, most men held jobs that enabled their wives to be full-time homemakers. At the same time, the private enterprise system produced many products that make household work and kiddie care easier (such as dryers, dishwashers, and disposable diapers).

The Pew Research Center refuted the Betty Friedan myth about the full-time homemaker's role being akin to a domestic slave. Pew's researchers say that in the typical American family, the woman makes the major decisions, and they have the numbers to back up their assertion: In 43 percent of American couples, the wife makes most decisions about finances, weekend activities, and home purchases. Husbands make the decisions for only 25 percent of couples, while 31 percent split decision making between husband and wife. Even if the husband earns more than his wife, the woman is still more likely to make the decisions about how the money is spent.

Another explanation for women's unhappiness could be the increase in easy divorce and illegitimacy, which means that millions of women are raising kids without a husband and therefore expect government to substitute as provider. The 2008 election returns showed that seven out of ten single women voted for Barack Obama, perhaps hoping to be beneficiaries of his "spread the wealth around" policies.

THE NEW SOCIAL REALITY

The feminists' determination to change our culture by pretending the interchangeability of male and female even includes revising our vocabulary. Ruth Bader Ginsburg's 1977 book, *Sex Bias in the U.S. Code*, identified hundreds of words in federal laws that she said must be changed in order to eliminate sex discrimination. She decreed that *husband* and *wife* must be changed to *spouse, mother* and *father* to *parent, widow* and *widower* to *surviving spouse, sister* and *brother* to *sibling*, and even *he or she* to *he/she*, and *her or him* to *her/him*.

About half of all US states have toadied to the feminists by adopting gender-neutral language in drafting bills and even changing state constitutions. Washington State spent six years performing the onerous task of changing thousands of words and phrases used in the state's laws. The final list of words to walk the plank included ombudsman (replaced by ombuds), penmanship, and freshman.

An *American Conservative* article describes similar vocabulary lunacy in the United Kingdom:

As part of the drive towards institutionalizing same-sex marriage—which is being spearheaded not by radical gays but by our posh, foppish Conservative prime minister, David Cameron—words such as "husband" and "wife" and "father" and "mother" are being airbrushed from much official government documentation. So welfare and immigration forms will shortly be scrubbed clean of any mention of the w-word or the h-word, in favor of more "neutral" terms such as "spouse" or "partner" because, as the *Daily Telegraph* reports, the government believes that once same-sex marriage is legalized "it would be confusing to refer to husbands and wives."

Fathers are already disappearing. At the end of May, the National Health Service, the largest employer in Britain—and the fifth largest in the world—took the decision to excise the six-letter f-word from a pamphlet on rearing children that it has been giving to mothers- and fathers-to-be for the past 14 years. The pamphlet will no longer refer to fathers following a complaint from one person—yes, that is all it takes to airbrush people from history in modern Britain—who was concerned that such terminology is "not inclusive of people in same-sex relationships." From now on the pamphlet will refer to mothers and "partners." Dads are so 20th century.[52]

That's the sad reality of family in the twenty-first century. Sadder still, Madeleine Schwartz writes enthusiastically about the "new social reality" in her article "The Anti-Family":

Teen motherhood, single motherhood, unmarried cohabitation—these are not plagues or social ills that pose a threat to the otherwise normal structures of everyday life. They are our new social reality. . . . There is nothing wrong with teenage or single motherhood. The things children need: economic livelihood, emotional support and an education, are not dependent on a nuclear family structure. Poverty is poverty whether it's endured by two people or four.

A couple cannot raise a child better than one can. Once we get rid of the idea that marriage is the privileged form of cohabitation and that women cannot raise children without the help of a man—ideas that the Left has been working to eradicate for decades—there is no reason that a teen should not be financially and emotionally assisted for her choice to have a family.[53]

Au contraire, there is overwhelming evidence that a married couple can raise a child better than an individual can. More of our social ills are traceable to single moms than to any other source. We need to build more prisons for their kids when they grow up.

Hanna Rosin wrote in the *Atlantic* magazine about how young women today pursue sexual promiscuity in lieu of permanent relationships, like marriage:

> What makes this remarkable development possible is not just the pill or legal abortion but the whole new landscape of sexual freedom—the ability to delay marriage and have temporary relationships that don't derail education or career. To put it crudely, feminist progress right now largely depends on the existence of the hookup culture. And to a surprising degree, it is women—not men—who are perpetuating the culture, especially in school, cannily manipulating it to make space for their success, always keeping their own ends in mind. For college girls these days, an overly serious suitor fills the same role an accidental pregnancy did in the 19th century: a danger to be avoided at all costs, lest it get in the way of a promising future.[54]

Unfortunately, this new societal paradigm is having another detrimental effect: childlessness. Childlessness has increased across most demographic groups but is highest among professionals. According to an analysis of census data conducted by the Pew Research Center, about one-quarter of all women with bachelor's degrees and higher in the United States wind up childless. The welfare queens, drug addicts, and illegal aliens seem to have no trouble having as many babies as they want, but rich women do not want the trouble until it is too late. This is a result of the incentives and disincentives that our society has created.

What's worse, when today's woman does decide to have a child, chances are high that she won't be married to the father. In 1960, only 11 percent of US children lived in households without fathers, but today's number is 15 million, or one in three children living without a father. The pathetic spiral of fatherlessness continues upward and is a principal cause of poverty and income inequality.[55]

Another factor fostering poverty is America's astronomical divorce rate. The Marriage and Religion Research Institute, a Washington, DC, think tank, has produced new research showing that the divorce revolution perpetually reduced US economic growth. Divorce removes a fourth of head-of-household productivity growth.[56] Here is the executive summary of how divorce, now the new normal in US society, constantly retards US economic growth:

- Human capital is one of the three major contributors to the growth of the U.S. economy.

- Marriage lends between one third to one quarter of the human capital contribution for adult men to economic growth.

- The "Divorce Revolution" (1960s and 1970s) tripled the rate of divorce in the United States thus imprinting, in a natural experiment, the effects of divorce on the economy.

- Through divorce men become less productive.

- Divorce *causes* this drop in productivity, thus contracting economic growth.[57]

On July 7, 2014, the language commissars got Governor Jerry Brown to sign a bill deleting the words *husband* and *wife* from California laws, replacing them with the word *spouse*. The bill's sponsor, state senator Mark Leno, bragged that this removes "outdated and biased language from state codes."

8

THE WAY HOME

So, who killed the American family? Was it the feminists, the judges, the "experts," the gays, or the politicians? Or maybe the media, or the schools and colleges? Gays, lesbians, and polygamists have received most of the publicity about the attacks on our marriage law, but they are vastly outnumbered by the other groups described in this book.

There are many others who just stood by and watched the decline of the family but did nothing to save it. Libertarians speak out against all sorts of liberty-depriving policies, but are silent about the offenses of the family court. Privacy advocates complain about NSA spying, but not about the obnoxious surveillance and supervision exercised by judges and busybody bureaucrats. Most psychologists refuse to criticize the courts and fail to denounce the corrupt practices of their fellow professionals.

Even advocates of traditional marriage fail to speak up for the rights of parents. If marriage means both parents have parental rights and responsibilities for their kids, then this calls for joint child custody in case of divorce. If a court relies on the personal discretion of a judge, or the judge imposes his or her bias in favor of custody by one parent, then the marriage does not secure parental rights but instead puts parents' rights under control of the "village."

Those who have religious or lasting marriages may be unconcerned with the problems of divorce and the family courts, but in reality, these problems affect us all.

It's so unfortunate that most churches have neglected their duty to remind their flocks of God's plan for marriage and children, and to emphasize the crucial importance of the nuclear family. Why are preachers so silent about the essential morality of marriage and the immorality of its redefinition by supremacist judges?

It should be clear that most social problems and many financial problems are caused by the absence of the nuclear family. The majority of suicides, runaways, school dropouts, kids using illegal drugs, teen pregnancies, and other social ills come from mother-headed homes. Likewise for those who end up in jail.

A long list of groups has worked to destroy the American family, and another long list just sat silently and watched it happen. This book is designed to jog them—and you—into action.

Do you want Congress to cut taxpayer spending and balance the federal budget? Do you want Congress to stop raising the debt limit and to start paying down the national debt? Do you want to reduce or even eliminate the handouts of cash and benefits for living expenses that are paid monthly to nearly half of all Americans, creating widespread dependency on government? Do you want to restore our traditional system of limited government, created by the Founding Fathers so that Americans can live in freedom without supervision by an intrusive government?

No way can any of that happen unless we restore the nuclear family as the lifestyle of the majority of Americans, so families can support themselves without welfare handouts and government infringement. The fiscal problems America faces today are caused by the social problem of the decline in the numbers of Americans living in a nuclear family. If the husband-father provider is not supporting his family, the women and children turn to Big Brother government.

The seventy-nine types of handouts, paid out monthly to nearly half of our population, are the cause of our unbalanced budgets. They are also to blame for our colossal national debt, which hangs like an albatross around the necks of our children and grandchildren. These entitlements have cultivated a growing attitude of dependence among a once very independent people. And they've provided justification for the prying eyes and ears of government busybodies who try to run our lives.

Just as damaging are the government's *dis*incentives to marriage and incentives to illegitimacy. When are we going to start the process of eliminating and/or at least reducing some or all of those seventy-nine varieties of incentives and disincentives?

When will we start teaching kids in school the social and economic (as well as moral) benefits of sexual abstinence until marriage and of making sure that marriage precedes pregnancy? When will we start teaching students that the moral lifestyle is the best route to rise out of poverty and eventually achieve the American dream? When will schools and churches teach girls that if their boyfriends aren't good candidates for marriage, they're not worth having babies with?

When will we reject the Left's efforts to change us into a totally secular nation? And when will we realize that Americans' commitment to God and His words in the Bible provide powerful support for the nuclear family?[1]

The majority of Americans have voted to uphold the nuclear family; thirty-seven states have passed state constitutional amendments or laws in support of traditional marriage.[2] So why do we tolerate social and fiscal policies that undermine marriage and provide taxpayer-paid incentives to people to avoid marriage? Why do we tolerate supremacist judges who are using their power to redefine marriage in violation of a clear vote by the people?

FRANK TALK ABOUT MARRIAGE

Marriage should have a privileged status in government's relations with individuals. The decision to marry someone is, of course, a private act, but marriage itself is an important public and social act. Marriage doesn't involve merely the two people marrying; it involves any children who may result. Marriage gives many social benefits to those who get married, to their children, and to society at large. Marriage is the best antidote to poverty and welfare dependency. The Census Bureau reported in 2001 that only 6 percent of married-parent families lived in poverty, compared to 33.6 percent of single-parent families.[3]

Our divorce laws are contrary to the American system that respects the rule of law. Current divorce laws in every state afford no rights to the spouse trying to maintain a marriage, but instead enable one spouse to terminate a marriage unilaterally. Many states have attempted divorce reform, but so far with no success.

There seems to be a conspiracy of silence on the value of marriage and the nuclear family. From the *London Daily Mail*, we read a statement by a leading British family lawyer:

> Marriage is as important to the future of the nation as climate change and poverty, a senior family lawyer said yesterday. Baroness Deech said the growing numbers of families without fathers was doing more harm to the next generation than other factors such as smoking, alcohol, poor diet and lack of exercise.
>
> And she warned that a conspiracy of silence surrounded the issue because political leaders were afraid to say married families were better for children than cohabiting families or single parent families. . . . Children of single mothers have greater problems than those of cohabiting parents, and children of cohabitees have greater problems than those of married parents.
>
> "Since this is so incontrovertible, why is it so brave, as Sir Humphrey would put it, to tackle the desirability of marriage over cohabitation, both for adults and children?" Lady Deech asked. The topic has become a no-go area.
>
> We live in a world where we are encouraged to take care of our own and our children's health: we are constantly admonished to take exercise, eat healthily, wear a cycle helmet, study the side

of the package, stop smoking, recycle, combat global warming, brush our teeth, control our drinking habits and have health checks.

But when it comes to the one issue that does more harm to the next generation than any of these—the absence of a father in the family—there is a conspiracy of silence.

Politicians fear to address it. It is time to place marriage issues up there along with climate change, poverty and peace as a topic pre-eminently relevant to the present and future happiness and health of all people.[4]

Some US commentators are trying to bring back the stigma of illegitimacy. James Taranto wrote in the *Wall Street Journal* about a New York City ad campaign shaming teen moms.

> At issue is a subway ad campaign by the New York City Department of Social Services. It features photos of grumpy-looking infants (carefully chosen for racial diversity), captioned by messages to their putative parents, written in a toddler-like scrawl. Examples: "Honestly Mom . . . chances are he won't stay with you. What happens to me?" "If you finish high school, get a job, and get married before having children, you have a 98% chance of not being in poverty." Viewers of the ad are invited to "text 'NOTNOW' to 877877 for the real cost of teen pregnancy."

The New York City ad campaign may be a step in the right direction, but it fails to get to the heart of the problem. Taranto explained:

> The ad campaign's focus on "teen pregnancy" rather than illegitimacy illustrates a class bias. The two may seem more or less interchangeable inasmuch as the idea of marrying and starting a family at 18 is today virtually unthinkable *within the educated class*. Today's privileged woman is expected to follow a life script in which high school is followed by college and a career. In that script, a period of sexual and romantic experimentation begins in college or before (made possible thanks to contraception, with abortion available as Plan C), and marriage and children are

expected to wait until after she is established in her career.

The "98%" poster alludes to that life script and makes the dubious supposition that following it—at least if one leaves out college—is realistic for all women. But an important reason women bear children out of wedlock is because they don't expect to find husbands. . . .

As this column has repeatedly noted, women are hypergamous, which means that their instinct is to be attracted to men of higher status than themselves. When the societywide status of women increases relative to men, the effect is to diminish the pool of suitable men for any given woman. If most women reject most men as not good enough for them, the effect is no different from that of a low sex ratio. High-status men, being in short supply, set the terms of relationships, resulting in libertine sexual mores and higher illegitimacy.[5]

STOPPING ANTI-MARRIAGE INCENTIVES

Gary D. Alexander explains in the *Philadelphia Inquirer* why we must fix the bloated welfare system:

Since the end of the Reagan presidency, the American welfare state has mushroomed beyond any proportion to actual need. More than 80 different "means-tested" programs are deeply embedded in at least nine federal departments; welfare expenditures have grown faster than the economy and population growth, faster than increases in the poverty rate, and faster than federal expenditures on defense, education, Social Security, and Medicare.

Counting programs such as Medicaid, TANF, food stamps, the Earned Income Tax Credit, housing aid, energy assistance, Head Start, and Supplemental Security Income, federal antipoverty spending has increased in real terms from 2.2 percent of GDP in 1989 to a projected 4.3 percent in 2013. You read that right: Nearly two decades after we "ended welfare as we knew it," welfare spending as a percentage of the national output has nearly doubled in real terms.

Including matching state funds, the welfare system is now a $1-trillion-a-year monstrosity. Judging from my experience managing the system in two states for nearly 15 years, I can attest that the myriad of assistance programs are riddled with fraud, waste, and abuse. The dysfunction is not merely enabled by recipients who game the system, or by noncitizens who shouldn't even qualify. The system also represents a cash cow for bureaucrats, caseworkers, service providers, and a host of consultants and peddlers who plan, implement, and allegedly evaluate these programs.[6]

A good example of US taxpayers' money subsidizing and incentivizing illegitimacy was illustrated on Sean Hannity's May 11, 2013, interview with a young man who has fathered twenty-two children with fourteen different mothers. Taxpayers, of course, are supporting them all. The man was proud of his achievement, didn't have a job, didn't pay child support, believes it is the taxpayers' duty to support his offspring, and defiantly looks forward to creating more kids with more women. The welfare system makes this possible.

All legal child-related incentives that encourage marriage have been systematically eliminated by either legislators or judges; as a result, marriage is no longer seen as a necessary prerequisite to having kids. We must undo enough of those changes so that those who undertake the rights and responsibilities of their own offspring will do so by marriage.

Our laws should encourage stable families. Kids have a right to their own parents, not people who are labeled parents by some judge's bias about the child's "best interest" or child-support orders. Ideally, parents should assume the rights and responsibilities of parenthood by getting married. Our society cannot force anyone to get married, but it can surely adopt policies that favor kids having parents who have voluntarily taken steps to act as parents.

The "Contract with America" adopted by Republican members of the House in 1994 recognized that the "welfare trap" was promoting dependency and illegitimacy. It offered these solutions: (1) AFDC (Aid to Families with Dependent Children) was denied to mothers ages seventeen and younger who had children out of wedlock. (2) Mothers age eighteen who gave birth to illegitimate children had to live at home to receive aid—unless the mother married the biological father or marries an individual who legally adopts the children. (3) Mothers already receiving AFDC were not to receive an increase in benefits if additional children were born out of wedlock. Those constructive proposals were never implemented. Although the "work" requirement significantly reduced the welfare rolls, President Obama, in defiance of the law, eliminated it with a stroke of his pen.

Our need to abolish taxpayer incentives that promote illegitimacy was spelled out by social scientist Charles Murray in his October 1993 article in the *Wall Street Journal*. His recommendations are more timely now than ever:

> Illegitimacy is the single most important social problem of our time—more important than crime, drugs, poverty, illiteracy, welfare or homelessness because it drives everything else. Doing something about it should be at the top of the American policy agenda. Here is what to do. . . .
>
> Bringing a child into the world is the most important thing that most human beings ever do. Bringing a child into the world when one is not emotionally or financially prepared to be a parent is wrong. The child deserves society's support. . . .
>
> Restoring economic penalties translates into the first central policy prescription: to end all economic support for single mothers. The Aid to Families With Dependent Children payment goes to zero. Single mothers are not eligible for subsidized housing or food stamps. An assortment of other subsidies and in-kind benefits disappear. . . .
>
> How does a poor young mother survive without government support? The same way she has since time immemorial. If she wants to keep a child, she must enlist support from her parents, boyfriend, siblings, neighbors, church or philanthropies. She must get support from somewhere, anywhere, other than the government. . . .
>
> Make adoption easy for any married couple who have the resources and stability to raise a child. . . .

Some small proportion of infants and larger proportion of older children will not be adopted. For them, the government should spend lavishly on orphanages. . . .

Make the tax code favor marriage and children. . . .

Little boys should grow up knowing that if they want to have any rights whatsoever regarding a child that they sire—more vividly, if they want to grow up to be a daddy—they must marry. Little girls should grow up knowing that if they want to have any legal claims whatsoever on the father of their children, they must marry.[7]

While it's true that we should make adoption easy for stable married couples, we should not look down our noses at orphanages. I personally know two men who grew up in an orphanage and were so successful as adults that they became billionaires.

RESTORING PARENTAL RIGHTS

The single biggest reform needed for the family court is to abolish the divisive "best interest(s) of the child" standard. That slogan drives a wedge between children and their parents. The law should only require parents to provide adequate care.

There can be no parental rights or family autonomy as long as some judge or other government official has the final say on a child's best interest. We have laws against child abuse and neglect, but unless there is evidence of some such crime, parental care is not the business of anyone outside the family. Family court disputes are burdened by the impossibility of determining what is best. It would be far simpler and more equitable if evidence and arguments about "best interest" were not allowed in court, and if only evidence about meeting the standard of adequate care were considered admissible.

When parents decide to let their kids play baseball, attend church, or be homeschooled, they should not be required to prove that these choices are best. Freedom must include the right to make choices that others may not consider best. No court should be allowed to consider whether any parenting is best, just as they cannot consider whether a religious choice is best.

The federal income tax system contains powerful incentives and disincentives. From 1948 until the 1970s, the incentives favored marriage and children raised by married couples. The incentives and disincentives are now profitable in the wrong direction—*against* marriage. The tax code now favors the unwed mother as "head of household" and her illegitimate children rather than parents who are raising their own children. The income tax system doesn't even require the single mom to report the income of her live-in boyfriend.

Every line in the income tax code reflects some public policy. There is no such thing as "neutral" tax policy. US public policy should support married couples and their obligation to raise their own children.

REFORMING CHILD SUPPORT

President Obama's Father's Day speech in 2013 included one provocative yet very declarative sentence: "We should reform our child support laws to get more men working and engaged with their children." Obama didn't elaborate, but, yes indeed, child support laws urgently need reform.

Many fathers work long hours and make incredible sacrifices for their families. Current child support formulas are based on the ridiculous notion that a father would make those same sacrifices for an ex-wife who is living with a new husband or boyfriend and for children he never or seldom sees. The formulas are also based on the unrealistic proposition that the father after divorce can support two households at the same comfortable level at which he formerly supported one.

Many fathers would happily do more to support their children if they were allowed to see them more often and were more engaged in their lives. But current child support laws include powerful disincentives: the more the mother prevents such contact, the more child support she receives.

Child support is not even really child support because the mother has no obligation to spend the money on the kids, and faithful payment of child support does not buy the father time with them. The unrealistic current purpose of child support is to allow the mother to maintain a separate household and standard of living comparable to the household the father supported when the family lived together.

Because of perverse incentives, unilateral divorce is often followed by a bitter child custody dispute with bogus allegations of domestic violence or child abuse, and the winner can get a huge child support windfall. Usually, a family court judge cannot know who is telling the truth. Reform should eliminate these bad incentives. No parent should collect money for denying kids the opportunity to see the other parent, and payments should not exceed reasonable documented child expenses. If both parents are willing and able to manage joint child custody, there may be little need for child-support payments.

Here are some other suggestions for reforming child support incentives and disincentives: Calculate child support based on taxable income instead of what a judge imagines a man earns or did earn or could earn; require that child support be spent on the kids; repeal the Bradley Amendment so child support obligations can be reduced when a man is sent overseas in the military, loses his job, has his pay reduced, is hospitalized, or is even sent to prison. We must abolish debtors' prisons, an un-American hangover from British law that we thought we'd abolished in the nineteenth century.

FEMINISTS ARE STILL WHINING

The feminists promote victimhood by a constant whine about a so-called gender gap in wages, repeating the false figure that women are paid only seventy-seven cents for the same work for which a man is paid a dollar. That's not only false; it's illegal, and a powerful federal agency, the Equal Employment Opportunity Commission, deals with law violators. The law doesn't require equal pay; it requires equal pay *for equal work*, and the feminists ignore the male-female work differentials in hours and other factors. US Labor Department statistics are based on full-time work as thirty-five hours a week; most men work more hours than that, and most women do not.

But, funny thing, as you'll recall from chapter 2, recent polling shows that many women don't object to the gender gap in wages because they are committed to hypergamy; that is, they want to marry men who earn more than they do. If a woman can't find a husband who meets that test, she often becomes another statistic of the unmarried.

Hanna Rosin's new book, *The End of Men: And the Rise of Women*, is her attempt to advise women about how they can succeed without marriage. "To put it crudely," which she surely does, "feminist progress is now largely dependent on [the] hook-up culture." Rosin's argument is that hookups, especially among college students, enable women to have all the fun of sex without allowing these one-night stands to develop into full-blown relationships that would "steal time away" from efforts to do well in college and advance a career in the workforce.[8] The woman's goal is financial independence from men, and Rosin thinks that having frequent sex with strangers enables women to gain that security, a non sequitur if there ever was one.

Rosin tries to make young women believe that the hookup lifestyle can lead to a successful marriage at some later date. But it's not the nuclear family that Rosin sees in her crystal ball. It's a new form of marriage she calls the "seesaw marriage" with "fluid" roles for the husband to do 50 percent of the dishes and the laundry.[9] It may be difficult to find the husband Rosin defines.

Feminists should terminate their war against Mother Nature because they are losing and will continue to lose. They had to admit in the *Atlantic*, as reported by Christina Hoff Sommers:

A recent Huffington Post/YouGov poll is typical: Only 23 percent of women and 16 percent of men identified as "feminist." . . . In a 2013 national poll on modern parenthood, the Pew Research Center asked mothers and fathers to identify their "ideal" working arrangement. Sixty-one percent of mothers said they would prefer to work part-time—or not at all. Fathers answered differently; 75 percent preferred full-time work.[10]

Girls take sex education classes in K–12 schools, and they learn how to have sexually active lives, but they do not learn some facts that become very important later. A new study reports: "Nearly half of women who became pregnant through in vitro fertilization (IVF) after age 40 say they were 'shocked' to discover they needed fertility treatments."[11]

In this study, researchers at the University of California San Francisco interviewed women from sixty-one families—including heterosexual couples, lesbian couples, and single women—who conceived and delivered children via IVF after age forty. The interviews were done between 2009 and 2011. "We found that women did not have a clear understanding of the age at which fertility begins to decline," the researchers wrote in their study, published online in the journal *Human Reproduction*. "Most women thought their fertility would last longer than it did," Rowan reported; "31 percent said they expected to get pregnant without difficulty at age forty."

"Very few participants had considered the possibility that they would need IVF," the researchers wrote, "and 44 percent reported being 'shocked' and 'alarmed' to discover that their understandings of the rapidity of age-related reproductive decline were inaccurate." When the researchers queried the participants about how they could be so mistaken, 28 percent said that incorrect information from friends, doctors, or the media had convinced them that older women could become pregnant easily. One forty-two-year-old woman remembers thinking, *everyone's having babies at forty-two . . . all the superstars are having them.*

"About a quarter of participants said their beliefs stemmed from messages about preventing pregnancy they had received since adolescence," Rowan continued. "One woman wrote, 'It's like, all of our lives we're terrified we're going to get pregnant too soon and have a child and ruin our lives . . . and, actually, it's not that easy.'"[12]

Although some of these participants were likely not feminists, the outcome was the same for those who never could get pregnant: childlessness. That's what the feminist movement has done to America. And all the impressive statistics you've ever read about women holding well-paying jobs and receiving college degrees will not produce happy women if they are remorseful about having rejected motherhood until after their biological clocks stopped ticking.

And one more glaring point: the lack of grandchildren isn't mentioned in feminist exposés of women's current unhappiness. In rejecting marriage and motherhood, most feminists also rejected the possibility of having grandchildren who could have provided a significant measure of older women's happiness.

Some Libertarians and others suggest getting the government completely out of marriage. But that not only won't work; it won't accomplish the goal of enhancing liberty and foreclosing busybody bureaucrats from running private lives.

Getting government out of who can get a marriage license doesn't get the government out of messy divorces and the problem of child custody. It's amazing how those who want to get the government off our backs are blind to the invasive supervision and control of private lives, children, homes, and property by the family courts.

Joanne Lipman, who has held several of the biggest jobs in publishing but still whines that "progress for women has stalled," nevertheless makes a couple of sensible comments. She writes that feminists define "progress for women too narrowly; we've focused primarily on numbers at the expense of attitudes." She's right about that. Attitude is the principal problem with feminists; as long as they believe they are victims of an oppressive patriarchy, they will never be happy or successful.

Lipman also urges feminists to "have a sense of humor." That's a very constructive proposal. Speakers who venture a joke during college lectures can easily identify the feminists by observing the students who are not laughing.[13]

MAKING PARENTHOOD RESPONSIBLE

Readers may get the impression that conservatives are just resistant to change and nostalgic for the good old days of the 1950s. On the contrary, we are advocating individual freedom, family autonomy, self-government, and other American values. Under these principles, citizens should be able to voluntarily assume the rights and responsibilities of marriage and parenthood, be able to rear their kids with minimal government interference, and have marriage law generally reflect popular views.

Our leaders are violating these principles. After the June 2013 US Supreme Court decision on two marriage cases, the liberals declared victory and celebrated, but they did not find the constitutional right to same-sex marriage that they wanted. The decision also did not affirm the marriage laws that were fairly passed by the US Congress and by California voters. So what did it do?

The Supreme Court opened the door for lower federal courts to finish the job. For example, a federal judge in 2013 ruled that the US Constitution now requires Ohio to recognize same-sex marriages from other states on Ohio death certificates, and the judge suggested that Ohio may later be required to fully accept out-of-state marriages even though Ohio law prohibits them.[14] The judge relied largely on the reasoning of *United States v. Windsor*,[15] the Supreme Court decision that struck down the federal Defense of Marriage Act (DOMA).

But as this book documents, the same-sex marriage debate is only a small part of the destruction of the American family. The bigger forces have been divorce law, illegitimacy, feminism, child support, judges overruling parents and deciding the best interest of children, cultural factors, and powerful financial incentives and disincentives.

We need laws and policies that restore marriage to being a voluntary union to assume the legal rights and responsibilities of the resultant kids. We already have made motherhood voluntary for women. They get free contraception under Obamacare, unrestricted abortion rights under *Roe v. Wade*, and even the right to give away the baby after birth. Single moms receive numerous welfare and child support benefits.

We should abolish all incentives for busting up families. One parent should not be allowed to make a court demand for both sole custody and child support. Kids need both parents. We should not be paying one parent to lock another parent out of his relationship with his own children.

Fathers should stop being intimidated by feminists and assert their rights as fathers. They should take a cue from Doris Lessing, the novelist, Nobel Prize laureate, and onetime feminist icon, who became a harsh critic of feminism in her later years (she died in 2013 at age ninety-four). In 2001 at the Edinburgh Book Festival, she attacked the "rubbishing of men which is now so part of our culture that it is hardly even noticed. . . . Men seem to be so cowed that they can't fight back, and it is time they did."[16]

Marriage has been the traditional mechanism by which men voluntarily become legal fathers. That is how our civilization has worked for centuries. Maybe some clever social engineers can figure out a better system for inducing parents to rear the next generation, but I doubt it. The American family system is the best, but it is broken and we need to restore it to prominence.

MARRIAGE IS THE ESSENTIAL UNIT

Marriage must be recognized as the essential unit of a stable society wherein husbands and wives provide a home and role models for the rearing of children. The American people and our elected representatives absolutely have a rational basis for concluding that marriage between a man and a woman should be protected and encouraged. Dr. Jennifer Roback Morse, president of the Ruth Institute, told the Illinois State Legislature on February 26, 2013:

> The essential public purpose of marriage is to attach mothers and fathers to their children and to one another. And the child is entitled to a relationship with and care from both of the people who brought him into being. Therefore, the child has a legitimate interest in the stability of his parents' union. But no child can defend these entitlements himself. Nor is it adequate to make restitution after these rights have been violated. The child's rights must be supported pro-actively, before harm is done. Marriage is adult society's institutional structure for protecting these legitimate interests of children.[17]

Various tax and welfare incentives for single moms should be reversed, so that incentives favor kids living with their own parents. Reform should get family courts out of the practice of pitting parents against each other, entertaining criminal accusations without evidence, assessing onerous support payments, sending dads to debtors' prison, and appointing so-called experts to make parenting decisions. Instead, the courts should protect the rights of parents.

There can never be family autonomy as long as judges, lawyers, and psychologists can second-guess ordinary parental decisions. All legal parents should have a right to joint custody of their kids unless evidence shows a parent to be unfit. Criminal accusations should be tried in a criminal court with due process. If both parents are willing and able to accept joint custody of the child, they should be free to negotiate an agreement for custody and child support and should not be overruled by judges, psychologists, or counselors.

We must restore the authority of both parents over their own children and remove that authority from officious judges, busybody bureaucrats, and pseudoexperts who pretend superior wisdom and exercise extraordinary power to dictate control over behavior, lifestyle, the family home, property, and money under the slogan "best interest of the child." That process always exacerbates the conflict between spouses. Parental authority should belong to parents, not to imposters.

REJECTING "THAT EMINENT TRIBUNAL"

The progressives and the anti-marriage factions are counting on supremacist judges to rule the family and non-family of future America. Having declared DOMA unconstitutional, the judges have already thrown out any chance that we can keep traditional marriage in some states but not others. The *Windsor* decision dashed the hopes of those who thought we could have a state's right solution for the definition of marriage.

We must count on grassroots Americans to reject the power that the courts—all the way from the Supreme Court to the family courts—have grabbed to define marriage and its relationship to children and to society.

It's time to learn a constitutional lesson from Abraham Lincoln when he rejected the rule of the Supreme Court's historic *Dred Scott* decision of 1857. Lincoln admitted that the court's ruling was personally binding on the man Dred Scott, but Lincoln expressed the hope that the "evil effect" of the court's bad decision would be "limited to that particular case, with the chance that it may be over-ruled and never become a precedent for other cases."

Thus, Lincoln accepted judicial review as binding in a specific case, but he rejected judicial supremacy—the notion that the Supreme Court could legislate new laws for the nation—because that would abolish self-government and submit us to the rule of judges. Lincoln said if we accept that concept, "the people will have ceased to be their own rulers, having to that extent practically resigned their government into the hands of that eminent tribunal."

Like Abe Lincoln, we should reject the power of "that eminent tribunal" to legislate or make public policy. The definition of marriage should be a legislative, not a judicial, issue. Laws and policies should be made by our elected representatives, not by supremacist judges.

NOTES

INTRODUCTION

1. Hillary Clinton, *It Takes a Village*, 10th anniv. ed. (New York: Simon & Schuster, 2006), xii.

CHAPTER 1: THE AMERICAN FAMILY WE ONCE KNEW

1. Alexis de Tocqueville, *Democracy in America*, trans. Henry Reeve, 3rd American ed. (New York: Adlard, 1839), 303.
2. See Andrew Cherlin, "American Marriage in the Early Twenty-First Century," *Marriage and Child Wellbeing* 15, no. 2 (Fall 2005), available at http://futureofchildren.org/publications/journals/article/index.xml?journalid=37&articleid=105&sectionid=674; and Jason DeParle and Sabrina Tavernise, "For Women Under 30, Most Births Occur Outside Marriage," *New York Times*, February 17, 2012, http://www.nytimes.com/2012/02/18/us/for-women-under-30-most-births-occur-outside-marriage.html?pagewanted=all&_r=0.
3. George Lakoff, "Metaphor, Morality, and Politics; or, Why Conservatives Have Left Liberals in the Dust," *Social Research* 62, no. 2 (Summer 1995).
4. George Lakoff, "The Santorum Strategy," *Huff Post Politics* (blog), March 12, 2012, http://www.huffingtonpost.com/george-lakoff/santorum-strategy_b_1338708.html.
5. Ibid.
6. Simone de Beauvoir, *The Second Sex* (New York: Alfred A. Knopf, 1952).
7. Christopher Ryan and Cacilda Jethá, Sex at Dawn: How We Mate, Why We Stray, and What It Means for Modern Relationships (New York: HarperCollins, 2010), 9.
8. Joseph Henrich, Robert Boyd, and Peter J. Richerson, "The puzzle of monogamous marriage," Philosophical Transactions of the Royal Society Biological Sciences 367 (2012): 657, http://www2.psych.ubc.ca/~henrich/pdfs/monogamousmarriage_2012.pdf?keytype=ref&ijkey=Veh7WiI1F7Thq0E.
9. David J. Ley, "Why Men Gave Up Polygamy," *Women Who Stray* (blog), February 8, 2012, http://www.psychologytoday.com/blog/women-who-stray/201202/why-men-gave-up-polygamy.
10. Natalie Angier, "Thirst for Fairness May Have Helped Us Survive," *New York Times*, Science, July 4, 2011, http://www.nytimes.com/2011/07/05/science/05angier.html.

11. Emmanuel Todd, *Explanation of Ideology: Family Structures and Social Systems*, trans. David Garrioch (New York: Blackwell, 1985).

12. Razib Khan, "Is Inbreeding Like Asexuality?" *Discover* (blog), July 23, 2012, http://blogs. discovermagazine.com/gnxp/2012/07/is-inbreeding-like-asexuality/.

13. Alex Tabarrok, "Cousin Marriage and Democracy," *Marginal Revolution* (blog), April 26, 2013, http://marginalrevolution.com/marginalrevolution/2013/04/cousin-marriage-and-democracy.html.

14. Margaret Mead, quoted in Steven Goldberg, "Feminism Against Science," *National Review* 43, no. 21 (November 18, 1991): 30, http://connection.ebscohost.com/c/articles/9111112620/feminism-against-science.

15. Betsey Stevenson and Justin Wolfers, "Marriage and the Market," *Cato Unbound: A Journal of Debate*, January 18, 2008, http://www.cato-unbound.org/2008/01/18/betsey-stevenson-and-justin-wolfers/marriage-and-the-market.

16. Betty Friedan, *The Feminine Mystique,* repr. ed. (New York: W. W. Norton, 2010), chap. 12, esp. 426.

17. Wikipedia, s.v. "familialism," accessed April 8, 2014, http://en.wikipedia.org/wiki/Familialism.

18. Jason DeParle, "Two Classes, Divided by 'I Do,'" *New York Times*, July 14, 2012, http://www.nytimes.com/2012/07/15/us/two-classes-in-america-divided-by-i-do.html.

19. Katie Roiphe, "*New York Times,* Stop Moralizing about Single Mothers: No, Their Households Are Not Always Sad and Falling Apart," *Slate,* July 16, 2012, http://www.slate.com/articles/double_x/roiphe/2012/07/single_mothers_always_falling_apart_.html.

20. John Zogby, "Demographics and the Election of 2012: The 'Marriage Gap,'" *Forbes*, July 12, 2012, http://www.forbes.com/sites/johnzogby/2012/07/12/zogby-demographics-and-the-election-of-2012-the-marriage-gap.

21. Ann Coulter, "Democrats' Ideal Voter: Illegal Alien, Convicted Felon," *Human Events* (blog), July 18, 2012, http://www.humanevents.com/2012/07/18/ann-coulter-democrats-ideal-voter-illegal-alien-single-mother-convicted-felon/.

22. Scott Rose, "Bombshell Letter: 200+ PhDs and MDs Question Scholarly Merit of Regnerus Study," *The New Civil Rights Movement*, June 29, 2012, http://thenewcivilrightsmovement. com/bombshell-letter-scores-of-ph-d-s-ask-for-retraction-of-regnerus-study/legal-issues/2012/06/29/42413.

23. Elizabeth Weil, "Unmarried Spouses Have a Way with Words," *New York Times*, Fashion & Style, January 4, 2013, http://www.nytimes.com/2013/01/06/fashion/unmarried-spouses-have-a-way-with-words.html.

24. Alessandra Stanley, "On Indian TV, 'I Do' Means to Honor and Obey the Mother-in-Law," *New York Times*, Television, December 25, 2012, http://www.nytimes.com/2012/12/26/arts/television/indian-soap-operas-ruled-by-mothers-in-law.html.

25. Gardiner Harris, "India's New Focus on Rape Shows Only the Surface of Women's Perils," *New York Times*, Asia Pacific, January 12, 2013, http://www.nytimes.com/2013/01/13/world/asia/in-rapes-aftermath-india-debates-violence-against-women.html.

26. Wikipedia, s.v. "2012 Delhi gang rape," accessed April 8, 2014, http://en.wikipedia.org/wiki/2012_Delhi_gang_rape_case.

27. "Rape in the World's Largest Democracy," *New York Times*, Opinion, December 28, 2012, http://www.nytimes.com/2012/12/29/opinion/rape-in-india.html.

28. Paul Bentley, "Muslim Abuser Who 'Didn't Know' That Sex With a Girl of 13 Was Illegal Is Spared Jail," *Mail Online*, News, January 25, 2013, http://www.dailymail.co.uk/news/article-2268395/Adil-Rashid-Paedophile-claimed-Muslim-upbringing-meant-didnt-know-illegal-sex-girl-13.html.

29. "China Orders Children to Visit Their Elderly Parents," BBC News, December 28, 2012, http://www.bbc.co.uk/news/world-asia-china-20860264.

30. Kathy Shinn, "Confucianism: A Brief History of Confucius and His Teachings," California State University, http://www.csuchico.edu/~cheinz/syllabi/asst001/fall97/11kshinn.htm, accessed March 17, 2014.

31. Charles Murray, "Why Aren't Asians Republicans?" *AEIdeas* (blog), November 26, 2012, http://www.aei-ideas.org/2012/11/why-arent-asians-republicans/; http://blog.eagleforum.org/2012/11/why-asians-voted-for-obama.html.

32. Diane Swanbrow, "Raising a Child Doesn't Take a Village, Research Shows," Phys.org, September 9, 2011, http://phys.org/news/2011-09-child-doesnt-village.html.
33. Alexis de Tocqueville, *Democracy in America*, vol. 2, trans. Henry Reeve (n.p.: Washington Square Press, 1899), 701.

CHAPTER 2: FEMINISTS DISAVOW THE FAMILY

1. Sabina Bhasin, "Second Southwest Florida Eagle Hatches as World Watches on Webcam," Naples News online, January 4, 2013, http://www.naplesnews.com/news/2013/jan/04/second-southwest-florida-eagle-hatches-world-watch/, 4.
2. "A Dialogue with Simone Beauvoir," in Betty Friedan, *It Changed My Life: Writings on the Women's Movement*, first Harvard University paperback ed. (Harvard University Press, 1998), 397.
3. Betty Friedan, *The Feminine Mystique,* repr. ed. (New York: W. W. Norton, 2010), 379; chap. 1, esp. 63.
4. Arthur S. Flemming, et al., *Sex Bias in the U.S. Code: A Report of the United States Commission on Civil Rights* (Washington, D.C.: U.S. Commission on Civil Rights, 1977), http://www.eagleforum.org/era/SexBiasBook/SexBiasBook.pdf, 206.
5. "Women in national parliaments: Situation as of 1st January 2014," http://www.ipu.org/wmn-e/classif.htm.
6. *Ellison v. Brady*, 924 F.2d 872, 879 (9th Cir. 1991).
7. Karl Marx and Friedrich Engels, *The Communist Manifesto* (London: Penguin, 2004), 27–28.
8. Wendy Goldman, "Family Code on Marriage, the Family, and Guardianship," in *Encyclopedia of Russian History* (2004), accessed March 18, 2014, http://www.encyclopedia.com/doc/1G2-3404100420.html.
9. Susan Faludi, "Death of a Revolutionary," *The New Yorker,* April 15, 2013, http://www.newyorker.com/reporting/2013/04/15/130415fa_fact_faludi?currentPage=all.
10. Bill Costello, "Education gender gap, boys are underachieving and girls are excelling," *News 4 Kids* (blog), November 8, 2010, http://www.juniorsbook.com/activity_workshop.asp?aid=467.
11. See Dave Gahary, "AFP Podcast & Article: Law Professor Promotes End of Black Race in America," *American Free Press,* March 18, 2012, http://americanfreepress.net/?p=3235; and Linsey Davis and Kinga Janik, "'Is Marriage For White People?': Stanford Law Professor's Views on Black Women, Marriage Deficit," abc News, October 19, 2011, http://abcnews.go.com/Health/stanford-law-professor-suggests-black-women-find-husbands/story?id=14620932.
12. Katie Roiphe, "More Single Moms. So What. The *New York Times* Condescends to Single Moms," *Slate,* February 22, 2012, http://www.slate.com/articles/life/roiphe/2012/02/the_new_york_times_condescends_to_single_moms_.html.
13. Rene Lynch, "Father-Daughter Dances Banned in R.I. as 'Gender Discrimination,'" *Los Angeles Times*, September 18, 2012, http://articles.latimes.com/2012/sep/18/nation/la-na-nn-father-daughter-dances-gender-discrimination-20120918.
14. "ACLU Issues Statement in Response to Father-Daughter Dance Controversy," American Civil Liberties Union of Rhode Island, September 18, 2012, http://www.riaclu.org/news/post/aclu-issues-statement-in-response-to-father-daughter-dance-controversy.
15. "Gender Revolution needs to destroy marriage," *Eagle Forum Legislative Alert,* June 8, 2012, http://blog.eagleforum.org/2012/06/gender-revolution-needs-to-destroy.html.
16. Sheryl Sandberg, *Lean In: Women, Work, and the Will to Lead* (New York: Alfred A. Knopf, 2013), 5.
17. W. Bradford Wilcox, "Moms Who Cut Back at Work Are Happier," *The Atlantic*, December 18, 2013, http://www.theatlantic.com/business/archive/2013/12/moms-who-cut-back-at-work-are-happier/282460/.
18. Margaret Sullivan, "Gender Questions Arise in Obituary of Rocket Scientist and Her Beef Stroganoff," *Public Editor's Journal* (blog), April 1, 2013, http://publiceditor.blogs.nytimes.com/2013/04/01/gender-questions-arise-in-obituary-of-rocket-scientist-and-her-beef-stroganoff/.

19. Douglas Martin, "*Yvonne* Brill, a Pioneering Rocket Scientist, Dies at 88," Science, *New York Times*, Space & Cosmos, March 31, 2013, http://www.nytimes.com/2013/03/31/science/space/yvonne-brill-rocket-scientist-dies-at-88.html.

20. Bennett Marcus, "Gloria Steinem: Sarah Palin and Michele Bachmann 'Are There to Oppose the Women's Movement,'" *Daily Intelligencer* (blog), August 11, 2011, http://nymag.com/daily/intelligencer/2011/08/gloria_steinem_sarah_palin_and.html.

21. F. Carolyn Graglia, *Domestic Tranquility: A Brief Against Feminism* (Dallas: Spence, 1998).

22. Maria Shriver and the Center for American Progress, eds. Heather Boushey and Ann O'Leary, *The Shriver Report: A Woman's Nation Changes Everything*, Center for American Progress, October 16, 2009, http://www.americanprogress.org/issues/women/report/2009/10/16/6789/the-shriver-report/.

23. Nancy Gibbs, "What Women Want Now," *Time*, October 14, 2009, "http://users.nber.org/~jwolfers/Press/WomensHappiness/WomensHappiness(Time).pdf.

24. Lisa Miller, "The Retro Wife: Feminists who say they're having it all—by choosing to stay home," *New York*, News & Politics, March 17, 2013, http://nymag.com/news/features/retro-wife-2013-3/, 1–3.

25. Taylor Marsh, "New York Magazine's Stepford Feminism Reworks the Feminine Mystique for the 21st Century," TaylorMarsh.com, March 20, 2013, http://www.taylormarsh.com/2013/03/new-york-magazines-stepford-feminism-reworks-the-feminine-mystique-for-the-21st-century/.

26. Samantha Ettus, "Why the 'Retro Wife' Threatens America's Economy," *Forbes*, March 20, 2013, http://www.forbes.com/sites/samanthaettus/2013/03/20/the-retro-wife-threatens-americas-economy/.

27. Jonathan Chait, "A Really Easy Answer to the Feminist Housework Problem," *New York* magazine, March 21, 2013, http://nymag.com/daily/intelligencer/2013/03/really-easy-answer-to-the-housework-problem.html.

28. David Brooks, "The Confidence Responses," *New York Times* Opinion Pages, May 2, 2013, http://www.nytimes.com/2013/05/03/opinion/brooks-the-confidence-responses.html.

29. Barbara Kay, "A Father's Day downer," *New York Daily News*, June 17, 2012, http://www.nydailynews.com/opinion/father-day-downer-article-1.1096613.

30. Neeru Tando, *Feminism: A Paradigm Shift* (New Delhi: Atlantic, 2008), 76.

31. Conservapedia, s.v. "Ruth Bader Ginsburg," accessed April 9, 2014, http://www.conservapedia.com/Ruth_Bader_Ginsburg.

32. "Do First Ladies' Opinions Matter," *Chicago Tribune News*, August 16, 1992, http://articles.chicagotribune.com/1992-08-16/news/9203130889_1_hillary-clinton-indian-reservation-system-examples-of-such-arrangements.

33. Wendy P. Warcholik, "'Freedom Feminism' and the Pursuit of Happiness," Oklahoma Council of Public Affairs, *Center for Family Prosperity* (blog), August 1, 2013, http://www.ocpathink.org/articles/2418.

34. 11 J. Legal Econ. 74 n. 17 (winter 2001).

35. General Services Administration, National Archives and Records Service, Office of the Federal Register, *Public Papers of the Presidents of the United States, Richard Nixon, 1971* (United States Government Printing Office), 1178.

36. Nancy Gibbs, "The State of the American Woman," Time, October 14, 2009, http://content.time.com/time/specials/packages/article/0,28804,1930277_1930145_1930309-2,00.html

37. Bernard Goldberg, *Bias: A CBS Insider Exposes How the Media Distorts the News* (Washington, DC: Regnery, 2001).

38. Jenet Jacob Erickson, PhD, *The Effects of Day Care on the Social-Emotional Development of Children* (Heritage Foundation, April 2011), http://www.scribd.com/doc/54439344/The-Effects-of-Day-Care-on-the-Social-Emotional-Development-of-Children.

39. Grover J. "Russ" Whitehurst, "New Evidence Raises Doubts on Obama's Preschool for All," *The Brown Center Chalkboard* (blog), November 20, 2013, http://www.brookings.edu/blogs/brown-center-chalkboard/posts/2013/11/20-evidence-raises-doubts-about-obamas-preschool-for-all-whitehurst.

40. Elizabeth Warren and Amelia Warren Tiagi, *The Two Income Trap: Why Middle-Class Mothers and Fathers Are Going Broke* (New York: Basic Books, 2003).

41. *Doe v. Bolton*, 410 U.S. 179, 221–22 (1973) (White, J., dissenting).
42. Kate Pickert, "Has the Fight for Abortion Rights Been Lost? Getting an Abortion Is More Difficult Today Than at Any Point Since the 1970s. Is the Pro-choice Movement Losing the Battle?" *Time*, Health & Science, January 2013, http://ideas.time.com/2013/01/03/has-the-fight-for-abortion-rights-been-lost/.
43. Gloria Steinem, "Revving Up for the Next Twenty-Five Years," in *Readings for Diversity and Social Justice: An Anthology on Racism, Sexism, Classism, Anti-Semitism, Heterosexism, and Ableism / Edition 1* (New York: Taylor & Francis, 2000), 256.
44. *Casey v. Planned Parenthood*, 505 U.S. 833, 856 (1992).
45. Prachi Gupta, "Sandra Day O'Connor's Very Dry Interview with Terry Gross," Salon.com, March 6, 2013, http://www.salon.com/2013/03/06/sandra_day_oconnors_very_dry_interview_with_terry_gross/.
46. Post Staff, "Man who allegedly tricked pregnant girlfriend into taking abortion drug charged with first-degree murder for death of fetus," *New York Post*, May 16, 2013, http://nypost.com/2013/05/16/man-who-allegedly-tricked-pregnant-girlfriend-into-taking-abortion-drug-charged-with-first-degree-murder-for-death-of-fetus/.
47. George A. Akerlof, Janet L. Yellen, and Michael L. Katz, "An Analysis of Out-of-Wedlock Childbearing in the United States," *Quarterly Journal of Economics* 111, no. 2 (1996): 314, available at http://www.washingtonpost.com/blogs/wonkblog/files/2013/10/outofwedlock.pdf.
48. Ibid., 279, 281.
49. Ani, "Women still want men who earn more," July 18, 2011, *Mid-day* (news blog), http://www.mid-day.com/articles/women-still-want-men-who-earn-more/128651.
50. Tiziana Barghini, "Educated Women Quit Work as Spouses Earn More," Reuters, March 8, 2012, http://www.reuters.com/article/2012/03/08/us-economy-women-idUSBRE8270AC20120308.
51. Ibid.
52. Lisa Belkin, "The Opt-Out Revolution," *New York Times Magazine*, October 26, 2003, 3, http://www.nytimes.com/2003/10/26/magazine/26WOMEN.html?src=pm&pagewanted=1.
53. Ibid., 1.
54. Anne-Marie Slaughter, "Why Women Still Can't Have It All: It's Time to Stop Fooling Ourselves . . . Here's What Has to Change," *The Atlantic*, June 13, 2012, http://www.theatlantic.com/magazine/archive/2012/07/why-women-still-cant-have-it-all/309020/.
55. "5 Health Hazards in Your Handbag," *RealBuzz*, December 13, 2012, http://uk.lifestyle.yahoo.com/5-health-hazards-handbag-051015229.html.
56. Myrna Blyth, Spin Sisters: How the Women of the Media Sell Unhappiness—and Liberalism—to the Women of America (New York: St. Martin's, 2005).

CHAPTER 3: OUTLAWING THE FAMILY

1. Defense of Marriage Act. H.R. 3396, 104th Congr. (1995–96).
2. Government Accountability Office, GAO/OGC-97-16 Defense of Marriage Act, January 31, 1997, Enclosure 1, http://www.gao.gov/assets/230/223674.pdf, 1, 3.
3. 2012 Republican Party Platform, on the American Presidency website, August 27, 2012, http://www.presidency.ucsb.edu/ws/?pid=101961.
4. U.S. Const. art. 2, § 3.
5. *United States v. Windsor, 133 S. Ct. 2675, 2718 (2013).*
6. Tamar Lewin, "Ideas & Trends: Untying the Knot; For Better or Worse: Marriage's Stormy Future," *New York Times*, November 23, 2003, http://www.nytimes.com/2003/11/23/weekinreview/ideas-trends-untying-the-knot-for-better-or-worse-marriage-s-stormy-future.html.
7. Michael Reagan, *Twice Adopted* (Nashville: Broadman & Holman, 2004), 44.
8. Ibid., 37.

9. F. Carolyn Graglia, "A Nonfeminist's Perspectives of Mothers and Homemakers Under Chapter 2 of the ALI *Principles of the Law of Family Dissolution*" (symposium on the ALI Principles of the Law of Family Dissolution, Brigham Young University's J. Reuben Clark Law School, Provo, UT, February 1, 2001), http://www.law2.byu.edu/lawreview/archives/2001/3/grac5.pdf, 998.

10. F. Carolyn Graglia, *Domestic Tranquility: A Brief Against Feminism* (Dallas: Spence, 1998), 136.

11. Leslie Bennetts, The Feminine Mistake: Are We Giving Up Too Much? (Hachette Digital, 2007).

12. Margaret F. Brinig and Douglas W. Allen, "'These Boots Are Made for Walking': Why Most Divorce Filers Are Women," *American Law and Economics Review* 2, no. 1 (2000): 126–69, http://www.unc.edu/courses/2010fall/econ/586/001/Readings/Brinig.pdf.

13. CH, "Comment of the Week," *Chateau Heartiste* (blog), December 14, 2012, http://heartiste.wordpress.com/2012/12/14/comment-of-the-week-13/.

14. *Principles of the Law of Family Dissolution*: Analysis and Recommendations (Tentative Draft No. 4, 2000). See http://scholarship.law.duke.edu/cgi/viewcontent.cgi?article=1040&context=djglp.

15. *Goodridge v. Dept. of Public Health*, 440 Mass. 309 (Mass. 2003); *Lawrence v. Texas*, 539 U.S. 558 (2003) (see http://supreme.justia.com/cases/federal/us/539/558/case.html); *Planned Parenthood v. Casey*, 505 U.S. 833 (1992).

16. Graglia, "A Nonfeminist's Perspectives of Mothers," note 72.

17. *Levy v. Louisiana*, 391 U.S. 68 (1968).

18. *Gomez v. Perez*, 409 U.S. 535 (1973).

19. *Goodridge v. Dept. of Public Health*, 798 N.E.2d 941 (Mass. 2003)

20. *Bowers v. Hardwick*, 478 U.S. 186 (1986).

21. *Lawrence v. Texas*, 539 U.S. 558 (2003)

22. See Natasha Mitchell's article "Why get married when you could be happy?" and the embedded audio file on the website of Radio National's podcast *Life Matters*, June 11, 2012, at http://www.abc.net.au/radionational/programs/lifematters/why-get-married/4058506.

23. David Boies on *Meet the Press*, NBC, March 26, 2013, http://www.nbcnews.com/video/meet-the-press/51309057#51309057.

24. Clifford Krauss, "Free to Marry, Canada's Gays Say, 'Do I?'," *New York Times*, August 31, 2003, http://www.nytimes.com/2003/08/31/international/americas/31CANA.html.

25. See David P. McWhirter and Andrew M. Mattison, *The Male Couple: How Relationships Develop* (n.p.: Prentice-Hall, 1985).

26. Phyllis Schlafly, "Equal rights for women: wrong then, wrong now," *Los Angeles Times*, April 8, 2007, http://www.latimes.com/la-op-schafly8apr08,0,3115449.story#axzz2yVAUJqMm.

27. *Idaho v. Freeman*, 529 F. Supp. 1107, 1155 (D. Idaho 1981), 2.

28. *NOW, Inc. v. Idaho*, 459 U.S. 809 (1982).

29. Melissa Wilt, "Forum: VAWA funds family breakups," *Washington Times*, September 24, 2005, http://www.washingtontimes.com/news/2005/sep/24/20050924-100322-8263r/?page=all.

30. Christina Hoff Sommers, *Who Stole Feminism?: How Women Have Betrayed Women* (New York: Simon & Schuster, 1994), 189–91.

31. "What is Domestic Violence?" Ferris State University Virtual Women's Center, accessed April 10, 2014, http://www.ferris.edu/HTMLS/studentlife/Minority/vwc/assault/faq/domestic.htm.

32. Lenore Walker, *The Battered Woman*, repr. (n.p.: William Morrow, 1980), xiii.

33. Ibid., xv.

34. Ibid., 98, 230.

35. Gloria Steinem, *Revolution from Within* (New York: Little, Brown, 1993), 259.

36. Andrea Dworkin, Our Blood: Prophecies and Discourses on Sexual Politics (n.p.: Perigee, 1981).

37. *United States v. Morrison*, 529 U.S. 598, 602 (2000). See http://www.law.cornell.edu/supct/html/99-5.ZS.html.

38. Martin S. Fiebert, "References Examining Assaults by Women on Their Spouses or Male Partners: An Annotated Bibliography," California State University, Long Beach, Department of Psychology, upd. June 2012, http://www.csulb.edu/~mfiebert/assault.htm.

39. See, for example, D. J. Whitaker et al., "Differences in frequency of violence and reported injury between relationships with reciprocal and nonreciprocal intimate partner violence," *American Journal of Public Health* 97 (2007): 941–47.

40. Sam Houston University, "Working couples face greater odds of intimate partner violence," *PsyPost* (blog), November 29, 2012, http://www.psypost.org/2012/11/working-couples-face-greater-odds-of-intimate-partner-violence-15236.

41. See http://www.acfc.org/acfc/assets/documents/research_pdf's/FamilyViolenceEdit.pdf; http://www.mediaradar.org/reports.php; http://www.mediaradar.org/press_releases.php;

42. See http://www.whitehouse.gov/sites/default/files/dear_colleague_sexual_violence.pdf.

43. Brent Griffiths, "Iowa Supreme Court ruling expands birth-certificate rights for lesbian couples," *Daily Iowan*, May 6, 2013, http://www.dailyiowan.com/2013/05/06/Metro/33183.html.

44. "Bill to Allow for More Than Two Parents" (transcript of *The Rush Limbaugh Show*), Rush Limbaugh's official website, July 2, 2012, http://www.rushlimbaugh.com/daily/2012/07/02/bill_to_allow_for_more_than_two_parents.

45. Senate Bill 1476: An act to amend Sections 3040, 4057, 7601, and 7612 of, and to add Section 4052.5 to, the Family Code, relating to parentage, http://www.leginfo.ca.gov/pub/11-12/bill/sen/sb_1451-1500/sb_1476_bill_20120831_enrolled.pdf, pp. 2–3.

46. Ken Ham, "The Evolution of the Family," *Around the World with Ken Ham* (blog), February 21, 2013, http://blogs.answersingenesis.org/blogs/ken-ham/2013/02/21/the-evolution-of-the-family/.

47. Abby Ellin, "Making a Child, Minus the Couple," *New York Times*, February 8, 2013, http://www.nytimes.com/2013/02/10/fashion/seeking-to-reproduce-without-a-romantic-partnership.html?pagewanted=all&_r=0.

48. Ibid.

49. Jennifer Roback Morse, "Why California's Three-Parent Law Was Inevitable," Public Discourse, September 10, 2012, http://www.thepublicdiscourse.com/2012/09/6197/.

50. Andrew Pollack, "Before Birth, Dad's ID," *New York Times*, Health, June 20, 2012, http://www.nytimes.com/2012/06/20/health/paternity-blood-tests-that-work-early-in-a-pregnancy.html?pagewanted=all.

51. Libertarian Party 2012 Platform, http://www.lp.org/platform.

52. Ibid.

53. "Platform of the Libertarian Party of California as amended in Convention, May 2009," http://webcache.googleusercontent.com/search?q=cache:http://ca.lp.org/wp-content/blogs.dir/1/files/2011/03/Platform-of-the-Libertarian-Party-of-California-May-2009.pdf, 11–12.

54. Mainwaring, interview by Kathryn Jean Lopez, "Undefining Marriage: What's Gender Got to Do With It?" *National Review Online*, July 2, 2013, transcript, http://www.americanthinker.com/2012/10/the_conservative_rationale_for_gay_marriage.html.

55. Republican Philadelphia: Republican Platform of 1856, http://www.ushistory.org/gop/convention_1856republicanplatform.htm; 2008 Republican Party Platform, American Presidency Project, http://www.presidency.ucsb.edu/ws/?pid=78545; Republican Platform, "We Believe in America," Preserving and Protecting America, 2012, http://www.gop.com/2012-republican-platform_Renewing/#Item1.

56. Jamie Glazov, "The ACLU vs. America," *Front Page* magazine, September 26, 2005, http://archive.frontpagemag.com/readArticle.aspx?ARTID=7151.

57. The full statement appears online at http://beyondmarriage.org/full_statement.html.

58. Richard H. Thaler and Cass R. Sunstein, *Nudge: Improving Decisions about Health, Wealth and Happiness*, rev. and exp. ed. (New York: Penguin, 2009), 223, 217.

59. *Brown v. Buhman*, 947 F. Supp. 2d 1170 (D. Utah 2013).

60. *Kitchen v. Herbert*, 961 F. Supp. 2d 1181 (D. Utah 2013).

61. United Nations Equity for Gender Equality and the Empowerment of Women Convention on the Elimination of All Forms of Discrimination Against Women (CEDAW). The full text can be seen at http://www.un.org/womenwatch/daw/cedaw/text/econvention.htm.

62. CEDAW, Article 2, http://www.un.org/womenwatch/daw/cedaw/text/econvention.htm#article2.

63. CEDAW, Article 5, http://www.un.org/womenwatch/daw/cedaw/text/econvention. htm#article5.
64. CEDAW, Article 10, http://www.un.org/womenwatch/daw/cedaw/text/econvention. htm#article10.
65. CEDAW, Article 11, http://www.un.org/womenwatch/daw/cedaw/text/econvention. htm#article11.
66. CEDAW, Article 16, http://www.un.org/womenwatch/daw/cedaw/text/econvention. htm#article16.
67. CEDAW, Article 17, http://www.un.org/womenwatch/daw/cedaw/text/econvention. htm#article17.
68. Wendy Wright, "CEDAW Committee Rulings," Concerned Women for America Legislative Action Committee website, August 27, 2002, http://www.cwfa.org/cedaw-committee-rulings/.
69. The text of this treaty can be viewed on the website of the United Nations Office of the High Commissioner of Human Rights, at http://www.ohchr.org/en/professionalinterest/pages/crc. aspx.
70. Ibid.
71. Ibid.
72. The text of the UN Convention on the Rights of Persons with Disabilities can be viewed at http://www.un.org/disabilities/convention/conventionfull.shtml.
73. Susan Yoshihara, "Clinton Promises Global Push for Abortion Rights," *The Corner* (blog), January 15, 2010, http://www.nationalreview.com/corner/192857/clinton-promises-global-push-abortion-rights/susan-yoshihara.

CHAPTER 4: FAMILY COURTS CONTROL THE FAMILY

1. William Glaberson, "New York Family Courts Say Keep Out, Despite Order," *New York Times*, N.Y./Region, November 17, 2011, http://www.nytimes.com/2011/11/18/nyregion/ at-new-york-family-courts-rule-for-public-access-isnt-heeded.html.
2. Ibid.
3. Rule 1915.11-1, Elimination of Parenting Coordination (Pa. 2013).
4. Barbara Kay, "A Father's Day downer," *New York Daily News*, June 17, 2012, http://www. nydailynews.com/opinion/father-day-downer-article-1.1096613.
5. *Parham v. J. R.*, 442 U.S. 584, 602 (1979).
6. *Fields v. Palmdale School District*, 427 F. 3d 1197, 1206–8 (9th Cir. 2005).
7. Ruth Bettelheim, "In Whose Best Interests?" *New York Times* Sunday Review, May 19, 2012, http://www.nytimes.com/2012/05/20/opinion/sunday/child-custody-in-whose-best-interests. html.
8. *Adoptive Couple v. Baby Girl*, 133 S. Ct. 2552, 2572 (2013).
9. "The Awesome Power of Family Courts," *Phyllis Schlafly Report* 43, no. 11 (June 2010), http:// www.eagleforum.org/psr/2010/june10/psrjune10.html.
10. Céleste Perrino-Walker, "A Right to Faith?" *Liberty* magazine, September/October 2010, http://www.libertymagazine.org/article/a-right-to-faith.
11. *Camreta v. Greene*, 131 S. Ct. 2020 (2011).
12. *Los Angeles County v. Humphries*, 131 U.S. 447 (2010).
13. Thomas Kasper, "Obtaining and Defending Against an Order of Protection," *Illinois Bar Journal*, June 2005, available on the website of the Alliance for Non-Custodial Parents Rights, at http://ancpr.com/obtaining_and_defending_against_.htm.
14. *Final Report of the Child Custody and Visitation Focus Group*, 1999, http://www. batteredmotherscustodyconference.org/Final%20Report%20of%20Child%20Custody%20 Visitation%20Focus%20Group1.pdf, 5.
15. Lisa Scott, "VAWA: Joe Biden's Shame," FatherMag.com, accessed April 11, 2014, http:// www.fathermag.com/0507/VAWA/.
16. Quoted on the website of the Alliance for Non-Custodial Parents Rights, accessed April 11, 2014, http://ancpr.com/amazing_nj_legal_journal_article.htm.

17. The Heritage Foundation, "Benefits of Family for Children and Adults," familyfacts.org, accessed April 11, 2014, http://www.familyfacts.org/briefs/6/benefits-of-family-for-children-and-adults.

18. David Finkelhor, Heather Hammer, and Andrea J. Sedlak, "Nonfamily Abducted Children: National Estimates and Characteristics," *NISMART (National Incidence Studies of Missing, Abducted, Runaway, and Thrownaway Children)*, October 2002, https://www.ncjrs.gov/pdffiles1/ojjdp/196467.pdf, 1.

19. American Bar Association Commission on Domestic Violence, "10 Custody Myths and How to Counter Them" (tip sheet), July 2006, available at http://apps.americanbar.org/abastore/index.cfm?pid=3480009&section=main&fm=Product.AddToCart.

20. David R. Usher, "ABA's Predatory Feminist Lawyers," WND Commentary, June 4, 2008, http://www.wnd.com/2008/06/66154/.

21. Bernard Goldberg, Bias: A CBS Insider Exposes How the Media Distort the News (n.p.: Regnery, 2002), 138.

22. Bill Rankin, "Court knew man jailed for a year for non-support was not child's father," *Atlanta Journal-Constitution*, July 14, 2009, http://www.ajc.com/news/news/local/court-knew-man-jailed-for-a-year-for-non-support-w/nQHxY/.

23. Bill Rankin, "Man jailed for child support, even though he was not the father, released," *Atlanta Journal-Constitution*, July 15, 2009, http://www.ajc.com/news/news/local/man-jailed-for-child-support-even-though-he-was-no/nQHyf/.

24. Stephanie Rice, "Children: Father didn't abuse us: Ex-Vancouver police officer spent nearly 20 years in prison," *Seattle Times*, July 11, 2009, http://seattletimes.com/html/localnews/2009456102_recantabuse11m.html.

25. Ethan Bronner, "Poor Land in Jail as Companies Add Huge Fees for Probation," *New York Times*, July 2, 2012, http://www.nytimes.com/2012/07/03/us/probation-fees-multiply-as-companies-profit.html.

26. American Civil Liberties Union of Ohio, *The Outskirts of Hope: How Ohio's Debtors' Prisons Are Ruining Lives and Costing Communities* (Cleveland: American Civil Liberties Union of Ohio, April 2013), http://www.acluohio.org/wp-content/uploads/2013/04/TheOutskirtsOfHope2013_04.pdf.

27. Dianna Thompson and Glenn Sacks, "Families and the War," *Washington Times*, November 21, 2002, archived on the website of the Military Parents Alliance, http://web.archive.org/web/20050413100236/http://militaryparents.org/dt_gs_families_and_the.php.

28. Phyllis Schlafly, "The Price Some Reservists Have to Pay," Eagle Forum, March 2, 2005, http://www.eagleforum.org/column/2005/mar05/05-03-02.html.

29. Leslie Kaufman, "When Child Support Is Due, Even the Poor Find Little Mercy," *New York Times*, February 19, 2005, http://www.nytimes.com/2005/02/19/nyregion/19support.html?pagewanted=all&position=.

30. Robert Seidenberg, "Minority Report: The Sci-Fi Movie Not as Chilling as Child Support Enforcement, Our Real 'PreCrime' Program," accessed April 11, 2014, http://www.fathersunite.org/ChildSupport/The_Liberator_minority_report.html.

31. Phyllis Schlafly, "Children Made Fatherless by Family Courts," Eagle Forum, January 12, 2005, http://www.eagleforum.org/column/2005/jan05/05-01-12.html.

32. Stephen Baskerville, "Divorced from Reality," 2, accessed April 11, 2014, http://www.archden.org/repository//Documents/MarriageFamily/Resources/Article_DivorcedfromReality.pdf?CFID=68812072&CFTOKEN=57908340.

33. Chris Johnson and Amy Sherman, "Midlands Voices: Family Law Reform is Needed," Omaha.com, January 17, 2014, http://www.omaha.com/article/20140117/NEWS08/140118942.

34. Michael Reagan, with Jim Denney, *Twice Adopted* (Nashville: Broadman & Holman, 2004), 27.

35. See William C. Duncan, "Waxing State, Waning Family: The Radical Agenda of the American Law Institute," *The Family in America* (Winter 2010), http://familyinamerica.org/journals/winter-2010/waxing-state-waning-family-radical-agenda-american-law-institute/#.U0f5DlVdWSo.

36. Appeal from the Dearborn Superior Court, the Honorable Brian D. Hill, Special Judge, Cause No. 15D02-1103-FD-84, January 17, 2013, http://www.in.gov/judiciary/opinions/pdf/01171301cds.pdf, 19–20.

37. Eugene Volokh, "Harshly Criticizing Judges (or Others) for Their Past Conduct = Crime?" The Volokh Conspiracy, January 22, 2013, in Freedom of Speech, http://www.volokh.com/2013/01/22/harshly-criticizing-a-judge-or-others-for-their-past-conduct-crime/

CHAPTER 5: INCENTIVES UNDERMINE THE FAMILY

1. Joyce A. Martin et al., "Births: Final Data for 2010," *National Vital Statistics Reports* 61, no. 1 (August 28, 2012): 8, http://www.cdc.gov/nchs/data/nvsr/nvsr61/nvsr61_01.pdf.
2. Robert J. Samuelson, "The Welfare State Wins This Budget War," *Washington Post*, Opinions, August 7, 2011, http://www.washingtonpost.com/opinions/the-welfare-state-wins-this-budget-war/2011/08/07/gIQA4fuE1I_story.html.
3. See Jake Tapper, "McCain to Attack for Public Radio Comments from 2001," *Political Punch* (ABC News blog), October 27, 2008, http://abcnews.go.com/blogs/politics/2008/10/mccain-to-attac/.
4. Arthur Laffer, "Work Disincentives, Still Crazy after All These Years: In the Spirit of Jack Kemp, a Pro-Growth Agenda Is Needed for America's Pockets of Poverty," *Wall Street Journal* Opinion, February 8, 2013, http://online.wsj.com/news/articles/SB10001424127887324235104578243373468081096.
5. Wilcox, interview by Kathryn Jean Lopez, "What's Marriage Got to Do with the Economy? Learning from the Demographics," *National Review Online*, October 27, 2011, transcript, http://www.nationalreview.com/articles/281387/what-s-marriage-got-do-economy-interview.
6. Melanie Phillips, "Britain's Liberal Intelligentsia Has Smashed Virtually Every Social Value," *Mail Online*, upd. August 11, 2011, http://www.dailymail.co.uk/debate/article-2024690/UK-riots-2011-Britains-liberal-intelligentsia-smashed-virtually-social-value.html.
7. See *Public Law 104–193—AUG. 22, 1996*, http://www.gpo.gov/fdsys/pkg/PLAW-104publ193/pdf/PLAW-104publ193.pdf.
8. Committee on Ways and Means, United States House of Representatives, *President's Fiscal Year 2006 Budget for the U.S. Department of Health and Human Services* (Washington, DC: U.S. Government Printing Office, 2006), 56.
9. "Statistics," *The Fatherless Generation* (blog), accessed April 11, 2014, http://thefatherlessgeneration.wordpress.com/statistics/.
10. Kerby Anderson, "Broken Homes, Broken Hearts—A Christian Perspective on Sex Outside of Marriage," Probe Ministries website, accessed April 11, 2014, http://www.probe.org/site/c.fdKEIMNsEoG/b.4219385/k.73CC/Broken_Homes_Broken_Hearts.htm.
11. Martin et al., "Births: Final Data for 2010."
12. Maggie Fox, "New voter bloc emerges: single women," *Today*, Health, November 7, 2012, http://www.today.com/health/new-voter-bloc-emerges-single-women-1C6904321.
13. Robert Rector, "Marriage: America's Greatest Weapon Against Child Poverty," Heritage Foundation, September 16, 2010, http://www.heritage.org/research/reports/2010/09/marriage-america-s-greatest-weapon-against-child-poverty.
14. Kathryn Wall, "Statistics reveal stark challenges for children raised in one-parent households," *Newsleader.com*, November 24, 2012, http://www.news-leader.com/article/20121125/NEWS01/311250054/.
15. *Strengthening the Safety Net: Hearing before the Committee on the Budget, House of Representatives*, April 17, 2012 (U.S. Government Printing Office), http://www.gpo.gov/fdsys/pkg/CHRG-112hhrg73801/html/CHRG-112hhrg73801.htm.
16. Rector, "Marriage: America's Greatest Weapon Against Child Poverty."
17. Ibid.
18. Stephanie Samuel, "Calif. Poll Shows Most Americans Believe in Traditional Marriage," *Christian Post*, Politics, October 14, 2011, http://www.christianpost.com/news/calif-poll-shows-most-americans-believe-in-traditional-marriage-58131/.
19. *Phyllis Schlafly Report* vol. 14, no. 9, April 1981.
20. Thaddeus Baklinski, "Pro-family groups applaud Supreme Court of Canada ruling in favor of marriage," LifeSiteNews.com, January 30, 2013, http://www.lifesitenews.com/news/pro-family-groups-applaud-supreme-court-of-canada-ruling-in-favor-of-marria.

21. Karen DeCrow, "Balance of Power," *New York Times*, May 31, 1992, http://www.nytimes.com/1992/05/31/magazine/l-balance-of-power-721892.html.

22. Loren Thompson, "Intelligence Community Fears U.S. Manufacturing Decline," *Forbes*, February 14, 2011, http://www.forbes.com/sites/beltway/2011/02/14/intelligence-community-fears-u-s-manufacturing-decline/.

23. Pam Fessler, "Record Number Of U.S. Households Face Hunger," NPR, November 15, 2010, http://www.npr.org/2010/11/15/131328286/record-number-of-u-s-households-face-hunger.

24. Fox, "New voter bloc emerges: single women."

25. Greenberg Quinlan Rosner Research Fund and Women's Voices: Women Vote Action Fund, "Unmarried Women On Health Care: Unmarried Women Driving Change on Leading Domestic Issue" (memo to "Interested Parties"), August 8, 2007, http://gqrr.com/articles/2066/3853_wvwv%20_health%20care%20memo_%200807m9_FINAL_.pdf.

26. Robert Rector, "The New Federal Wedding Tax: How Obamacare Would Dramatically Penalize Marriage," Heritage Foundation, January 20, 2010, http://www.heritage.org/research/reports/2010/01/the-new-federal-wedding-tax-how-obamacare-would-dramatically-penalize-marriage.

27. Jim Angle, "Obama's Health Care Law Penalizes Marriage, Analysts Say," Fox News Politics, October 27, 2011, http://www.foxnews.com/politics/2011/10/27/obamas-health-care-law-penalizes-marriage-analysts-say/.

28. Ibid.

29. Robert J. Samuelson, "An economy that's tearing our society apart," *Washington Post*, April 14, 2013, http://www.washingtonpost.com/opinions/robert-samuelson-family-meltdown-and-economic-decline/2013/04/14/f0d4b6d2-a388-11e2-82bc-511538ae90a4_story.html.

30. Jessica Silver-Greenberg, "Perfect 10? Never Mind That. Ask Her for Her Credit Score," *New York Times*, Business, December 26, 2012, http://www.nytimes.com/2012/12/26/business/even-cupid-wants-to-know-your-credit-score.html.

31. Jordan Weissman, "53% of Recent College Grads Are Jobless or Underemployed—How?" *The Atlantic*, April 23, 2012, http://www.theatlantic.com/business/archive/2012/04/53-of-recent-college-grads-are-jobless-or-underemployed-how/256237/.

32. Jennifer Liberto, "I will graduate with $100,000 in loans," CNN Money, June 19, 2013, http://money.cnn.com/2013/06/19/pf/college/student-loan-debt/.

33. "Student Debt Levels—Now Averaging More Than $35,000—Surprise to Half of 2013 College Grads: Fidelity Study Finds Nearly 40 Percent Would Have Made Different Choices Had They Better Understood Costs," Fidelity.com, May 16, 2013, http://www.fidelity.com/inside-fidelity/individual-investing/college-grads-surprised-by-student-debt-level-exceeds-35000.

34. Glenn Harlan Reynolds, "What's Really 'Immoral' About Student Loans: It's Not So Much the Interest Rates Charged. It Is, Rather, the Principal of the Thing," *Wall Street Journal*, Opinion, June 28, 2013, http://online.wsj.com/news/articles/SB10001424127887324688404578541372861440606. See also his book *The Higher Education Bubble* (New York: Encounter, 2012).

35. Stephen J. Dubner, "The Cobra Effect: A New Freakonomics Radio Podcast," *Freakonomics*, October 11, 2012, http://freakonomics.com/2012/10/11/the-cobra-effect-a-new-freakonomics-radio-podcast/.

36. Anonymous commenter to the blog post "Facing Reality About Social Issues," *Eagle Forum*, October 4, 2012, http://blog.eagleforum.org/2012/10/facing-reality-about-social-issues.html.

37. Rick Stengel, interview by Rush Limbaugh, "Another Journalist Joins the Regime," *The Rush Limbaugh Show*, September 13, 2013, transcript, http://nation.foxnews.com/time-person-year/2012/12/19/limbaugh-obama-time-s-person-year-because-he-symbolizes-new-stupid-people-demographic.

38. Maureen Dowd, "A Lost Civilization," *New York Times*, Opinion, December 8, 2012, http://www.nytimes.com/2012/12/09/opinion/sunday/dowd-a-lost-civilization.html.

39. Ann Coulter, Guilty: Liberal "Victims" and Their Assault on America (New York: Crown Forum, 2008).

40. Ann Coulter, "America Nears el Tipping Pointo," Ann Coulter website, December 5, 2012, http://www.anncoulter.com/columns/2012-12-05.html.

41. Ibid.
42. Jonathan Last, "A Nation of Singles: The Most Politically Potent Demographic Trend Is Not the One Everyone Talked about after the Election," *Weekly Standard*, December 10, 2012, http://www.weeklystandard.com/articles/nation-singles_664275.html?page=3.
43. Laura Wood, "The Fluke Vote," *The Thinking Housewife: On the Common Good and the Good That Is Common* (blog), December 5, 2012, http://www.thinkinghousewife.com/wp/2012/12/the-fluke-vote/.
44. Steve Sailer, "Happy White Married People Vote Republican, So Why Doesn't the GOP Work on Making White People Happy?" *VDare.com*, February 28, 2013, http://www.vdare.com/articles/happy-white-married-people-vote-republican-so-why-doesnt-the-gop-work-on-making-white-peopl.

CHAPTER 6: EXPERTS REDEFINE THE FAMILY

1. Robert E. Emery, Randy K. Otto, and William O'Donohue, "Custody Disputed," *Scientific American*, October 2005, http://www.scientificamerican.com/article.cfm?id=custody-disputed. See also, Leslie Eaton, "For Arbiters in Custody Battles, Wide Power and Little Scrutiny," *New York Times*, May 23, 2004.
2. Carol Tavris, "How Psychiatry Went Crazy," *Wall Street Journal*, May 17, 2013, http://online.wsj.com/news/articles/SB10001424127887323716304578481222760113886.
3. Daniel Goleman, "Scientist At Work: Allen J. Frances; Revamping Psychiatrists' Bible," *New York Times*, April 19, 1994, http://www.nytimes.com/1994/04/19/science/scientist-at-work-allen-j-frances-revamping-psychiatrists-bible.html.
4. Allen J. Frances, "DSM 5 is Guide Not Bible—Ignore Its Ten Worst Changes," *DSM 5 in Distress* (*Psychology Today* blog), December 2, 2012, http://www.psychologytoday.com/blog/dsm5-in-distress/201212/dsm-5-is-guide-not-bible-ignore-its-ten-worst-changes.
5. Ibid.
6. Mike Adams, "Psychiatry goes insane: Every human emotion now classified as a mental disorder in new psychiatric manual DSM-5," Natural News, December 13, 2012, http://www.naturalnews.com/038322_DSM-5_psychiatry_false_diagnosis.html.
7. Mike Adams, "When Students Cheat Liberals Retreat," Townhall.com, September 14, 2012, http://townhall.com/columnists/mikeadams/2012/09/14/when_students_cheat_liberals_retreat/page/full.
8. Stephen A. Diamond, "End of Men: The 'Feminization' of Psychotherapy," *Evil Deeds* (blog) (*Psychology Today*, October 5, 2012), http://www.psychologytoday.com/blog/evil-deeds/201210/end-men-the-feminization-psychotherapy. See also Cassandra Willyard, "Men: A Growing Minority? Women Earning Doctoral Degrees in Psychology Outnumber Men Three to One. What Does This Mean for the Future of the Field?" American Psychological Association, http://www.apa.org/gradpsych/2011/01/cover-men.aspx (this article was recommended by Dr. Diamond in "End of Men").
9. California Supreme Court Case No. S107355, Appellant's and Dr. Judith Wallerstein's replies to *Amici* Briefs Submitted by Leslie E. Shear and Richard A. Warshack, October 17, 2003, http://www.thelizlibrary.org/site-index/site-index-frame.html#soulhttp://www.thelizlibrary.org/lamusga/.
10. Leslie Ellen Shear, "Application Per CRC, Rule 29.1(F) for Leave to File Amicus Brief (and Word-Count Certification and Request)," *The Liz Library*, http://www.thelizlibrary.org/lamusga/ShearFinal.pdf, v.
11. Denise Grady, "Judith S. Wallerstein, Psychologist Who Analyzed Divorce, Dies at 90," *New York Times*, Health, June 20, 2012, http://www.nytimes.com/2012/06/21/health/research/judith-s-wallerstein-psychologist-who-analyzed-divorce-dies-at-90.html.
12. Brian Palmer, "How to Diagnose a Toddler with ADHD: Don't all little kids have short attention spans?" *Slate*, October 17, 2011, http://www.slate.com/articles/health_and_science/explainer/2011/10/adhd_in_toddlers_how_can_you_tell_.html.

13. "LaViolette Combative on the Stand," *My Crime Time* (Jodi Arias murder trial blog), April 8, 2013, http://mycrimetime.blogspot.com/2013/04/laviolette-combative-on-stand.html.

14. "LaViolette's 'The Continuum of Aggression & Abuse' Explained," *My Crime Time* (blog), March 26, 2013, http://mycrimetime.blogspot.com/2013/03/laviolettes-continuum-of-aggression.html.

15. R. Mark Rogers, "Presenting Your Case," Guideline Economics, http://www.guidelineeconomics.com/fightcase/legalbasis.html.

16. Lois M. Collins and Marjorie Cortez, "Why Dads Matter," *The Atlantic*, February 23, 2014, http://www.theatlantic.com/health/archive/2014/02/why-dads-matter/283956/.

17. *Marriage of Adams* (2012) 209 Cal.App.4th 1543.

18. Custody Care Inc. (home page), the website of David J. Jimenez, EdD, accessed April 16, 2014, http://custodycareinc.com/.

19. Custody Care Inc., "About Us," http://custodycareinc.com/index_files/Page348.htm.

20. Custody Care Inc., "Abbreviated Curriculum Vitae," http://custodycareinc.com/index_files/Page294.htm.

21. *Christina Adams v. Jack A.*, No. G045920 (quoting Super. Ct. No. 05D011298).

22. Rachel Aviv, "Where Is Your Mother? A Woman's Fight to Keep Her Child," *The New Yorker*, December 2, 2013, 52.

23. Margo Howard, "I Vote for Symbolism," Creators.com, accessed March 26, 2014, http://www.creators.com/advice/dear-margo/i-vote-for-symbolism.html.

24. Margo Howard, "Cheating and the Computer," Creators.com, accessed March 26, 2014, http://www.creators.com/advice/dear-margo/cheating-and-the-computer.html.

25. Margo Howard, "Brothers Might Never Warm to Divorced Sis," *Columbus Dispatch*, December 2, 2012, http://www.dispatch.com/content/stories/life_and_entertainment/2012/12/02/brothers-might-never-warm-to-divorced-sis.html.

26. Annie, "Married 25 Years and Longing for Love," Boston.com, Lifestyle, March 23, 2011, http://www.boston.com/lifestyle/relationships/articles/2011/03/23/married_25_years_and_longing_for_love/.

27. David Brooks, "The Limits of Empathy," *New York Times*, September 29, 2011, http://www.nytimes.com/2011/09/30/opinion/brooks-the-limits-of-empathy.html.

28. "Empathy Represses Analytical Thought, and Vice Versa," Medical Xpress, October 30, 2012, http://medicalxpress.com/news/2012-10-empathy-represses-analytic-thought-vice.html.

29. Michael Gaynor, "The empath-in-chief versus the Bible on judges," RenewAmerica, May 14, 2009, http://www.renewamerica.com/columns/gaynor/090514.

30. Joanne Lipman, "Why Tough Teachers Get Good Results," *Wall Street Journal*, September 27, 2013, http://online.wsj.com/news/articles/SB10001424052702304213904579095303368899132.

31. Christina Hoff Sommers and Sally Satel, *One Nation Under Therapy: How the Helping Culture Is Eroding Self-Reliance* (New York: St. Martin's Press, 2005).

32. Ibid.

33. *Double Tongued Dictionary*, s.v. "therapism," accessed April 16, 2014, http://www.waywordradio.org/?s=therapism&submit=search.

34. Sommers and Satel, *One Nation Under Therapy*.

35. Cecil Adams, "Are Shrinks Nuts?" *Straight Dope*, September 28, 2012, http://www.straightdope.com/columns/read/3072/are-shrinks-nuts.

36. Robert Epstein and Tim Bower, "Why Shrinks Have Problems," *Psychology Today*, July 1, 1997, http://www.psychologytoday.com/articles/200909/why-shrinks-have-problems.

37. Tara Haelle, "Few Answers on How to Effectively Help Children Cope with Trauma: Evidence Supports the Effectiveness of Some Cognitive Behavioral Therapies, but . . . Children Exposed to Traumatic Events," *Scientific American*, February 11, 2013, http://www.scientificamerican.com/article/research-offers-few-answers-trauma-children/.

38. Benedict Carey, "Drugs Used for Psychotics Go to Youths in Foster Care," *New York Times*, November 20, 2011, http://www.nytimes.com/2011/11/21/health/research/study-finds-foster-children-often-given-antipsychosis-drugs.html.

39. Moe Tkacik, "Why Big Pharma is Causing the Adderall Shortage," *The Fix* (addiction and recovery blog), November 17, 2011, http://www.thefix.com/content/pay-attention-adderall-add-big-pharma7004.

40. Brinda Adhikari, Joan Martelli, and Sarah Koch, "Doctors Put Foster Children at Risk with Mind-altering Drugs," ABC News, December 3, 2011, http://abcnews.go.com/Health/doctors-put-foster-children-risk-mind-altering-drugs/story?id=15064560.

41. Jennifer Kahn, "Can You Call a Nine-Year-Old a Psychopath?" *New York Times*, May 11, 2012, http://www.nytimes.com/2012/05/13/magazine/can-you-call-a-9-year-old-a-psychopath.html?pagewanted=all.

42. John Horgan, "What Are Science's Ugliest Experiments?" *Scientific American*, May 14, 2012, http://blogs.scientificamerican.com/cross-check/2012/05/14/what-are-sciences-ugliest-experiments/.

43. Steven M. Berman et al., "Potential Adverse Effects of Amphetamine Treatment on Brain and Behavior: A Review," *Molecular Psychiatry* 14, no. 2 (February 2009): 123–42; available on the website of the US National Library of Medicine and National Institutes of Health, http://www.ncbi.nlm.nih.gov/pmc/articles/PMC2670101/.

44. "S. 1877—Speak Up to Protect Every Abused Kid Act," HSLDA website, December 12, 2011, http://www.hslda.org/Legislation/National/2011/S1877/default.asp.

45. Lawrence Summers, "Remarks at NBER Conference on Diversifying the Science & Engineering Workforce" (transcript), Cambridge, MA, January 14, 2005, http://www.harvard.edu/president/speeches/summers_2005/nber.php.

46. George H. Will, "Harvard Hysterics," *Washington Post*, January 27, 2005, http://www.washingtonpost.com/wp-dyn/articles/A40073-2005Jan26.html.

47. Frank Furedi, "It's Time to Expel the 'Experts' From Family Life: In Repackaging Parenting . . . a Gaggle of Experts Hopes to Colonise Our Personal Lives," FrankFuredi.com, September 12, 2011, http://www.frankfuredi.com/index.php/site/article/492/.

48. Bob Unruh, "Psychologists Blacklist Conservative Colleagues: 'The More Liberal Respondents Are, the More Willing They Are to Discriminate,'" WND, August 19, 2012, http://www.wnd.com/2012/08/psychologists-blacklist-conservative-colleagues/.

CHAPTER 7: CULTURE MOCKS THE FAMILY

1. Phyllis Schlafly, "How the Government Influences Our Culture," *Northwestern University Law Review* 102, no. 1 (Winter 2008): 491, http://www.law.northwestern.edu/lawreview/v102/n1/491/LR102n1Schlafly.pdf.

2. Secular Humanism, http://secular-humanism.com/; accessed April 15, 2014.

3. Victor Dorff, "Education's Cheating Epidemic: Many Kids Today See Dishonesty as a Crucial Part of Any Path to Success," *Los Angeles Times*, July 17, 2012, http://articles.latimes.com/2012/jul/17/opinion/la-oe-dorff-cheating-20120717.

4. *Meyer v. Nebraska*, 262 U.S. 390 (1923).

5. *Pierce v. Society of Sisters*, 268 U.S. 510 (1925).

6. *Wisconsin v. Yoder*, 406 U.S. 205 (1972).

7. *Troxel v. Granville*, 530 U.S. 57 (2000).

8. *Fields v. Palmdale School District*, 427 F. 3d 1197, 1206–8 (9th Cir. 2005).

9. *Morrison v. Board of Education*, 419 F. Supp. 2d 937 (E.D. Ky. 2006). See http://www.ca6.uscourts.gov/opinions.pdf/08a0146a-06.pdf and https://www.aclu.org/sites/default/files/images/asset_upload_file855_24216.pdf.

10. *Parker v. Hurley*, 474 F. Supp. 2d 261 (D. Mass 2007).

11. *Fields*, 427 F.3d 1197; *C.N. v. Ridgewood Board of Education*, 430 F.3d 159 (3d Cir. 2005).

12. *Brown v. Hot, Sexy & Safer Productions*, 68 F.3d 525 (1st Cir. 1995).

13. *Kitzmiller v. Dover Area School District*, 400 F. Supp. 2d 707 (M.D. Pa. 2005).

14. *Eklund v. Byron Union School District*, Case No. C 02-3004 PJH, 2003 U.S. Dist. LEXIS 27152 (N.D. Cal. Dec. 5, 2003), aff'd, 154 Fed. Appx. 648 (9th Cir. 2005).

15. Kevin D. Williamson, "That's Indoctrination! Everything Your Suburban Fourth Grader Needs to Know about Gay Marriage," *National Review Online*, December, 4, 2012, http://www.nationalreview.com/articles/334702/s-indoctrination-kevin-d-williamson.

16. "Ad Protests Toronto Schools," *Eagle Forum*, October 9, 2011, http://blog.eagleforum.org/2011/10/ad-protests-toronto-schools.html.

17. Scott Adams, "The War on Parents," *The Scott Adams Blog*, March 19, 2012, http://stage.dilbert.com/blog/entry/the_war_on_parents/.

18. Eric Brodin quoting an anonymous British journalist, "Destroying the Family: Swedish Style" (speech), Washington, DC, September 21, 1985, http://blog.eagleforum.org/2011/11/destroying-family-swedish-style.html or http://nkmr.org/pl/om-nkmr/stadgar/130-notifications-and-decisions.

19. Phyllis Schlafly, *The Supremacists: The Tyranny of Judges and How to Stop It* (Dallas: Spence, 2004). See also Phyllis Schlafly, "The Morality of First Amendment Jurisprudence," *Harvard Journal of Law & Public Policy* 31, no. 1 (Winter 2008), http://www.law.harvard.edu/students/orgs/jlpp/Vol31_No1_Schlaflyonline.pdf, 95–103.

20. Wikipedia, s.v. "Familialism," http://en.wikipedia.org/wiki/Familialism.

21. Wikipedia, s.v. "Complementarianism," last modified March 23, 2014, http://en.wikipedia.org/wiki/Complementarianism.

22. Carol Morello, "Married couples at a record low," *Washington Post*, December 14, 2011, http://www.washingtonpost.com/local/married-couples-at-a-record-low/2011/12/13/gIQAnJyYsO_story.html%22%20title=%22.

23. D'Vera Cohn et al., "Barely Half of U.S. Adults Are Married—A Record Low: New Marriages Down 5," Social & Demographic Trends, *Pew Research*, December 14, 2011, http://www.pewsocialtrends.org/2011/12/14/barely-half-of-u-s-adults-are-married-a-record-low/.

24. Morello, "Married couples at a record low."

25. Sheela Kennedy and Larry Bumpass, "Cohabitation and Children's Living Arrangements: New Estimates from the United States," *Demographic Research* 19 (September 19, 2008): 1686.

26. *Hawkins v. United States*, 358 U.S. 74, 75 (1958).

27. Ibid., at 81–82 (Stewart, J. concurring).

28. *Trammel v. United States*, 445 U.S. 40, 53 (1980).

29. Kate Taylor, "Sex on Campus: She Can Play That Game, Too," *New York Times*, Fashion & Style, July 12, 2013, http://www.nytimes.com/2013/07/14/fashion/sex-on-campus-she-can-play-that-game-too.html?pagewanted=all.

30. Tracy Clark-Flory, "Stop Calling us Wives and Moms: A Petition Calls on President Barack Obama to Drop His Retro Rhetoric about Women," Salon.com, February 13, 2013, http://www.salon.com/2013/02/13/stop_calling_us_wives_and_moms/.

31. Suzi Parker, "It's Time for Women to Take Back the Word 'Feminism,'" *Washington Post*, February 8, 2013, http://www.washingtonpost.com/blogs/she-the-people/wp/2013/02/08/its-time-for-women-to-take-back-the-word-feminism/.

32. Peggy Orenstein, "Should the World of Toys Be Gender-Free?" *New York Times*, Opinion, December 29, 2011, http://www.nytimes.com/2011/12/30/opinion/does-stripping-gender-from-toys-really-make-sense.html.

33. Elizabeth Sweet, "Guys and Dolls No More?" *New York Times Sunday Review*, December 21, 2012, http://www.nytimes.com/2012/12/23/opinion/sunday/gender-based-toy-marketing-returns.html.

34. Kay S. Hymowitz, "The Black Family: 40 Years of Lies," *City Journal,* Summer 2005, http://www.city-journal.org/html/15_3_black_family.html.

35. Kate Bolick, "All the Single Ladies," *The Atlantic*, September 30, 2011, http://www.theatlantic.com/magazine/archive/2011/11/all-the-single-ladies/308654/.

36. Suzanne Venker, "Is the 50/50 Marriage the Ideal?" *The Home Front* (blog), December 4, 2011, http://www.nationalreview.com/home-front/284855/5050-marriage-ideal/suzanne-venker.

37. David Brooks, "Why Men Fail," *New York Times* Opinion Pages, September 10, 2012, http://www.nytimes.com/2012/09/11/opinion/brooks-why-men-fail.html.

38. Hanna Rosin, "The End of Men," *The Atlantic*, June 8, 2010, http://www.theatlantic.com/magazine/archive/2010/07/the-end-of-men/308135/.

39. GuestPoster, "Guestpost: Oooh, My Oocytes! Or, My Experience With Freezing My Eggs," *corporette* (blog), December 19, 2011, http://corporette.com/2011/12/19/guestpost-oooh-my-oocytes-or-my-experience-with-freezing-my-eggs/.

40. Jason DeParle and Sabrina Tavernise, "For Women Under 30, Most Births Occur Outside Marriage," *New York Times*, February 17, 2012, http://www.nytimes.com/2012/02/18/us/for-women-under-30-most-births-occur-outside-marriage.html.

41. Christina Hoff Sommers, "The Boys at the Back," *Opinionator* (blog), February 2, 2013, http://opinionator.blogs.nytimes.com/2013/02/02/the-boys-at-the-back/.

42. Bill Costello, "Where the Education Gender Gap is Leading America," *Education Reporter*, December 2008, http://www.eagleforum.org/educate/2008/dec08/gender-gap.html.

43. Conservapedia, s.v. "Title IX," http://www.conservapedia.com/Title_IX; accessed April 15, 2014.

44. Suzie Lechtenberg, "Women Are Not Men: A New Freakonomics Radio Podcast" (transcript), *Freakonomics*, January 25, 2013, http://freakonomics.com/2013/02/24/women-are-not-men-a-new-freakonomics-radio-podcast/.

45. "Women Are Not Men," *Eagle Forum Blog*, February 28, 2013, http://blog.eagleforum.org/2013_02_01_archive.html.

46. Emily Lambert, "When Women Earn More Than Their Husbands," University of Chicago Booth School of Business website, February 18, 2013, http://www.chicagobooth.edu/about/newsroom/news/2013/2013-02-18-bertrand.

47. See Marianne Bertrand, Emir Kamenica, and Jessica Pan, *Gender identity and relative income within households*, October 2013, http://faculty.chicagobooth.edu/emir.kamenica/documents/identity.pdf.

48. Bella DePaulo, "Shriver's 'Woman's Nation' is Actually a Wife and Mother's Nation: The Evidence," *Living Single* (blog), October 23, 2009, http://www.psychologytoday.com/blog/living-single/200910/shriver-s-woman-s-nation-is-actually-a-wife-and-mother-s-nation-the-evidence.

49. Betsey Stevenson and Justin Wolfers, *The Paradox Of Declining Female Happiness* (Cambridge, MA: National Bureau of Economic Research, 2009), http://languagelog.ldc.upenn.edu/myl/StevensonWolfers.pdf, 3.

50. Rebecca Walker, "How my mother's fanatical views tore us apart," *Mail Online*, upd. May 23, 2008, http://www.dailymail.co.uk/femail/article-1021293/How-mothers-fanatical-feminist-views-tore-apart-daughter-The-Color-Purple-author.html.

51. Kate Bolick, "All the Single Ladies," *The Atlantic*, November 2011, http://www.theatlantic.com/magazine/archive/2011/11/all-the-single-ladies/308654/.

52. Brendan O'Neill, "Britain Abolishes Itself," *The American Conservative*, July 30, 2012, http://www.theamericanconservative.com/articles/britain-abolishes-itself/.

53. Madeleine Schwartz, "The Anti-Family," *The New Inquiry*, November 12, 2012, http://thenewinquiry.com/essays/the-anti-family/.

54. Hanna Rosin, "Boys on the Side: The Hookup Culture . . . Driven by Women Themselves," *The Atlantic*, August 22, 2012, http://www.theatlantic.com/magazine/archive/2012/09/boys-on-the-side/309062/.

55. Luke Rosiak, "Fathers Disappear from Households Across America: Big Increase in Single Mothers," *Washington Times*, December 25, 2012, http://www.washingtontimes.com/news/2012/dec/25/fathers-disappear-from-households-across-america/?page=all.

56. Henry Potrykus and Patrick Fagan, "The Divorce Revolution Perpetually Reduces U.S. Economic Growth," MarriResearch, accessed April 15, 2014, http://marri.us/the-divorce-revolution-perpetually-reduces-economic-growth.

57. Ibid.

CHAPTER 8: THE WAY HOME

1. See Phyllis Schlafly and George Neumayr, *No Higher Power: Obama's War on Religious Freedom* (Washington, DC: Regnery, 2012).

2. The Capital-Journal, "Huelskamp to seek constitutional amendment defining marriage: Kansas congressman says Supreme Court decision undermines marriage and family," CJOnline.com, June 26, 2013, http://cjonline.com/news/2013-06-26/huelskamp-seek-constitutional-amendment-defining-marriage.

3. Family Research Council, "Why Marriage Should Be Privileged in Public Policy," April 30, 2003, http://www.frc.org/insight/why-marriage-should-be-privileged-in-public-policy.

4. Steve Doughty, "Conspiracy of silence on value of marriage: Politicians frightened to admit fathers are vital, says top family lawyer," *Mail Online*, February 15, 2013, http://www.dailymail.co.uk/news/article-2279326/Decline-marriage-children-growing-fathers-doing-harm-smoking-global-warming-poor-diets-says-Baroness.html.

5. James Taranto, "The Limits of Moral Suasion," *Wall Street Journal*, March 12, 2013, http://online.wsj.com/news/articles/SB10001424127887324281004578356422222235976?mg=reno64-wsj&url=http%3A%2F%2Fonline.wsj.com%2Farticle%2FSB10001424127887324281004578356422222235976.html.

6. Gary D. Alexander, "Fix Bloated Welfare System," Philly.com, May 22, 2013, http://articles.philly.com/2013-05-22/news/39448122_1_tanf-welfare-system-food-stamps.

7. Charles Murray, "The Coming White Underclass," accessed April 16, 2014, http://www.sullivan-county.com/racism/murrey.htm.

8. Hanna Rosin, *The End of Men: And the Rise of Women* (New York: Riverhead, 2012), 21, 23.

9. Ibid., 47–78, 7.

10. Christina Hoff Sommers, "How to Get More Women (and Men) to Call Themselves Feminists," *The Atlantic*, June 25, 2013, http://www.theatlantic.com/sexes/archive/2013/06/how-to-get-more-women-and-men-to-call-themselves-feminists/277179/.

11. Karen Rowan, "Fertility Drop-off Surprises Women Over 40," Live Science, December 10, 2012, http://www.livescience.com/25386-fertility-decline-surprises-women.html.

12. Ibid.

13. Joanne Lipman, "The Mismeasure of Woman," *New York Times*, October 23, 2009, http://www.nytimes.com/2009/10/24/opinion/24lipman.html?pagewanted=all.

14. *Obergefell v. Wymyslo*, Case No. 962 F. Supp. 2d 968 (S.D. Ohio 2013).

15. *United States v. Windsor*, 133 S. Ct. 2675 (2013).

16. Fiachra Gibbons, "Lay off men, Lessing tells feminists," The Guardian (UK), August 13, 2001, http://www.theguardian.com/uk/2001/aug/14/edinburghfestival2001.edinburghbookfestival2001.

17. "Dr. Morse's testimony on preserving natural marriage, delivered at the Illinois State Capitol on Tuesday, February 26," *Ruth Institute Newsletter* 8, no. 9 (February 28, 2013): http://www.ruthinstitute.org/newsletters/2013/Feb13/illTestimony.html.

INDEX

OTHER BOOKS BY PHYLLIS SCHLAFLY

A Choice Not An Echo (1964)

The Gravediggers (1964)

Strike from Space (1965)

Safe Not Sorry (1967)

The Betrayers (1968)

Mindszenty the Man (1972)

Kissinger on the Couch (1975)

Ambush at Vladivostok (1976)

The Power of the Positive Woman (1977)

The Power of the Christian Woman (1981)

Equal Pay for UNequal Work (1984)

Child Abuse in the Classroom (1984, rev 1985, rev 1993)

Pornography's Victims (1987)

Who Will Rock the Cradle? (1989)

Stronger Families or Bigger Government? (1990)

Meddlesome Mandate (1991)

First Reader (1994)

Allegiance (2000)

Turbo Reader (2001)

Feminist Fantasies (2003)

The Supremacists (2004, rev 2006)

The Flipside of Feminism (2011)

No Higher Power (2012)